D0672701

Geopolitics of hunger

Geopolitics of hunger

USING HUNGER AS A WEAPON...

© Presses Universitaires de France 1999

This book is the English edition of *Géopolitique de la faim*, first published by
Presses Universitaires de France, 108 Bd Saint-Germain, Paris, in October 1998

ISBN 0 9535018 09

Publisher: Action Against Hunger
1 Catton Street, London WC1R 4AB

Cartography: Carl Voyer
Translation: Iesha Singh and Isabel Brenner
Production: Sayce Publishing, London, UK
Printer: Ebenezer Baylis, The Trinity Press, Worcester, UK

This book is dedicated to the local and expatriate volunteers who have lost their lives in the course of work with Action Against Hunger. Their commitment and their courage will remain inscribed in the memory of all our volunteers, volunteers who today are pursing the same fight to protect those made victim by the use of hunger as a weapon, in conditions that are often difficult, sometimes extreme.

Contents

PART 2
HOW TO FACE THE HANGMAN?

Preface

Hunger has its uses, and famine is not only a disaster but also a system which may be beneficial for some. Drawing on the field experience of Action Against Hunger workers across the world, this book convincingly documents the use of hunger as a weapon. It is at once a powerful indictment of governments and factions who manipulate or tolerate hunger, and an eloquent reaffirmation of the legal right to food and security set out in the United Nations Charter of 1945.

Perhaps most striking in this catalogue of unnatural disasters is the sheer diversity of uses to which hunger has been put, many of them going beyond the simple use of hunger as a counter-insurgency tactic. Not all of these uses can be mentioned here. But the reader is taken, for example, to north-eastern Brazil, where successive droughts have spawned a kind of 'drought industry' in which relief and State subsidies are appropriated by politically dominant large landowners who are thereby able to pose as benefactors (boosting their chances of re-election) and to benefit from public works that secure reservoirs for their cattle ranches. In turn, deprivation in the north-east has encouraged many poor people to risk clearing land in the Amazon district. But here, too, hunger has been functional, as harsh and unrelieved conditions have repeatedly forced the cheap sale of newly cleared land, often to large cattle ranchers or mineral companies. In addition, violence – in the form of militia attacks or planned forest fires – has routinely been used to eject the impoverished colonisers as well as long-resident Indians.

In Somalia, too, land hunger has helped fuel suffering among those displaced (in this case, very often by international fruit companies and their local allies). Paradoxically, those living in Somalia's most fertile areas have been hardest hit by famine, since these areas have been coveted the most by multinationals, militias and State officials. In Burma, where the oppressed Rohingyas have been systematically deprived of citizenship, the right to land and freedom of movement, one cannot point the finger simply at 'ethnic hatred' or wanton cruelty; rather, the oppression is part of a complex system serving a number of functions, including deflecting the discontent of neighbouring Buddhist Arakanese through tactics of 'divide and rule', lining the pockets of underpaid security officials and civil servants through a range of punitive taxes, and weakening the Rohingyas to a point where they are forced to concentrate on survival rather than political organisation. Meanwhile, the international community has colluded in the return of Rohingya refugees from neighbouring Bangladesh to unsafe conditions in Burma.

In addition to links between hunger and economic exploitation, the book documents the use of hunger as a crude military weapon (for example, by the government in Sudan and by the Soviet Union and then the Taliban in Afghanistan) and, still more perversely, the starving of 'their own people' by military factions. In Afghanistan's Hazarajat region, for example, and parts of southern Sudan, such 'own goals' appear to have served a dual purpose: to attract maximum aid, which can then be appropriated; and to allow the portrayal of opponents in the worst possible light. Even governments – and North Korea seems to be an example – may actively intensify the suffering of some regions in pursuit of international resources for areas with a high political priority. If all this were not bad enough, religious ideology has added another dangerous element to the mix: in Burma, it has helped to justify the oppression of Muslims; in Sudan, it has helped to justify the starvation of non-Muslims (and even, bizarrely, of Muslims in rebel areas); and in Afghanistan, the Taliban have imposed draconian restrictions on women's access to employment, education, health care and even humanitarian relief.

It is one thing to condemn the use of hunger as a weapon; quite another to recognise that you yourself (or a government you support) may also be manipulating hunger for political purposes.

International sanctions on Iraq have led to enormous human suffering. Before the oil-for-food deal was finally struck with Baghdad in May 1996, Unicef and the World Food Programme estimated that 4,500 children were dying from lack of food every month. In the case of Rwandan refugees in Zaire in 1996–97, international relief was quite inadequate and mortality rates were extremely high. Whilst it is true that the refugees were being used as pawns of Hutu extremists who were responsible for genocide and were recovering in Zaire with the help of international aid, can this justify the gross insufficiency of relief to what were seen, in some quarters, as 'pariah' refugees? In Sierra Leone, after a military junta seized power in May 1997, blocking humanitarian aid became, in practice, part of the international sanctions against the regime.

The issue is hardly a simple one. Sanctions – as the book acknowledges – are an alternative to war. They seemed to work in South Africa. And in the case of Iraq, some of the responsibility for the suffering of Iraqis lies with the manipulation of this suffering by Saddam Hussein, who for a long time refused to accept food and medical aid as 'humanitarian exceptions' to the sanctions whilst simultaneously imposing his own embargo on the Kurdish north. Moreover, throwing aid at abusive regimes or factions may reinforce their power and reinvigorate their abuses.

Even so, the book makes a strong case for looking again at the morality – and efficacy – of sanctions. It is particularly critical of the withholding of relief assistance, arguing that this is contrary to international law. And it points out that sanctions may bring political as well as human costs: elites may flourish both politically and economically not only despite sanctions but also because of them. Control of smuggling can be very profitable. And the control of the media can allow an autocratic ruler (a Slobodan Milosovic or a Saddam Hussein) to pose as the saviour of his people in the face of an international 'conspiracy'.

If anything, the thawing of the Cold War has encouraged the use of hunger as a weapon, as civil wars have increasingly funded themselves through attacks on civilians and as ideological agendas have dovetailed into theft, organised crime and the manipulation of scarcity and aid.

Yet at the same time, public cereal stocks have been declining, with production falling in the former eastern bloc and, simultaneously, the EC following the US policy of reducing agricultural subsidies. Funding for emergency relief has been cut significantly. And these trends appear to have encouraged an increasing international indifference to suffering and malnutrition in countries with long-standing crises such as Somalia, as well as to more dramatic crises such as those in Zaire. It has become increasingly tempting for international donors to withhold food on the grounds that it is fuelling local abuses. While this book provides no easy answers, it will make a vital contribution if it helps to raise awareness that hunger is being manipulated for political ends, perhaps not least by those surprisingly close to home.

DAVID KEEN
(Author of *The Benefits of Famine: Famine and Relief in Southwestern Sudan, 1983–89*, Princeton, 1994)

Foreword

The present book forms the first 'Geopolitics of Hunger' report which will in future be published by Action Against Hunger on an annual basis. It is the fruit of a joint effort by all the organisation's members and, as such, has the characteristic of not having been written by professional researchers (as a result of which, there may be certain imperfections which we hope you will forgive). Instead, the book has been written by both men and women from the field, those working in countries where hunger has struck and running programmes aiming to eradicate it, and often faced with hypocrisy or deliberate actions to impede their work by those in whose interest it is that hunger persists.

We have chosen to give this first report the subtitle 'Using Hunger as a Weapon', for as our volunteers have unfortunately and all too often realised, the suffering of hunger victims is not the result of chance. It is the result of a deliberate process undertaken for geopolitical and economic reasons, and aimed at placing certain populations in a situation of extreme poverty and dependence. The question, then, is what can be done in view of such base behaviour? How can we accept that such suffering be inflicted on human beings when we have the effective and technical means with which to alleviate it? Rather, the issue is one of finding a strategy that allows us to act effectively but without playing into the hands of such hangmen.

This book, then, presents a series of analyses made by our volunteers – whether doctors, nutritionists, agronomists or hydrologists – of a number of 'hunger-stricken countries', those on which a certain light can be shed. Having fought in these countries for months on end so as to run their programmes, these volunteers have provided us with their own framework of analysis and their own conclusions, based on personal experience. A number of jurists, economists and political experts were also keen to support our efforts by contributing to this first report, both enriching it and further developing the analyses in it. For this, we would like to thank them very much.

No doubt the reader will have realised by now that this report does not claim to be exhaustive; it does not claim to be a 'directory' of world hunger, nor a country-by-country description of the different forms of malnutrition afflicting each. Other institutions, such as Unicef, the United Nations Development Programme (UNDP), the World Food Programme (WFP) or the European Commission, with all of whom we work in partnership, would be much better placed than Action Against Hunger to provide such documents to those wishing to have the full statistics at their fingertips.

The sustainable removal of hunger from the planet cannot, in effect, be the task of one lone humanitarian organisation, nor for that matter of several organisations united by the same cause. Only the firm determination of States from both the North and the South can possibly put an end to the scandals caused by famines. Only through their support for the efforts of major organisations working for global co-operation, and only through their implementation of mechanisms to effectively sanction the hangmen, can this be done. Unfortunately, however, States remain insensitive to a number of human tragedies unless public opinion is mobilised, unless it shows compassion and its desire for justice. As sentries of hunger, humanitarian organisations have a role to play in fostering such mobilisation – by issuing warnings and by furnishing explanations. We hope that this report will make its own modest contribution.

JOSÉ BIDEGAIN AND JEAN-LUC BODIN

PART 1
CURRENT FAMINES

Emergency situations

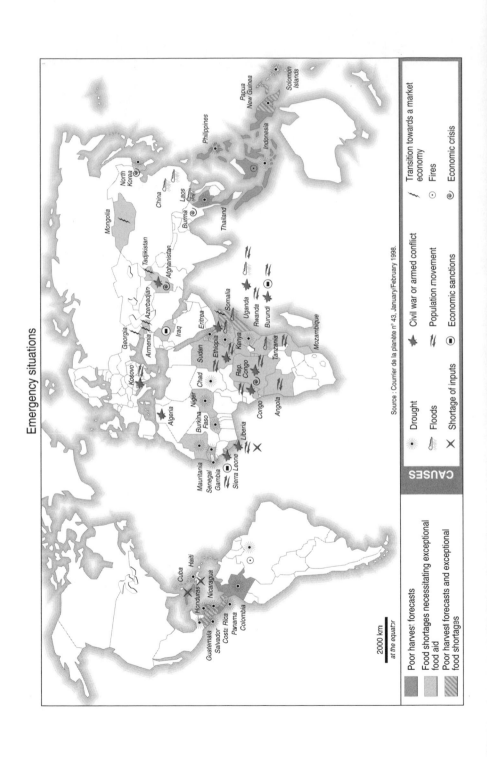

Source : *Courrier de la planète nº 43, January/February 1998.*

CAUSES

☀ Drought	✹ Civil war or armed conflict	∿ Transition towards a market economy
🌡 Floods	⫶ Population movement	⊙ Fires
✕ Shortage of inputs	Ⅰ Economic sanctions	ⓔ Economic crisis

Poor harvest: forecasts

Food shortages necessitating exceptional food aid

Poor harvest forecasts and exceptional food shortages

2000 km
at the equator

The new geopolitics of hunger

SYLVIE BRUNEL

The 'geopolitics of hunger'. This was the eye-catching title of a book published almost 50 years ago by a Brazilian doctor, Josué de Castro. The book deplored the injustices suffered by some sectors of the population, essentially deprived of access to food for political reasons. The analysis remains relevant today, both in Brazil (source of the original inspiration) and elsewhere. Far from being explained by over-population or a lack of food, hunger is due to the inability of certain groups to obtain food due to unjust socio-economic structures – structures that are deliberately unjust.

Even today, nothing has changed in north-east Brazil. Each drought only reinforces the political power of those who rule, of those who oppose all structural reform for fear that this challenges the very foundations of their power. Similarly in the Amazon, the forest fires that cause misery and malnutrition among the indigenous Indians and small-scale settlers are a blessing for large landlords and businesses, who are allowed to move ever deeper into the forest and gain ever more land for livestock raising.

Today more than ever, hunger is a political weapon. The early warning systems that constantly monitor the state of the Earth, notably through satellite observations, should be able to warn of impending famines and to prevent droughts already predicted from generating widespread death, by sending food through targeted food distributions and by the establishment of effective preventative systems. There is enough food. In fact, to feed the world's population of six billion and given the resources that exist in most continents, there should even be enough food for tomorrow when population figures are expected to stabilise around 10–11 billion.

FAMINES THAT NO LONGER FALL FROM THE SKIES

Halting a famine becomes easy from the moment that action is made possible. Specialised humanitarian organisations such as Action Against

Hunger can 'rescue' a malnourished child in less than a month. Only they must be able to intervene in time. They must be able to reach the victims of hunger (that is, those forming the most vulnerable groups of a population – above all, minorities, and within these, women and children). And they must be able to work freely to ensure that the food aid definitely reaches those who are most in need.

Yet famines continue to decimate entire populations. The pages that follow describe some of those affecting a number of countries in 1998. And in this, there is no getting away from the fact that the conditions listed above, while apparently simple, are rarely all present. If they are, it takes time, and during this time, people die. That is to say, *some* people die, while others calculate the benefits to be had from their deaths, benefits which would allow them to negotiate their position, their power and their recognition.

No famine today occurs by chance. It is too simple to accuse destiny when people die of hunger or when help does not arrive in time to save them. It is too simple to accuse the devastation caused by climatic crisis, the consequences of overpopulation, the lack of food resources, the incompetence of local authorities or the inadequacy of local transport infrastructures. Obviously none of these factors facilitates the work of rescuers, and sometimes even prevents them from being as efficient as they might wish. However, they are never the real determinants. Nor do they ever suffice as an explanation of sudden mass starvation. Whenever action can be taken, tragedy can be averted.

If hunger is still a problem in this world of plenty, it is because it has become a weapon. Admittedly, this weapon has always been used by a number of governments and a number of armed movements – whether to eliminate irritating populations or to conquer land, often through the latter's destruction (scorched-earth policies). However, one would have hoped that with the end of the Cold War, such conflicts would have become something of the past: the world would be pacified and armed hostilities would end.

A SHORT TYPOLOGY OF FAMINES

Not only has none of this come true, but the rise in the use of humanitarian aid (a new form of aid 'by default', given the collapse in the geopolitical utility of public aid) has given rise to a new practice: the use of hunger as a weapon and a means to political recognition. It is no longer the enemy or those to be conquered who are starved, but rather the very population of those party to the conflict and wishing to benefit from it. This they can do through extensive media coverage and the concomitant international compassion thereby stirred – an inexhaustible source of money, food and political forums allowing them to exercise their claims. 'Charity-business' has, therefore, permitted hunger to become a weapon of war for movements deprived of their traditional geopolitical support and obliged to search for the means with which to perpetuate their struggle *in situ*.

After 20 years of existence, 20 years of fighting against hunger on all fronts, Action Against Hunger has had the time to put technical tools into place for fighting hunger (from treating the effects of malnutrition to reviving agricultural production). In addition, having come across so many famines and so much (often insensitive) manipulation of the starving, the organisation's field workers are now able to draw up a typology of famines as well. Based uniquely on those which have given grounds for intervention over the past year, a number may be identified.

'Classical' famines are created to eliminate 'irritating' members of the population. They have by no means disappeared but rather continue to wreak death – as in Sudan against the rebels of the south, or in Burma against minorities on the periphery. The situation is all the more insidious in Burma where forced labour and progressive deprivation have compelled families to emigrate in order to avoid starving to death – and this is helping the government in Rangoon to achieve its goals. The existence of such famines tends to be denied by those who organise them, up until the moment when the process takes on such proportions that it can no longer be concealed and its objectives already fulfilled: that is, the elimination of all those who represent an obstacle to the search for absolute power.

Other strategies are more recent, more perverse and also more subtle. They consist of 'exposing' the terrible drama of people suffering from hunger – people, in fact, who have deliberately been left to suffer from hunger in the pursuit of another cause. The origin of the Iraqi tragedy, for example, lies in the embargo having been lifted and the declaration of the government as a victim, when the latter has in fact refused to apply any measure that might mitigate its peoples' hardship. Sometimes, the method is exploited with even more insensitivity, with civilians being intentionally deprived of their means of subsistence through the destruction of their crops and a reign of terror in the countryside. Meanwhile, the towns in which they are forced to take refuge turn out to be traps to which food supplies cannot be guaranteed. Inevitably, when the situation reaches dramatic proportions, journalists are invited to discover the horrors (obviously attributed to the tragic consequences of war), and so mobilise international humanitarian aid. This aid is then meticulously diverted to feed the soldiers and support the war effort. Such famines, then, have quite literally been created in what are usually favourable natural environments. They are then exposed, as was the case in Liberia not so long ago (where, exhausted by the reign of terror and due to fears of a renewed upsurge of the war, the people ended up voting for their principal enemy), and as is the case at present in Sierra Leone, where those who control the rice distributions subsequently hold the reins of power.

Such a small typology of famines would not be complete without mentioning those that are most absurd. That is, those that result from the incompetence of governments blinded by ideology – whether that of communism as currently in North Korea (and previously in China, where the Great Leap Forward resulted in the death of 30 million people at the beginning of the 1960s), or that of Islamic fundamentalism as in Afghanistan, where thousands of households have been deprived of an income simply because they are female-headed.

As Josué de Castro once stated: 'It is not enough to produce food. Instead, it must be possible for this to be purchased and consumed by those in need.' Today, the evolution of the world food situation makes this proposition all the more relevant. As we will see in the last part of the book, the use of hunger as a weapon does not exist only within the new conflicts of poor countries. It is increasingly coming to the forefront in the relationship between North and South, with the depletion of wheat stocks and their privatisation, and with the growing dependence of the South on food imports – for all of which the North holds the key.

At the dawn of the 21st century, a new geopolitics of hunger is beginning to take shape, making reflection on the ethics of North-South relations and on new forms of co-operation all the more urgent. Consideration needs also to be given to respect by humanitarian NGOs for principles of action making them all the more aware of attempts to divert their assistance and to effectively counter the strategies of – as Ahmedou Ould Abdallah put it – these 'new pharaohs who are starving their people'. The right to food must be defended more than ever.

Food and terror in Sierra Leone

PASCAL LEFORT
JONATHAN LITTELL

Chronology

27 April 1961	Sierra Leone achieves independence
1968	Siaka Stevens comes to power
1985	Siaka Stevens hands power over to his chef d'état-major, General Joseph
23 March 1991	First RUF offensive in Kailahun district, Eastern province
29 April 1992	Military coup d'état. Captain Valentine Strasser takes power at the head of the NPRC
16 January 1996	Valentine Strasser is 'gently' overthrown by General Julius Maada Bio who promises to set the path for a transition to democracy
15 March 1996	Ahmad Tejan Kabbah is democratically elected as President of Sierra Leone
26 March 1996	Ceasefire agreement between the RUF and the armed forces of Sierra Leone
25 May 1997	Military coup d'état. President Kabbah flees to Guinea. Establishment of a military junta, the AFRC, led by Major Johny Paul Koromah
28–29 August 1997	ECOWAS summit in Abuja. Implementation of an embargo on Sierra Leone
23 October 1997	Conakry Accords provide for the return to power of President Kabbah on 22 April 1998
6 February 1998	Launch of the ECOMOG offensive on Freetown. Flight of the junta
10 March 1998	Return of President Kabbah to Freetown

Sierra Leone

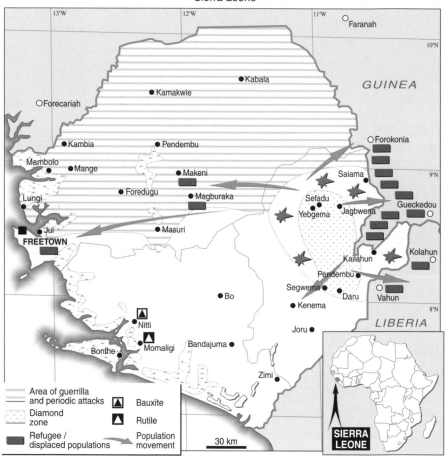

13°W   12°W   11°W

○ Faranah

10°N

GUINEA

● Kabala

● Kamakwie

○ Forecariah

● Kambia   ● Pendembu

Mambolo

● Mange   ● Makeni

Lungi   ● Foredugu   ● Magburaka

● Jui

FREETOWN

● Masuri

○ Forokonia

Saiama ●

9°N

Sefadu

Yebgema   Jagbwena

Gueckedou ○

Kolahun ○

Kailahun ●

Pendembu ●

Segwema ●   Daru ●   Vahun ○

● Bo

LIBERIA

8°N

▲ Nitti

▲ Momaligi

Bandajuma ●

Bonthe ●

● Kenema

Joru ●

Zimi ●

Legend	
Area of guerrilla and periodic attacks	▲ Bauxite
Diamond zone	▲ Rutile
Refugee / displaced populations	Population movement

30 km

SIERRA LEONE

'Rice is a weapon of war'
Ahmad Tejan Kabbah
President of Sierra Leone, February 1998

In Sierra Leone, nothing relating to food is innocent: whether humanitarian organisations want it or not, they always become ensnared in the games played by those around them. From August 1997 until February 1998 (when Freetown was 'liberated' by ECOMOG's Nigerian troops and the democratically elected President Ahmad Tejan Kabbah returned to power), Sierra Leone was subject to a total embargo imposed by ECOWAS. Although the texts clearly made provisions for the exemption of humanitarian aid (the free passage of food, according to the principle of the 'filtering embargo'), not one sack of food was able to be transported to the country during this period. The Guinean authorities who were entrusted with supervising this free passage always found a reason to block it: delays due to administrative obstacles, procedural problems requiring clarification and so on. Should this have been seen as a deliberate strategy or simply an accumulation of circumstances and incompetence? The United Nations, while still protesting, has seemed more than happy to accept the second hypothesis. The fall of the military junta, however, has put an end to a farce that was on the verge of becoming a tragedy. The results remain to be seen.

This said, in Sierra Leone political manipulation of food aid is not new. However, before looking at the embargo, certain basic principles might be remembered.

SIAKA STEVENS AND THE APC:
FOOD AS AN INSTRUMENT OF POWER

In the majority of African countries, clientelism – that is, privileged relationships between patron and client with the extension of this network across a whole society – forms the basis of power. Whether displayed beneath the banner of democracy or of Marxism, whether the 'great leader' is the author of a military coup or one of the IMF's best pupils selected in accordance to rules, the method and the model of governance tend to remain the same. In most of these countries, behind the façade that is presented to the West, one tends to find the same 'networks linking informal business and politics' that William Reno describes as the *Shadow*

State.[1] Sierra Leone, under the regime of Siaka Stevens and his successor Joseph Momoh, has seen itself became quietly but systematically and completely gangrened by this Shadow State. This to the point that the country has become nothing more than an empty shell that a group of officers, hardly beyond adolescence, would be able to crush between two fingers – for mere distraction.

The two principal forces of this Shadow State, the fuel that ran the engine, were diamonds and food, more specifically white rice, 'the medium of exchange for a client state'.[2]

Corruption, under the regime, can be understood not only as the thirst for personal enrichment, but also as the accumulation of resources with a view to redistribution. At the lower end of the scale, the civil servant or the policeman receiving his *kidogo* or his daily *tchai* has to feed a whole network of relatives: his immediate family, his brothers- and sisters-in-law, his cousins and so on. At the intermediate level, a local politician will base his power on the allocation of jobs, exploitation licences and payments to dozens of similar subordinates. The same applies at the national level, ministerial and presidential. 'A personal fortune', according to Richards, is 'a political bank account.'[3] The political elite gains and maintains power by building up a network of clients across the country, people whose own economic survival entirely depends on the length of time their patron remains in power. And the patron, this 'Big Man', not only has to ensure a maximum redistribution of any resources under his control, but also needs to verify that no-one is either treated unfavourably or offended (should they then turn against him) and, above all, that his source does not run dry.

In Sierra Leone, as in Zaire, the system was pushed to the extreme by President Siaka Stevens and his All-People's Congress (APC). Stevens (after a turbulent period during which his election was revoked by a military coup d'état, itself soon overthrown) came to power in 1968. To do this, he drew on the support of client networks that had been established in regions later neglected by his predecessors from the Sierra Leone People's Party (SLPP), who subsequently gained the support of the Mende

1. William Reno; 1995; *Corruption and State Politics in Sierra Leone*; Cambridge University Press, Cambridge, UK; p. 8.
2. Paul Richards; 1996; *Fighting for the Rain Forest, War, Youth and Resources in Sierra Leone*; James Currey/Heinemann, Oxford, UK.; p. 158.
3. Richards, *op cit.*, p. 35.

ethnic minority (Sir Milton Margai, President of Independence, and his brother Albert, in particular).[4] The interested reader might refer to the book by William Reno for details about the extraordinary deals between local politicians, Lebanese negotiators, foreign companies and the IMF/UNDP, organised by Stevens in order to construct his Shadow State. What concerns us here, however, is the introduction into the circuit of rice, more specifically white rice, the 'political food' of Sierra Leone, as it was called by one of Stevens' ministers.[5]

Rice – that is, locally grown brown rice – is the staple food in the region. However, the massive demand for labour power generated by the relatively crude exploitation of diamond fields in the east and south of the country (the principal source of revenue for Stevens' regime) has caused an 'exodus of miners', so significantly diminishing the labour available for agriculture. Hence, as Richards remarks: 'One of the major interventions of the State consisted in ensuring cheap rice imports from abroad.'[6] This white rice, mainly from South-East Asia, was redistributed in several ways.

Direct distributions occurred firstly to the miners, so as to guarantee the flow of diamonds, then to the security forces and members of the police, and finally to the civil servants whose dependence on rice had grown as a result of the economic recession that had hit the country at the end of the 1970s. In 1982, Stevens even resorted to paying civil servants in kind (in rice, of course) so as to compensate for State budget deficiencies.

The remainder of the rice was put, in large quantities and at subsidised prices, at the disposal of Stevens' political clients (and later those of Momoh). Ministers, members of parliament, merchants and senior officers all gained considerably, reselling the rice at market prices through a vast network of small *traders*. Certain more impressive aspects of this '*politique du ventre*', as J-F. Bayart has called it,[7] should not be ignored, among them the whole drama that surrounded the distributions and forms one of the keys to understanding the embargo.

Thus, the murmurs of discontent among the urban population impoverished by the recession were appeased through rice distributions. In this, Stevens is a 'Crafty Old Man [who] emphasises his personal control,

4. This privileged relationship between the SLPP and the Mende was seen again with the arrival in power of A.T. Kabbah, in 1996, with the same kickbacks as a result.
5. Reno, *op. cit.*, p.144.
6. Richards, *op. cit.*, p.51.
7. Quite literally: 'politics of the stomach'. J-F. Bayart; 1989; *L'État en Afrique*; Fayard, Paris; p. 257.

reveals his munificence [in] distributing rice and money to the suppli-
cants.'[8] By doing this, concludes Richards: 'The government of the APC
locked itself into a cycle of dependence on diamonds and white rice.'[9] This
dependence was made all the more important by the automatic effect that
such massive imports of subsidised rice had on national production.
Unable to counter this unfair competition, national production declined,
resulting in the impoverishment of the rural population.

This is what ultimately led to the fall of the APC regime. In 1991,
enraged by the support offered by Momoh to ECOMOG, the Liberian war
leader, Charles Taylor, decided to destabilise the regime by forming a
guerrilla movement in the east of Sierra Leone. This was to be the Rebel
United Front (RUF) of ex-corporal Foday Sankoh which soon managed to
distance itself from its Liberian sponsors and become an effective rebel
movement. Among the RUF's principal targets were, of course, the diamond
fields. Faced with the degree of violence adopted by the RUF, the APC's last
source of income rapidly whithered away, and with it, easy access to
subsidised rice. Humanitarian aid was to take its place, but too late for
Momoh, who was easily overthrown in April 1992 by a group of young
officers who had come to Freetown to protest against the non-payment of
army wages and material conditions at the front.

FODAY SANKOH AND THE RUF: FOOD AND TERROR

Self-proclaimed hero of the struggle for democracy and the fight against
the corruption and clientelism of the APC regime, Foday Sankoh hoped to
rally the populations to the east of the country to his cause. However, the
atrocities committed by RUF fighters (and notably by the Liberian and
Burkinian mercenaries who joined them) were soon to alienate him from
civilian support. Without the active support of the population and without
external backing (as from the end of 1992, the border zone with Liberia
came under the control of the hostile ULIMO faction), the RUF rapidly
abandoned all ideas of controlling and administering territories. Instead, it
adopted a guerrilla strategy based on the movement's capacity to withdraw
into the depths of the forests, on preying on rural communities and on
destabilising the private economy. The strategy drew its strength from the

8. Reno, *op. cit.*, p. 143.
9. Richards, *op. cit.*, p. 51.

break-up of fighters into small groups benefiting from a significant degree of autonomy and from systematic recourse to terror as a weapon of war.

All too often described as free, terror is used by the RUF as an instrument of control and propaganda. It forms the axis of the movement's bid to procure food from rural communities which, quite naturally, do not support it. Beyond this coercion, the extent of the violence committed also acts to deter resistance, although assailants tend to be few and poorly equipped.

In this, the burning of houses represents a double threat: not only the loss of a shelter, but just as often the loss of food and any hidden seeds as well. As a result, food security is compromised for two seasons. Similarly, at the end of 1994, the amputation campaign waged against women involved in harvesting rice in the Mayamba district was implemented essentially with a view to expropriating the crops, but also to scar the women for the rest of their lives. The impact was immediate: the harvesting stopped even in villages where amputations had not taken place. The crops were these communities' only means of subsistence and self-sufficiency, and the ability to store seeds was a further and crucial precondition of their survival. The RUF employed the same strategy on the eve of the elections at the end of 1995, amputating the hands of potential voters as a way of demonstrating their outright rejection of the elections. After having been ousted from power by ECOMOG troops in February 1998, the RUF once more reverted to barbaric practices. In attacking isolated villages in the north, it combined a scorched-earth policy with massacre, rape, amputation and the destruction of villages by fire. This time, the message was even more explicit: 'Remember that the RUF is here and ask ECOMOG to return your hands.' Once again, these atrocities led to huge population movement.

Beyond being for the procurement of food, the RUF uses terror to chase rural populations from supposedly hostile areas, or from areas of strategic interest, towards the large urban conglomerations. It is also used to erode these people's confidence in a government incapable of guaranteeing their security (Bo, 1995, for instance) or to counter ECOMOG's claims to victory (1998, for example). There is also an internal objective. In view of the iron discipline imposed on combatants, the terror to which communities are subject provides a clear indication to any potential deserters that the situation is not much better in the villages.

But the struggle for power equally involves weakening the adversary. The clientelist system established by Siaka Stevens, and which proved more than a match for the clean-up desires of the NPRC regime under

Captain Valentine Strasser, is very much dependent on the private economy for its survival. To attack the latter, then, is to attack the very foundations of power. By concentrating its offensive on the country's eastern area, the RUF primarily tried to target the diamond fields in Kono and Tongo Field districts. Driven out of Koidu in 1993, and then held at bay from the main diamond-mining areas due to the deployment of foreign mercenaries (British and then South African), the RUF eventually came to attack the weakest link in the chain: food imports. Attacks were then concentrated on the food convoys that brought rice from Freetown to the major towns of the east.

For reasons of a complex mechanism of compensation, the exploitation of diamonds and the trading of imported rice are closely linked. Faced with a chronic currency shortage on the foreign-exchange markets, the work of rice importers and diamond dealers is complementary. Rice importers, whose merchandise is paid for mostly in local currency, are in desperate need of foreign exchange to pay their foreign suppliers. Diamond dealers, on the other hand, require the local currency, Leones, to pay prospectors for the stones collected; yet the sale of their diamonds results in an income in a foreign currency that cannot be repatriated since most stones are exported illicitly. In the field, Lebanese traders tend to hold both functions concurrently, acting, moreover, as 'bankers' for prospectors by offering them food and equipment as credit in return for promises to sell their stones. By blocking rice imports, diamond mining thus becomes paralysed.

Despite a well-functioning strategy and an exceptional capacity for survival, the reappearance of the RUF in 1994–95 cannot be attributed to their military prowess alone. Although the army enjoyed the support of several hundred mercenaries from South Africa's 'Executive Outcomes', at the end of 1994 the town of Bo came under direct threat from the RUF, with announcements that the rebels were less than 20 km away from Freetown. Throughout the conflict, the role of the military was more than ambiguous, making the war something of an enormous fool's game – a huge game of deceit – in which civilians became both spectators and victims.

THE NPRC AND THE 'SOBELS' PHENOMENON: FOOD AND PILLAGING

The arrival in power of the young officers of the NPRC on 29 April 1992 should have put a rapid end to the war. This at least was one of the main objectives of the new President, 27-year-old Captain Valentine Strasser, heir to a power vacuum left by President Momoh who had fled to Guinea as soon as the first shots had been fired. Five years later, on the 25 May 1997, President Kabbah (democratically elected only one year earlier) was overthrown by an alliance between the military and RUF rebels. For most, this represented the explosion into broad daylight of a masquerade that had begun in 1992, at the expense of the civilian population.

Having come to power with the firm intention of putting an end to the corruption undermining the State and to the clientelism of the APC regime, the NPRC was soon confronted by dissension within the army. The increasingly ostentatious accumulation of wealth by the junta's leaders, busy reaping the dividends to be had from diamond exploitation, stood in stark contrast to the living conditions of their somewhat abandoned soldiers. The Sobel phenomenon emerged as a result of this double dichotomy: the junta's leaders had too much to lose from a transition to democracy, while the soldiers had no other choice but to survive by preying on civilian populations and concluding local agreements with RUF rebels. Attacks by the RUF on garrisons that were well armed multiplied and, each time, substantial stocks of arms and ammunition disappeared. At the same time, atrocities on the roads and in the villages increased to the extent that it was not possible to attribute all of these to the RUF. The phenomenon, then, had been magnified by the presence of volunteers (often very young boys) among the military who, generally lacking status, had no other means of survival than pillaging. As of 1994, the Sobel phenomenon began to intensify, with the distinction between RUF rebels and disaffected soldiers becoming ever more confused. As a result, civilian self-defence militia groups began to spring up in the north and south of the country. Organised around the traditional hunting groups of the Mende ethnic minority, the Kamajors, they aimed to protect communities from the atrocities committed not only by the RUF but also by the military.

The tragic deterioration in the humanitarian situation in 1995 provided terrible evidence of the connivance between the rebels and the military.

At the beginning of 1995, an estimated one and a half million people were found to be displaced in the Sierra Leonean interior. In the province of the south, the RUF rebels had been imposing a reign of terror for over one year – the amputation of hands providing the most striking evidence of this. Guerrilla tactics such as this led to an abrupt fall in agricultural production and large-scale migration towards the regional capital, the town of Bo, where the displaced population found itself gathered into camps thrown up around the periphery. The town was also subject to a blockade, although cereal supplies were vital to its survival. The multiplication of attacks on the Freetown-Mile 91-Bo Road quickly became more of an organised racket. For example, on New Year's Eve 1995, when rebel pressure on Bo was at its height, the military succeeded in entering a convoy of 53 trucks of rice and fish into the town. Transporters admit to having been paid by the military for free passage. Yet the level of confiscation and destruction of convoys was such that transporters had to suspend their activities. In parallel, NPRC confiscation of much of the income from diamond mining (given its anxiety over maintaining tight control over rice sales – with price controls being instituted at the peak of the crisis in August 1995) caused a sharp decline in the amount of imported rice available in the interior and aggravated the food crisis. At the height of the crisis 7,000 children, of which 1,000 were severely malnourished, were treated by Action Against Hunger. During this time, sacks of rice that had been stolen on the roads – some still stained with blood – could be found in the markets in the diamond-mining areas.

KABBAH, ECOWAS AND THE UNITED NATIONS: FOOD AS AN INSTRUMENT FOR RECONQUERING POWER

Democratically elected on 15 March 1996, President Ahmad Tejan Kabbah swore the oath two weeks later. As a former senior civil servant of the UN, he was expected to reconcile Sierra Leoneans. However, despite a ceasefire agreement with the RUF, fighting continued and Kabbah, lacking confidence in his army, instead reinforced the Kamajor militia groups, appointing their leader, Inga Norman, as Vice-Minister of Defence. At the same time he revived traditional SLPP networks, promoting the Mende populations in the south. On 25 May 1997, he was overthrown by a military coup d'état which forced him into exile in Guinea.

An attempt by ECOMOG troops based in Freetown at a counter coup d'état was immediately put down by the officers of the military coup, grouped within the Armed Forces Ruling Council (AFRC). They soon received the backing of the RUF. The Nigerians, meanwhile, poorly prepared and badly equipped, were driven back with a resounding echo and heavy losses to bases in Lungi and Jui, from where the junta never managed to dislodge them. Over the following weeks, Freetown was looted. With the exception of MSF and the ICRC, both of which left a few expatriates in Freetown, humanitarian workers were evacuated 'en masse'. Action Against Hunger returned two months later to re-open its bases in

Freetown, Bo and Makeni and remained one of the only NGOs to have a permanent expatriate presence in Sierra Leone throughout the AFRC period.

On 26 June, the 14 member States of ECOWAS gathered together in Conakry to discuss the situation in Sierra Leone. The final communiqué issued from the Conference stated that the principal objective was: 'the rapid return to power of the legitimate government of President Kabbah'. Three types of measures were envisaged to achieve this objective: dialogue, the imposition of sanctions and an embargo, and the use of force. A Committee of Four (C4), comprising Nigeria, Guinea, Côte d'Ivoire and Ghana, was established to follow the situation and implement the chosen measures (the Committee was later enlarged to include Liberia).[10]

However, a legal framework for the embargo was not drawn up until the end of August. The resolution adopted by the Heads of State and ECOWAS' governing body was harsh: in addition to a total embargo on 'the export of all goods to Sierra Leone' (Article 4), it stipulated that: 'Member States would neither send nor deliver humanitarian items to the illegal regime, unless with the authorisation...of ECOWAS' (Article 5).[11] Anxious to obtain the approval of the international community for this, ECOWAS turned to the UN Security Council to support and confirm its decision.

On 8 October 1997, the Security Council voted in Resolution 1132 on Sierra Leone. The text, without explicitly endorsing the embargo decreed by ECOWAS, expressed 'strong support for the efforts of ECOWAS in the resolution of the crisis in Sierra Leone' (Article 3). The Resolution then reiterated a number of the sanctions declared in the ECOWAS resolution, including a ban on the import of fuel, weapons and ammunition, and the suspension of visas for members of the junta and their families. Article 8 delegated the application of these sanctions to ECOWAS. Lastly, Article 14 stipulated that: 'All those concerned, including ECOWAS, the UN and other international humanitarian agencies, should establish appropriate arrangements for the provision of humanitarian aid, and ensure that this aid responds to local needs and is delivered and used in all security by the beneficiaries targeted.'[12]

Despite this clear distinction and irrespective of the evaluation mission sent by the UN Department of Humanitarian Affairs (OCHA) to Conakry,

10. UNDHA; 2 July 1997; *Sierra Leone Humanitarian Situation Report;* ref. DHAGVA – 97/0239.
11. ECOWAS; 28–29 August 1997; *Decision on Sanctions Against the Junta in Sierra Leone.*
12. *Security Council Resolution 1132 (1997) on the Situation in Sierra Leone*; 8 October 1997.

humanitarian organisations never obtained the authorisation necessary to transport their assistance to Sierra Leone, while the trucks of Lebanese or Sierra Leonean merchants passed through, with rice, other food, fuel, etc.

Mainly targeted were food distributions. Since food affected the very nerve-centre of power as conceived in Sierra Leone, it was also a major stake in the legitimisation of parties claiming power. Unable to distribute food directly, as during the golden age of Stevens, the warring parties expropriated humanitarian food distributions as a way of demonstrating to the people their capacity to provide them with food and, by implication, their legitimacy. Hence, it was normal that President Kabbah did not want his people to receive a single sack of food which could not be credited to him. The junta played the same game by banking upon, after the first few months, the honest collaboration of NGOs and by using the radio to publicise the distributions undertaken.

President Kabbah made it quite clear, declaring to the press: 'The embargo will be lifted once I return to the country...this is all part of the suffering that [my people] must endure in order to drive out the junta.'[13] Those around him were even more explicit: when a journalist from AFP described to one of them the situation in the capital, the latter simply replied: 'So much the better...in suffering, they will learn not to question us.'[14] On the other side, the message was clear and well understood. 'I believe that our enemies want to use rice as a political weapon to give a bad image of our government and the impression that we are incapable of providing the people with the essentials,' Lieutenant Colonel Eldred Collins, Minister of Trade for the AFRC and number three within the RUF, declared to an AFP reporter.[15]

During a meeting with the UN evaluation mission, President Kabbah went on to drive the message home: 'In Sierra Leone rice is used as a weapon of war.'[16]

The blocking of food aid during President Kabbah's period of exile had a somewhat curious but logical corollary: from the moment he was restored to power, food had to arrive quickly and in waves. Before fighting had even come to an end in Freetown, not just President Kabbah, but also the UN Special Envoy, Francis Okelo, together with the British Ambassador, Peter

13. AFP; 13 November 1997; *Bulletin Quotidien de l'Afrique*; no. 15077.
14. *Ibid.*
15. AFP; 8 December 1997; *BQA*; no. 15093.
16. UN Security Council; 10 February 1998; *Interim Report...*; p. 4.

Penfold, stepped up calls to UN and NGO humanitarian agencies urging them to effect a general distribution in Freetown as soon as possible, a distribution which was, according to information collected by Action Against Hunger, not only useless, but even harmful to the local economy.

The manifest opportunism of the President and his allies scandalised the humanitarian community, with agencies soon deciding, on the proposal of Action Against Hunger, to limit food distributions to those most vulnerable in the town. The same approach was taken following ECOMOG's capture of the country's principal towns; the British government, meanwhile, went as far as to put a military helicopter at the disposal of humanitarian agencies so as to transport food to the towns of Bo and Kenema, which had remained loyal to President Kabbah.

In this, the more 'dramatic' aspect (to take up the point made by Richards) of the food distribution, as of the embargo, can be seen. Rather than acting as a means of economic pressure, or conversely, as concrete help, the two operations were *gestures*, demonstrations that were strongly symbolic. In the eyes of the people, power resides in the one who gives or holds back the food. The equation *no Kabbah = no food; Kabbah = food* had to be hammered into the head of each Sierra Leonean.

In this enterprise, President Kabbah was able to take advantage of British Government support and of his privileged relations within the UN. From the moment the coup d'état took place, Britain was at his side, supplying him with the means to establish a government-in-exile and a secret radio station near Freetown, whilst also promising to secure political support within the UN. At the same time, the British decided to play the humanitarian card: immediately after the coup, the government announced the suspension of all its aid programmes to Sierra Leone. On 6 June 1997, a group of British NGOs addressed a letter to Clare Short, Secretary of State for International Development, requesting clarification on 'the present policy of the Department for International Development (DfID) on funds for humanitarian aid in Sierra Leone'.[17]

Clare Short replied: 'Existing plans for co-operation in development, put into place with the government of President Kabbah, will not be continued under present circumstances.' As for humanitarian aid as such, this depended on security conditions: 'We must be sure that the aid will not

---

17. CARE UK *et al.*; 6 June 1997; letter to Clare Short, Secretary of State for International Development.

be diverted or used in such a way as to prolong the current crisis.'[18] In fact, not one evaluation of humanitarian aid was made by DfID throughout the crisis. 'As from October,' explained one official from the Foreign Office involved in the Sierra Leone crisis, 'Ambassador Penfold has decided that humanitarian aid should be blocked. NGO activities should be discouraged.'[19] However, as soon as ECOMOG launched its attack on Freetown, a delegate from DfID arrived in Conakry to assess the needs and the conditions for a resumption in aid. It was later discovered that London's commitment to President Kabbah also extended to military support of his movement, in violation of the embargo imposed on Sierra Leone.

'In practice,' says Philippa Atkinson *'humanitarian aid became part of the sanctions. The cancellation by DfID of the majority of its funding to British NGOs, the restriction of UN operations by a top security rating, and the holding up of cross-border deliveries of relief goods due to 'administrative' difficulties, demonstrate the united stance of the international community on this issue.'*[20]

To be fair, the position of the international community, within ECOWAS as much as within the UN, was far from being unanimous, but before such hawks no-one was able to impose an alternative solution. The UN agencies opposed to the *de facto* blockade of humanitarian aid were unable to take any action due to a permanent *security rating* of phase 5, prohibiting the presence of expatriate personnel in the field. Despite the somewhat late despatch of an evaluation mission to assess humanitarian needs, the importance of the Department of Political Affairs and the UNDP – where President Kabbah enjoyed widespread support – relative to the Department of Humanitarian Affairs was interred, with alarmist reports from the WFP or Unicef changing nothing.

In Sierra Leone, humanitarian food aid was thus deliberately checked for eight months, quite clearly due to the will of President Kabbah, but also due to ECOWAS, ECOMOG and the Guinean government – and due to Britain and a part of the UN system as well. The fact that Kabbah and his regional colleagues used 'rice as a weapon of war', even if unacceptable, might almost seem normal: his adversaries did not do much better. However, UN participation in such manipulation represents an attack on the principles of neutrality and impartiality on which humanitarian aid is

18. Clare Short; 21 June 1997; letter to Will Day, Chief Executive, CARE UK.
19. Private telephone conversation with the authors.
20. Philippa Atkinson; 1998; *Sierra Leone: an Attack on Humanitarianism*; RRN No. 10; p. 3.

founded. Some within the UN are conscious of this problem and are trying to learn from the consequences. But their opinions are hard to swallow. By manipulating humanitarian aid, or by tacitly complying with such manipulation, the UN has simply allowed its moral authority to sap away.

The Great Lakes tragedy

Rwanda

SYLVIE BRUNEL

CHRONOLOGY OF A PLANNED AND PROGRAMMED GENOCIDE

– *One single nation, two antagonistic peoples*. Hutus and Tutsis have always lived together and spoken the same language, Kynarwanda. The distinction between the Tutsi nobility, considered to be a race of Hamitic lords originally from Egypt, and the Hutu 'people' believed to be of Bantu origin only emerged during the course of Belgian colonisation after 1900. Rwandan identity cards institutionalised this ethnic divide for 60 years, distinguishing Hutus (who made up 85% of the population before the genocide in 1994) from Tutsis (14%) and Twas (1%). In the 1950s, however, having always been dependent on Tutsi support, the Belgians turned against the latter when they began agitating for freedom from colonial rule. When the country achieved independence, power was therefore handed over to the Hutus. In 1959, 1963–64, 1973 and 1990, anti-Tutsi 'pogroms' caused mass migration to neighbouring countries, particularly Uganda.

– *The Tutsi offensive*. In October 1990, the Rwandan Patriotic Front (RPF), including the Ugandan Tutsi refugees who had helped President Museveni come to power in 1986, launched an offensive aimed at reconquering Rwanda. On the basis of military cooperation agreements concluded between the French government and the Rwandan government under Juvenal Habyarimana (in power since 1973), France supported the Rwandan government's forces in its efforts to drive the assailants back, also helping to train Forces Armées Rwandaises (FAR) soldiers. Under the operation code-named 'Noroît', some 700 French soldiers were mobilised between 1990 and 1993. According to initial results from the Parliamentary fact-finding commission, the operation was steered directly by the French government, as indeed were all relations between France and Rwanda, notably at the time of the 1994 genocide. In 1993, as the RPF reached the outskirts of Kigali, thousands of people were displaced due to fighting in the north.

– Under pressure from the international community, France in particular, a peace agreement was concluded between the RPF, the Rwandan government and the opposition in Arusha on 4 August 1993. The agreements were to pave the way for a government of national reconciliation together with elections monitored by the United Nations. The UN Assistance Mission to Rwanda (UNAMIR) was deployed in Rwanda with some 3,000 soldiers, but ethnic tensions remained strong, with certain media organisations, among them the Radio Television Libre des Milles Collines (RTLMC), continuing to transmit hostile anti-Tutsi propaganda. The result was mounting violence, while NGOs and local Rwandan organisations vainly tried to warn the international community of looming tragedy.

– *Planned genocide.* On 6 April 1994, the Rwandan president and his Burundi counterpart, Cyprien Ntaryamira, were killed. Their plane, returning from a regional summit on the Rwandan and Burundi crises in Dar-es-Salaam, was shot down by rockets just as it was about to land in Kigali. The incident, the perpetrators of which have yet to be identified (the RPF? Hutu extremists rejecting the Arusha peace agreements?), gave the signal for an organised massacre of Tutsis and moderate Hutus across the country. Ten Belgian Blue Helmet soldiers were assassinated by the Presidential guard as they vainly tried to protect the Prime Minister, a moderate Hutu. Both the Interhamwe (extremist Hutu militia groups) and President Habyarimana's party, with the support of part of the Hutu population (women included), began systematically to massacre Tutsis, in most cases on the basis of pre-established lists.

With contributions from French and Belgian soldiers, together with the US marines, France then launched operation 'Amaryllis' (9–17 April 1994), which involved the evacuation not only of Europeans from Rwanda, but also of some of the regime's most prominent people, notably President Habyarimana's family. Despite their pleas, Tutsis, embassy personnel included, were abandoned there and then, some being killed before these same military who had been ordered not to intervene.

Rwanda: population decrease in the different provinces, April 1994 to November 1994

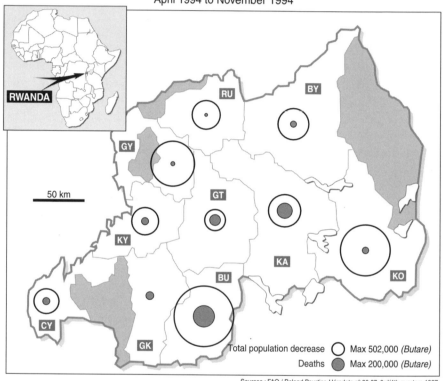

RWANDA

50 km

RU
BY
GY
GT
KY
KA
KO
BU
CY
GK

Total population decrease ○ Max 502,000 *(Butare)*

Deaths ● Max 200,000 *(Butare)*

Sources : FAO / Roland Pourtier, Hérodote n° 86-87, 3rd/4th quarters 1997.

Refugee camps in Kivu, August 1996

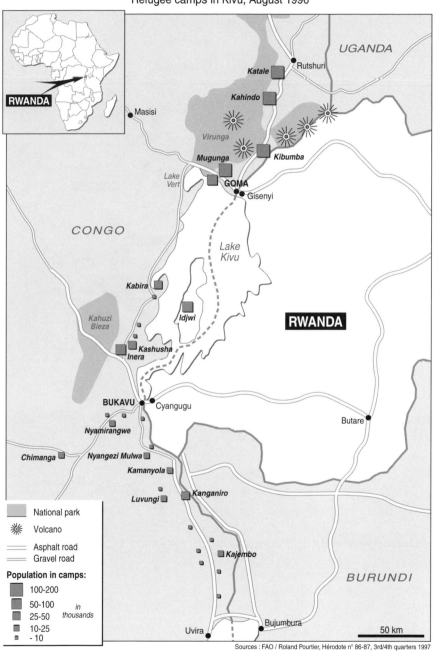

RWANDA

UGANDA
Rutshuri
Katale
Kahindo
Masisi
Virunga
Mugunga
Kibumba
Lake Vert
GOMA
Gisenyi
CONGO
Lake Kivu
RWANDA
Kabira
Idjwi
Kahuzi Bieza
Kashusha
Inera
BUKAVU
Cyangugu
Butare
Nyamirangwe
Chimanga
Nyangezi Mulwa
Kamanyola
Luvungi
Kanganiro
Kajembo
BURUNDI
Uvira
Bujumbura

National park
Volcano
Asphalt road
Gravel road
Population in camps:
100-200
50-100   *in thousands*
25-50
10-25
- 10

50 km

Sources : FAO / Roland Pourtier, Hérodote n° 86-87, 3rd/4th quarters 1997

Exodus of Hutu refugees

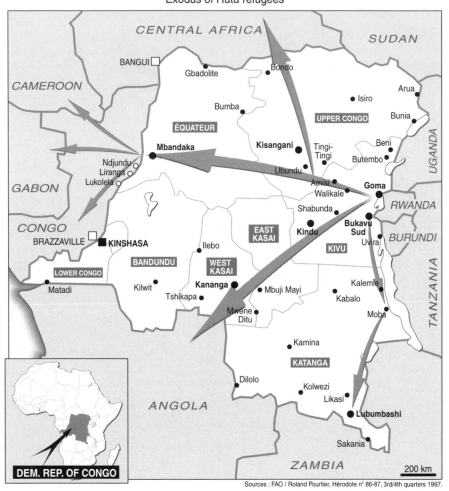

Sources : FAO / Roland Pourtier, Hérodote n° 86-87, 3rd/4th quarters 1997.

– Between 6 April 1994 and the end of June, at least 800,000 people (out of a total Rwandan population of 7.5 million!) were killed, victims of a planned genocide against the Tutsis. The massacres were committed using traditional weapons such as sticks, machetes, knives, etc. The few who survived suffer from atrocious mutilations.

– On 21 April, the UN withdrew, claiming that they had neither the resources nor the mandate to fight the massacres (the UN only started using the term 'genocide' in July). The RPF continued its violence, moving towards Kigali. A massive exodus of the Rwandan population towards the borders of neighbouring Tanzania, Burundi and especially Zaire resulted.

– A *'humanitarian' response from France*. On 22 June 1994, the UN Security Council voted on Resolution 929, mandating France to launch operation 'Turquoise' with a view to creating a 'safe haven' in south-western Rwanda. Effective as of 23 June (lasting until 22 August, when UNAMIR II began), access to this demilitarised zone was forbidden to the RPF troops who took over Kigali on 4 July. The zone made it possible to provide protection for thousands of displaced people – even if the worst of the genocide was over. However, it also offered sanctuary to countless perpetrators of the genocide, the Interhamwe and FAR included.

– Cholera, dysentery and a lack of drinking water in the Zairean refugee camps caused 50,000 people to die in Goma over the summer months, just as humanitarian organisations from all over the world, propelled by strong media coverage, began to descend upon Rwanda. In September, the UNHCR estimated the number of Rwandan refugees in other countries to number some 2.1 million: 1.3 million in Zaire; 850,000 in Goma; 450,000 in Bukavu and 30,000 in Uvira. In these camps, villagers tended to be grouped together according to their community of origin either under the leadership of their traditional leaders or that of militia groups, so underlining the fact that the exodus was organised. Executions of Tutsi families continued, especially at night.

– *Justice late in implementation*. On 8 November 1994, the UN decided to set up an International Criminal Tribunal for Rwanda to bring to justice the perpetrators of the genocide committed between 1 January and 31 December 1994. The Tribunal, based in Arusha, Tanzania, became operational in November 1995, almost a year later.

On 14 November 1994, MSF-France suspended its humanitarian operations in the Rwandan refugee camps of Bukavu, claiming control by the genocide's perpetrators. They also closed their operations in Tanzania on 20 December 1994.

– *Retaliation*. On 22 and 23 April 1995, the Rwandan army (APR) opened fire on a crowd of 100,000 people, mostly women and children, in the displaced camp of Kibeho in Gikongoro district, part of the former operation 'Turquoise' zone. This they did after having forced them together on a hill and deprived them of food and water for several days. Four thousand people were killed and countless injured. On 22 May, the European Union suspended its aid to Rwanda.

On 6 December 1995, 38 international NGOs were expelled from Rwanda by the government, while another 18 saw their activities 'suspended'. Having refused to open a nutrition programme for children in Kigali, in the belief that there was a greater humanitarian emergency elsewhere, Action Against Hunger was among them.

In March 1996, UNAMIR II withdrew from Rwanda at the request of the Rwandan government. The situation in the country began to deteriorate. The government lacked the resources required to rebuild a society which had lost a good number of its elite and qualified personnel. The prisons had started to fill up with alleged perpetrators of the genocide (more than 120,000 people in 1997). Some of them were no doubt responsible, others tended to be victims of neighbourhood conflicts, particularly where their dwellings and fields had been coveted by the thousands of former Tutsi emigrants returning from Uganda.

The shortage of legal professionals means that it has not been possible to investigate the cases of the many detainees who have died due to a lack of health care and minimal space in overcrowded prisons. The refugee camps, meanwhile, fed as they are by international humanitarian aid, promote insecurity through countless cross-border raids. This is particularly the case around Kivu in Zaire where 'Hutu power', under restoration with the help of humanitarian aid and the discrete support of countries such as France, is preparing a comeback.

– *A new political configuration*. In November 1996, the Rwandan army, with support from Uganda, decided to clear the camps on the border with Zaire, using force. In order to flee from their bombing, some 600,000 to 800,000 people returned to Rwanda, despite fears of revenge attacks. Another 300,000 fled towards the west. Under the leadership of Laurent Désiré Kabila, Mobutu's long-time opponent, the Alliance of Democratic Forces for the Liberation of Congo (ADFL) launched an offensive throughout Zaire heading towards Kinshasa. The ADFL was a heterogeneous coalition composed of RPA soldiers, Ugandans and Banyamulenges, a large Tutsi community originally from Rwanda but having lived for several generations in Kivu, where they had been denied Zairean nationality at the beginning of the 1980s and had since come into confrontation with the indigenous inhabitants. The ADFL also had the support of US counselors. Mobutu, an ageing dictator under medical treatment in Europe due to serious illness, witnessed his power collapse: the Zairean forces fled without resistance, pillaging and plundering as they went.

– On 16 May, President Mobutu left Kinshasa. On 17 May, Laurent Kabila proclaimed himself President of the Democratic Republic of Congo in Lubumbashi. On 20 May, he entered Kinshasa. Between 200,000 and 300,000 people disappeared in the Zairean forest, killed not only by disease and starvation, but also by the ADFL forces who massacred thousands of people in their forward advance. The new President systematically opposed any enquiry commission.

– On 16 May 1998, Seth Sendashongo, a moderate Hutu who had taken part in the first government of Paul Kagame in Kigali, but had been forced to resign in 1995 due to his condemnation of repeated human rights violations in Rwanda, was assassinated in Nairobi. He had just founded the Democratic Resistance Force (DRF), an opposition movement condemning the mounting Tutsi ethno-fundamentalism in Rwanda.

– In summer 1998, Kivu burst into open rebellion, with support from Rwanda and Uganda. Although benefiting from the armed support of Angola and Zimbabwe, Kabila had lost control over his country.

AN EXPLOSIVE POLITICAL CONFIGURATION

The file on the Great Lakes region is thus far from being closed, with civilians across all countries concerned continuing to pay the price of an upheaval which has fundamentally shaken the region.

Rwanda remains a country traumatised by its experiences, described by Remy Ourdan in an article in *Le Monde* on 18 March 1998 as 'the country of dead souls'. The number of executions, after summary justice, of alleged perpetrators of the genocide is increasing, almost as if having to compensate for the lengthiness of procedures and the difficulties in investigating the files of the 130,000 accused – detained in prisons full to the brim, where sanitary conditions are appalling. Those described as 'escapees of the genocide', who have returned from exile or escaped from – or survived – the 1994 massacres, are trying hard to find their place in Rwanda's new society. They suffer from a feeling that they have been denied justice, from the loss of loved ones, from a lack of understanding by those Tutsis returning from Uganda and from the loss or destruction of their houses – and sometimes of their belongings, too – and they feel curiously guilty at having survived when so many disappeared. As for those Hutus who have returned from the camps or who stayed, they are the victims of repeated atrocities committed by the Rwandan armed forces and the police using the persistent cross-border forays by the former regime's forces as a pretext to massacre entire families or even entire villages in retribution. While the nature of the civil war may have changed, it nonetheless continues.

The problem of Hutus and Tutsis living side by side has been resolved in neither Rwanda nor Burundi. The media, politicians and small groups of extremists continue to foster an ethnic hostility which regularly breaks out into appalling massacres, the main victims of which are the peasant populations. In Burundi, as underlined by Ahmedou Ould Abdallah during his two-year mediation mission for the UN, the social and political climate has been 'poisoned' by fear. It is a fear shared by both individuals and communities. Florence Daunis has also described a situation tense to the extreme, where the embargo and the forced resettlement policy practised by the new regime have placed large numbers of people – displaced persons, refugees or simple villagers – in a state of acute vulnerability.

In the new 'democratic' Congo, violence and corruption reign in a way that leaves no comparison with the last years of the Mobutu regime. From 1997 to 1998 the country's self-proclaimed President, Laurent Kabila, opposed any enquiry commission on human rights, for fear that his own responsibility in the tragic fate of the 200,000 Rwandan refugees who disappeared in his territory in 1996 might come to light.

In Arusha, Tanzania, the International Criminal Tribunal charged with the prosecution and sentencing of those responsible for the Rwandan genocide is having to work under difficult conditions: inadequate funding, witnesses who fear reprisals against either themselves or their families and the difficulties in identifying and bringing to justice the genuinely guilty, many of whom have sought refuge abroad or benefit from protection.

Throughout the year in France, a Parliamentary fact-finding commission has been gradually investigating the French government's role in the Rwandan genocide, by collecting statements from both reticent military or political players, as well as the virulent accusations of researchers and NGOs. For the latter, the constant support given by the French government to that of Habyarimana and then to the 'Hutu power' being reconstituted on the country's borders – a support motivated by a determination to thwart Anglo-Saxon influence over areas considered part of the French 'realm' – is responsible for much in the Great Lakes tragedy.

Nevertheless, faced with the Rwandan genocide, the international community is today looking to commit an act of 'repentance' – including American repentance as expressed by President Clinton on a visit to Rwanda at the end of March 1998 and UN repentance as voiced by Kofi Anan, Secretary General of the UN. Indeed, Kofi Anan was himself the victim of humiliation only a few weeks later in Kigali, given his leadership of the UN peace-keeping forces which had left the country in the middle of the 1994 'massacres'. Yet while repentance may be fashionable, contrition cannot erase the crimes committed, especially if one bears in mind the discrepancy between the 'never again', repeated to saturation point during the 50th anniversary commemorations of Jewish extermination in Auschwitz, and an African genocide which left the world completely and utterly indifferent.

The result is a political configuration which is more explosive than ever. It is the consequence, according to Gérard Prunier, of a succession of unresolved crises, the international community having preferred a humanitarian response to what first of all required a political and legal solution.

Successive and unresolved political crises

GÉRARD PRUNIER

Each unresolved political crisis in the Great Lakes region tends to form the basis of the one that follows. The roots of the present problem, then, may be found in the Rwandan crisis, a crisis which has spilled over into the entire region.

The first and related unresolved crisis is that of the Tutsi massacres which took place in Rwanda between 1959 and 1963, and caused thousands of people to flee into exile. The response of the international community was somewhat fatalistic, due to the recent creation, under Belgian influence, of a state dominated by the Hutu ethnic group and where the Tutsis were considered survivors of a bygone aristocratic age no longer having a place in the new Africa of Independent States. The refugee problem was therefore never resolved, the Tutsis remaining foreigners in Zaire, Uganda and even Burundi, despite it being a Tutsi-dominated State. Only Tanzania allowed them to integrate to some extent, granting them Tanzanian citizenship status.

The diaspora, left to itself, was given a second chance in Uganda through participation in the guerrilla war led by Museveni, who came to power in 1986. Within these forces the Tutsis formed their own core group, their own secret society and their own structure for retaking power. Thus, all was set for a new crisis to be triggered following their armed return to Rwanda in 1990.

When the genocide first started in April 1994, no-one recognised it as such, at least not initially. The UN bent over backwards just to avoid using the term, since most of its member States were signatories to the 1948 Convention on the Suppression of Genocide which placed them under an obligation to intervene – France, a country which for many years supported the regime at the root of the genocide, included. The most cruel and atrocious farce was that of UNAMIR, the UN force present in Rwanda after 1993, which numbered 3,700 soldiers, one third of whom were

Belgian, one third Ghanian and one third Bangladeshi. Romeo Dallaire, the Canadian General then commander of the troops, continually asked permission to intervene, requiring only a modification of his mandate and 20 armoured vehicles. Yet just as the genocide was reaching its apogee, the UN Security Council decided to withdraw most of its troops from Rwanda, so making a mockery of a mission supposed to prevent a renewed upsurge of violence in the country just at the time when the Arusha Peace Agreements were about to be implemented! The genocide had reached such staggering proportions that it took even me, reputed expert on the Great Lakes region, three days to fully realise, after President Habyarimana's assassination, what the world was actually witnessing. This was exactly the kind of pre-meditated and organised genocide of which the world had been afraid and which it had never really dared believe could happen. The shameful retreat of forces supposed to guarantee the population's security was therefore all the more frightening.

The fourth unresolved crisis is obviously that of the situation in the camps on the Rwandan border where some two million people took refuge. It is in understanding this crisis that we can really begin to understand how events began to spiral and how each one ushered in the next. Some of these refugees were fleeing the advance of the RPF, aware of their responsibility in the genocide; others were fleeing simply because the traditional Rwandan authorities whom they were used to obeying ordered them to leave the country. Indeed, contrary to much opinion, Rwandans are an extremely obedient people: over-organised, Rwanda could almost be considered the Prussia of Africa.

Yet, what did the international community do about these camps? Essentially nothing. It simply put food into the open mouths of the starving. The political problem posed by persistent camp supervision by Hutu forces responsible for the genocide was not considered, not even in Zaire, from where cross-border Hutu raids were orchestrated. While Tanzania acted swiftly and managed to shortcut and deflate the politico-military nexus operated within the camps by the Rwandan Armed Forces, Zaire on the other hand not only did nothing, but Mobutu even tried to draw upon refugee support in order to win elections destined for 1996 or 1997, elections that he had been compelled to promise the international community. This he did by distributing Zairean identity cards. The Rwandan refugees thus became part of Mobutu's political game in an area, eastern Zaire, long hostile to him. The international community did not intervene, particularly France, which was still dreaming about Rwanda's reconquest by 'Hutu power' (a reconquest that was to enable the reconstruction of a small part of France's defeated empire).

The fifth unresolved crisis obviously lies in the Arusha Tribunal – another farce, albeit not a bloody one. With 20 accusations in three years, it has broken all records for being slow, all the more so since those accused are, except for one or two cases, not the real orchestrators of the genocide, but rather those who were simply carrying out orders. If one had wanted to send a signal to Kigali to make its rulers understand they were alone and would have to manage by themselves as best as possible, there could not have been a better way to do it. Those responsible for the genocide, having taken refuge in Cameroon, Gabon, Kenya, Canada or France, some with false identities, could rest assured, able to end their days in peace. Faced with such a denial of justice, the reaction of the Tutsis was simple: 'Since no-one else will take those responsible into hand, we'll kill them ourselves.'

So we come to the sixth issue: when the Rwandan Tutsi forces penetrated Zaire, they had only one aim – to remove the abcess at its borders which the international community was not only tolerating but had been keeping alive for three years. All methods were welcome: either people returned to Rwanda or they would be forced to flee. The derisory efforts of the ex-FAR to oppose the offensive, to the extent of massacring those who tried to return, revealed that their grip over the camps had finally become sufficiently fragile to be dismantled relatively easily, even if without the mercenaries that the Zairean army had employed in 1995–96, in its first attempt to do this. Meanwhile, those who fled westwards to escape camp shelling were soon caught in something of a political Bermuda triangle, with the international community rapidly coming to consider the problem as resolved and even denying their very existence. Once again, the multinational deployment force – one minute envisaging coming to their aid, the next minute abandoning the idea – hid behind the skirts of humanitarian assistance. This was the result of a hidden agenda. The French wanted to block the offensive led by Kabila and Kagame due to the threat it posed to their ally, Mobutu. America wanted to block the force so that their friends might reach Kinshasa. The refugees were the least of their worries. Put simply, the Americans were forced to disguise their intentions by lying about the nature of aerial exploratory missions and satellite photos, while the French brandished their photos with an ardour supposed to legitimise their pseudo-humanitarian discourse.

As for those who disappeared in eastern Zaire – figures suggest 200,000 missing people – it is certain that not all of them were killed directly. Some

15–20% of them were, no doubt, the victims of mass executions. The others were deliberately deprived of medical assistance and food, and forced to walk long hours through a hostile forest environment where they died of exhaustion, hunger and disease. Today, we are waiting for the next episode, and there will almost certainly be one. It is no use believing that a regime based on an ethnic minority, like that of the Rwandan Tutsis, can last forever through the use of repression, after having dropped all political links with its Hutu compatriots.

Bibliography

African Rights: Files: *Witnesses of Genocide*.
Mehdi Ba; 1997; *Rwanda, un Génocide Français*; L'esprit frappeur.
Colette Brackman; 1994; *Rwanda, Histoire d'un Génocide*; Fayard.
Rony Brauman; 1994; *Devant le Mal, Rwanda, un Génocide en Direct*; Arlea.
Hérodote; 1997; Géopolitique d'une Afrique médiane; no. 86/87.
Jean-Pierre Chrétien (ed); 1995; *Rwanda, les Médias du Génocide*; Karthala.
Jean-Pierre Chrétien; 1997; *Le Défi de l'Ethnisme: Rwanda et Burundi: 1990–96*; Karthala.
Alain Destexhe; 1994; *Rwanda: Essai sur le Génocide*; Complexe.
Jean-François Dupaquier (ed); 1996; *La Justice Internationale Face au Drame Rwandais*; Karthala.
Dominique Franche; 1997; *Rwanda, Généalogie d'un Génocide*; Mille et Une Nuits.
André Guichaoua; 1995; *Les Crises Politiques au Rwanda et au Burundi*; Karthala.
Omaar-Waal (eds); 1995; *Rwanda, Death and Defiance*; African Rights.
Gérard Prunier; 1997; *Rwanda 1959–1996, Histoire d'un Génocide*; Dagorno.
Filip Reyntjens; 1998; *Rwanda, Trois Jours qui ont fait Basculer l'Histoire*; Harmattan.
François-Xavier Vershave; 1994; *Complicité de Génocide? La Politique de la France au Rwanda*; La Découverte.

Burundi

Legend:
- Severe nutritional problems
- National park
- Conflict zone

RWANDA

TANZANIA

DEM. REP CONGO

South Cyohoha Lake

Lake Rweru

○ Butare

● Kirundo

KIRUNDO

MUHINGA

● Cibitoke

CIBITOKE

NGOZI

● Muhinga

● Kayanza

● Ngozi

3°S

KAYANZA

BUBANZA

● Bubanza

● Muramvya

Karuzi ●

KARUZI

CANKUZO

● Cankuzo

○ Uvira

■ BUJUMBURA

MURAMVYA

BUJUMBURA

● Gitega

RUYIGI

● Ruyigi

GITEGA

○ Kibongo

BURURI

● Bururi

RUTANA

● Rutana

TANZANIA

○ Nundu

30 km

Lake Tanganyika

Makamba ●

MAKAMBA

4°S

○ Kamonanira

○ Kasulu

29°

30°

BURUNDI

Burundi: a hostage population

FLORENCE DAUNIS

Chronology

April 1993	First general elections. Melchior Ndadaye, Hutu member of FRODEBU, wins the elections with 64% of the vote.
21 October 1993	Assassination of President Ndadaye during an attempted military coup. Prime Minister Sylvie Kinigi, as well as several members of the government, repair to the French embassy which becomes the *de facto* seat of government, while the Minister of Health, J. Minani, proclaims a 'provisional Burundi government in exile' in Kigali. A series of killings in the hills leave 50,000 dead and nearly one million refugees and displaced persons.
November 1993	The OAU decides to send a contingent of 200 men for a period of six months and to establish an international investigation commission 'on the failed coup d'état and the assassinations which took place'.
April 1994	The second Hutu President, Cyprien Nyaryamira, is killed as Rwandan President Juvénal Habyarimana's airplane explodes.
September 1994	Inauguration of President Sylvestre Ntibantuganya (Hutu of FRODEBU) and of a Prime Minister (Tutsi of UPRONA). Signing, following from the initiative of UN Secretary General envoy, Ahmedou Ould Abdallah, of a convention on the allocation of seats between parties of the presidential camp and parties of the opposition.
March 1995	The international conference on refugees in Bujumbura ends with the resignation of Prime Minister A. Kanienkilo, under pressure from UPRONA. Appointment of a new Prime Minister, A. Nduwayo. Massive exodus from Bujumbura leaves the town virtually mono-ethnic.
April 1996	Negotiations between FRODEBU and UPRONA delegates in Tanzania. Julius Nyerere, former President of Tanzania, presides.

June 1996	President Ntibantuganya seeks international military assistance.
10 July 1996	The OAU approves, in principle, the sending of an international force to Burundi.
16 July 1996	Beginning of a forced resettlement policy for several thousand Rwandan refugees in the north (ends on 23 July).
25 July 1996	Coup d'état by Major Buyoya
31 July 1996	Regional summit Arusha II with the Presidents of Kenya, Rwanda, Uganda and Tanzania and the Prime Minister of Zaire; the embargo is maintained
20 August 1996	Rwandan refugee camps closed by the armed forces; forced repatriation to Rwanda.
6 September 1997	The Arusha II summit brings together six regional Presidents. Sanctions arc renewed and the government in Bujumbura is asked to cooperate in the mediation efforts of Julius Nyerere
2 October 1997	Mounting tension between Burundi and Tanzania along the shores of Lake Tanganyika. Violent shooting between the two sides.

CONTEXT: STRUCTURAL PROBLEMS UNDERLYING
A DIFFICULT SITUATION

Burundi is one of the most densely populated countries in Africa. In 1990, the population was estimated at 5.4 million, inhabiting a land area of 27,834 sq. km, which corresponds to an average of 182 persons per sq. km. However, the figure rises to 197 persons per sq. km if only highlands, not prone to flooding, are taken into consideration. It is estimated that the population of Burundi would double every 25 years were the annual population growth rate of 3% to remain stable over a given period.[1]

Such land pressure has gradually led to the cultivation of pasture and fallow land, although plots are becoming smaller and smaller in size due to continual subdivision across the generations. At present, the average size

1. Faculté des Sciences Agronomiques, Centre Universitaire de Recherche et de Développement en Agro-Economie (CERDA); Université du Burundi; *Autosuffisance et Sécurité Alimentaire*; Dr Ir Ndimira Pascal Firmin.

of a farm in Burundi is 1.5 hectares per family (usually made up of six to seven members); in short, an area hardly sufficient to guarantee survival.

An essentially monodependent economy

The Burundi economy is agriculture-based, with agriculture accounting for 50% of GDP prior to the crisis in 1993, and contributing to nearly 90% of export earnings.[2] In 1995, coffee accounted for 81% of export earnings,[3] so making the country extremely vulnerable to fluctuating world market coffee prices, as well as dependent on its own export capacities.

The Structural Adjustment Programme (SAP), introduced in 1986 to promote changes in the organisation of the country's economy (reduction of institutional expenditure, diversification of subsistence economies by stimulating private investment and exports, production of substitutes in order to reduce imports, etc.), did not bring concrete and satisfactory results. While Burundi remains predominantly dependent on agriculture, production techniques have not developed. Annual per capita income has stagnated at around US$210.

The road infrastructure is not even sufficiently developed to facilitate trade and so reduce costs between the various provinces where different foodstuffs are produced. Transportation is not accessible to farmers at reasonable prices. The range of tools available is also very limited and hardly adapted to the diverse forms of farming to be found in the country.

Few markets other than the agricultural

About 80% of the country's population works in agriculture such that, given the conditions described above, land represents even more of a scarce resource. As a result, land possession often leads to friction and tension.

Taken altogether, in a country considered to be one of the ten poorest in the world,[4] these factors have engendered the same feelings of despair

2. International Bank for Reconstruction and Development; 1996; *Country Briefs*; Volume 1. *Africa Region, Europe and Central Asia Region*; Washington, 1996, annex.
3. World Bank; 1996; *Special Programme of Assistance. Status Report for Burundi. Prepared for the Fall 1996 SPA Meeting*. November 1996.
4. Burundi has been categorised by the United Nations as one of the Least Developed Countries.

among the rural people that can be found in most predominantly agricultural societies, where the country's population growth exceeds its production capacity – at least as long as farming techniques remain the same.

Such despair among a rural population that has lost all hope in the future is exacerbated by the poverty which has struck more than 90% of the population living just outside the urban centres. The worst affected are female-headed families, as well as people who are uneducated and have no access to income other than that to be gained from farming.

Public sector jobs often represent the sole means of access to the sphere of wealth distribution and power, thus very much limiting the possibilities of breaking out of such a poverty trap.

In a relatively small country, where industrial production is virtually non-existent and economic activity is limited to the agricultural sector, rural exodus cannot therefore really be considered as a viable solution. The lack of employment prospects, coupled with a somewhat bleak future, has provided fertile ground for all kinds of extremist agitation.

AN ALREADY DIFFICULT SITUATION EXACERBATED BY CIRCUMSTANCES

A country in latent conflict since 1993

Although Burundi's post-colonial history has been marked by waves of repression and violence time and time again, there is no doubt that the failed military coup of 21 October 1993, and the subsequent period of unrest, are events which sparked the civil war between the army and opposition forces.

Regardless of whether it was before or after the coup d'état of 15 July 1996, successive and brutal cycles of rebellion by insurgents, followed by military retaliation, have wreaked havoc across Burundi's north-western provinces, Cibitoke, Bubanza and rural Bujumbara. This, in turn, has forced numerous people to take refuge in the surrounding forests and swamps, leaving behind a brother, a husband or a father killed on the grounds of suspicion that he might have been allied to one or other of the forces present, or simply out of sheer delight. These violent events, hyped by the media and qualified at each stage as 'the onset of a coup d'état', or 'genocide drop-by-drop', have cost the lives of at least 200,000 people over the past three years and provoked significant displacement.

For several months, if not years, these internally displaced people had limited access to food and medical assistance. However, at the end of 1996, after Laurent Kabila's Alliance expelled the rebels from their bases in northern Kivu, a degree of stability was restored, enabling a growing number of sick and malnourished to come out of hiding in a final attempt to reach these 'safe' areas and so obtain access to food and health care.

Nevertheless, despite the relative security in Burundi in the last few months of 1996, most other countries in the region remained unstable. While Kabila's troops advanced ever deeper into the Zairean forest, Rwanda was forced to receive and absorb one million returning refugees.

In an attempt to take advantage of this relatively calm period, the Burundi government decided to implement a population resettlement policy in the areas of insecurity, to facilitate ethnic-cleansing in the forest and hills. Thus, they forced the peasants to leave their hills for resettlement in camps under strict military control.

The policy, launched in Karusi during 1996, was introduced in most of Burundi's northern provinces, including Cibitoke, Bubanza and Kayanza, in April 1997. The number of peasants forced to relocate to these camps has *officially* exceeded 270,000, out of a total of 600,000 displaced persons across the whole of Burundi.[5]

At the same time, while the various negotiation processes had reached a standstill, and the Burundi population was still awaiting the removal of the embargo, an armed rebellion was being reorganised, particularly in Rwanda and to a lesser extent in Tanzania. Thus, attacks were relaunched such that, today, the area around Kibira/Nyungwe forest has once again become one of permanent insecurity. Large areas of Cibitoke, Bubanza and rural Bujumbara provinces, as well as Bururi and Makamba, have once again become inaccessible to humanitarian agencies.

The harmful effects of the embargo

Following on from more than four years of civil war, the combined effects of resettlement and the economic embargo imposed by neighbouring countries have exacerbated an already precarious situation, depriving some 10% of the population of regular access to their fields and causing severe malnutrition almost everywhere in the country.

---

5. Department of Humanitarian Affairs statistics, 4 June 1997.

The embargo imposed on Burundi was initially a regional embargo imposed after the coup d'état of 25 July 1997. In the first instance, it was voted in during the Arusha summit of 31 July 1997. Participants in the regional summit (Cameroon, Ethiopia, Rwanda, Tanzania, Uganda, Zaire and the OAU) called for the restoration of 'constitutional order', in particular that of parliament together with an authorisation to re-legitimise the existence of all political parties. They also called on the new regime to enter into negotiations with *all* parties involved in the conflict, including the various armed factions, so that the peace agreement might be signed. The embargo, then, imposed without the preliminary agreement of the UN Security Council, was implemented only by neighbouring African countries.

As a result, shipments to and from Burundi were blocked, in theory, at the ports of Mombasa (Kenya) and Dar-es-Salaam (Tanzania). This was at a time when arabica coffee from Burundi represented 80% of the country's exports and when all its fuel as well as most manufactured products were imported.

Nevertheless, while the embargo has officially reduced government revenue by at least 50%, products can still be found in the markets of Bujumbura and those of major towns throughout the country, although prices are now so high that few can afford to buy.

According to an economic survey commissioned by Action Aid in February 1997,[6] inflation had already increased by an estimated 40–50%. The annual review of market prices produced by FAO shows an average price increase of 92.7%.[7] The price of certain vital products, such as milk and bananas, has doubled.

The country's borders have also proved quite porous with regard to military equipment and weapons. Provision of arms to the rebels has continued, most notably through the intermediary of Rwandan Hutu refugee camps in Zaire, and then through the former Rwandan Interhamwe after their return to Rwanda in December 1996. The armed forces, on the other hand, have received support from the Rwandan army and other neighbouring countries, as well as from wealthy families in Bujumbura.

The embargo has, in fact, strengthened the position of large families specialising in black market trade. With part of the tea and coffee harvests

6. Sanctions in Burundi – Independent Survey commissioned by Action Aid; February 1997.
7. Price Monitoring Statistics; July 1996 – July 1997; FAO.

being transferred to Rwanda or the Democratic Republic of Congo, proceeds contribute to a continuation of the war and the purchase of export products, resold at exhorbitant prices on the market. The governing classes profit from the embargo as much as a number of neighbouring countries. Kenya, Uganda and Tanzania impose high customs duties, storage costs and air freight charges – aimed, *inter alia*, at humanitarian aid. The embargo, then, has become an end in itself, a sanction 'of principle', allowing certain people to get rich.

A national budget dominated by military expenditure

A special report by FAO and WFP[8] in 1997 revealed continued deterioration in the average quantity of food consumed since 1994, whilst a 'strategic study' published by Unicef in the same month estimated that 60% of health services in the country were barely functioning. The civil war has devastated a national health care system that was once efficient, based on a network of rural health centres grouped around provincial reference hospitals. One quarter of the country's doctors and nurses have either been killed or fled. Bujumbura aside, government statistics have further estimated that for every 75,000 people, there is only one doctor!

At the same time, the government has been using the lack of export earnings due to the embargo – a loss estimated at about 50% – as a pretext to curb the health budget (4% of the total budget). This has led to delays, or even failure, in paying for health personnel and medicines, and further hindering the re-opening of some health structures, with 40% of the domestic budget being reserved for national defence!

Before the crisis and the large-scale population displacements it provoked, severe malnutrition was not really a problem given a country as fertile as Burundi. According to some of the most recent findings, since the previous public and private health care centres dealing with chronic malnutrition were neither sufficient in number nor adapted to the extent of the crisis, health service personnel still remaining in the country have not been able to respond to the country's rapidly spiralling needs or to adopt more efficient techniques.

Finally, even where such personnel are working in the few structures which still function, treatment of malnutrition in public health centres is

8. Crop and Food Supply Assessment, March 1997.

on the basis of a fee (100 Fbu per consultation), so rendering it inaccessible to low-income families – those most likely to suffer from hunger.

DISASTROUS CONSEQUENCES FOR CIVILIANS

Today, some areas of Burundi appear more secure than others, to the extent that food security programmes and agricultural rehabilitation activities are being envisaged. However, the situation in those areas in which Action Against Hunger works, around the forest of Kibira in the north-west of the country, is such that medium- or long-term programmes are hard to imagine.

Chronic instability and waves of insecurity caused by fighting between Hutu rebels and government forces in the hills means that these are in a continual emergency state as far as food is concerned. Our programme beneficiaries are not currently in a position to re-establish food self-sufficiency. These are populations who have no access to land or cannot obtain a sufficient income from it, due to racketeering, pillaging and abduction, etc., all further exacerbated by recent adverse weather conditions. Against such a backdrop, the possibility of implementing rehabilitation or food security programmes is somewhat restricted, if not actually negated.

Decapitalisation leads to increasing civilian impoverishment

While the civilian population in general has been the conflict's first victim, not all individuals have been affected in the same way. In this regard, three groups might be distinguished among the rural population.

– The resettled population
Population resettlement took place under extremely precarious health conditions: no water sources nearby and no sanitary structures in sufficient number, such as latrines, showers, etc. Diets, meanwhile, were reduced to mainly cassava, which is very poor in certain vitamins and proteins. The appalling quality of water also engendered a number of health problems, including dysentery, intestinal worms and so on. Consequently, overcrowding in the resettlement camps, coupled with an inadequate sanitary infrastructure, has led to a proliferation of diseases,

especially pneumopathies, further exacerbated by the anaemic state of much of the population. In the same way, diseases typical of such precarious conditions, among them cholera, typhus, measles, and scabies, have also spread. There has, in parallel, also been a rapid decline in the population's nutritional status, affecting adults and children alike and resulting in an ever-increasing mortality rate (in some places, 5–10 children out of every thousand die every month).

Resettlement has been accompanied by severe restrictions on the freedom of movement. In some provinces, including Kayanza where Action Against Hunger works, restrictions were, however, later relaxed, following pressure from the UN and NGOs. This subsequently enabled access to the nearest health centres (feeding centres and medical consultation clinics), as well as to fields a few days per week. However, the latter were often too far away to permit a return journey in one day, and where this was feasible, the exactions of the military forces also came into play.

Today, most of these resettlement camps are closed, the civilian population having returned to their places of origin – the strategy not having proved successful in terms of security improvements. While there is no denying that most of these people previously subsisted on somewhat poor levels of production and that their nutritional intake was not always sufficient, it would be fair to say that their presence in these makeshift camps dramatically exacerbated deficiencies and caused many deaths.

– The displaced
Part of the civilian population living in the hills was voluntarily displaced, fleeing fighting and the frequent passage of armed forces, and mostly resettling around urban centres and major towns in the province from where they originally came. With more than 140,000 people crammed into camps around Bubanza, for instance, the town no longer resembles the small town pencilled in on the maps of Burundi by the IGN. The nutritional situation here has reached almost unprecedented proportions, again for reasons of over-crowding and the lack of sanitary facilities. The accumulated deprivation suffered over more than five years has effectively reduced these communities to walking skeletons, fragile and susceptible to any infection.

This population does not have access to cultivable land, since the surrounding hills are either controlled by rebels or riddled with landmines. When they do have access to the surrounding land, they possess neither the seeds nor the tools necessary for its cultivation. In fact, these displaced persons tend to have no goods in their possession (having left behind their small livestock and long exhausted any modest food supplies taken with them). As a result, they have no other choice but regularly to sell part of their humanitarian aid distribution to pay for transport, medicine and other basic needs. An inability to look towards the future, and a general apathy with regard to what lies ahead for Burundi and their own survival, has also been noted among these people – something that makes them all the more vulnerable.

– *The peasant population*
Another sector of the population, particularly in the country's centre and south, did not leave their land or banana plantations. Over the past three years, a large number of these households have been forced to sell their belongings, goats, pigs and sometimes even their tools in return for food or seeds which they were unable to plant in time due to insecurity or adverse weather conditions. The process cannot be reversed in one single harvest.

While the 1998 harvest appears to be a good one, asset depletion has reached such proportions that the Burundi peasant and farmer dependency is of major concern. Under present security conditions in Burundi, it is impossible for those groups of the population still living on their own land to produce enough to survive, let alone generate a surplus which could be sold or exchanged for other products, now unaffordable due to the embargo.

Obstacles and limits to humanitarian relief activities

The veil of silence which has cloaked a number of areas in Burundi, together with the inability of NGOs to gain access to populations threatened by death, are cause for much concern. Insecurity is still the main obstacle to humanitarian aid, not only because this limits local and expatriate movement, but above all because it inhibits the civilian population from receiving adequate food aid and nutritional treatment.

The therapeutic nutritional recovery of a patient is significantly more effective if monitored over 24 hours in a centre specifically designed for that, death often being the consequence of hypothermia or hypoglycemia, both of which often occur during the night. In Burundi, Action Against Hunger is not permitted to keep such centres open at night: thus, most function for a maximum of 10 hours per day only. When the government does give us authorisation – for centres near an urban area, within a provincial hospital, etc. – it tends to be patients, accompanying families and local personnel who refuse to stay for fear that they might become the target of an attack or be too far away from their families and home should any problems arise.

Security is also the ideal excuse for preventing NGOs, generally considered as far too curious or moralistic anyway, from witnessing the reign of terror encouraged by each of the warring factions.

In general, the Burundi authorities show a singular unwillingness to cooperate with humanitarian organisations. A number of obstacles inhibit us from rapidly responding, in even the smallest of ways, to the needs of the civilian population. Ministerial structures responsible for monitoring humanitarian activities are such that they have, among other things, led to a multiplication of procedures necessary for humanitarian organisations and long delays in obtaining the number of authorisations required.

These procedures, sometimes contradictory and often vague, make us lose valuable time in an emergency situation requiring immediate response. For instance, Action Against Hunger spent an incredible amount of wasted energy on attempts over at least four months to obtain (in January 1998) the necessary authorisation required to open a nutrition programme in Bubanza, although our organisation had officially responded to an appeal by the Ministry of Health in October 1997, declaring Bubanza province an 'absolute priority' and calling upon the assistance of international humanitarian organisations, most notably those specialised in nutrition.

The embargo, meanwhile, hinders humanitarian organisations from importing medicines, specific foodstuffs such as therapeutic milk and basic items such as blankets, all of which would help us to ensure the effective treatment of diseases or victims of hunger. This results in important delays to emergency activities. Moreover, even when foodstuffs and logistical equipment (such as radios) do arrive, they are subject to further delays at Burundi customs. It usually takes more than two months to clear basic medical supplies and more than three weeks for therapeutic milk – by which time our teams have completely run out of stocks.

For our organisation, Burundi is, in terms of the crisis in the Great Lakes region and in terms of the areas in which we work, one of the countries which best represents the way in which, even today, a civilian population can be held hostage by those obsessed with power and wealth, and in total disdain of the population's well-being.

Sudan: accomplices to an organised famine?

SYLVIE BRUNEL

Chronology

1956	Sudanese Independence. Civil war ravages the South in its own bid for independence.
1969–85	Military government of Jaafar al-Numeiri.
1972	Civil war ends (1955–72) with signature of the Accords of Addis Ababa. Numeiri accepts the autonomy of three provinces in the South, united as one, and grants them religious and cultural liberty.
1983	Violation of the 1972 Accords. Creation of the Sudanese People's Liberation Movement (SPLM) under John Garang. Civil war breaks out again following the promulgation of the Shari'a (Islamic law) throughout the country.
1986–89	Government of Sadiq al-Mahdi.
1988	Admission of Islamists to the government.
1989	Signature of agreements creating the humanitarian operation, 'Operation Lifeline Sudan' (OLS). Coup d'état by Omar Hassan Ahmad al-Bashir and installation of government.
1991	Fissure of southern opposition (SPLM/A led by J. Garang) and creation of a new group, SSIM/A, led by Riek Machar.
November 1992	In search of food and security, 4.5 million persons (around 75% of the population of the South) flee their homes to other areas in Sudan, Ethiopia and Uganda.
June 1995	Assassination attempt of Egyptian President Hosni Mubarak. Khartoum is accused.
November 1995	Resumption of peace negotiations under the auspices of IGADD, but no advances made.
December 1996	Creation of an opposition movement based in Asmara (Eritrea), named the National Democratic Alliance (NDA) and composed of the SPLM and the North's principal opposition movement.

21 April 1997   Signature of a peace plan by the different parties present, excluding the SPLM and John Garang.

September 1997   Expulsion of Action Against Hunger from South Sudan.

Spring 1998   Drought and fighting provoke serious famine in South Sudan.

15 July 1998   Signature of a truce among the different parties to the conflict to allow the delivery of humanitarian aid.

In North Sudan as in the South, the strategies used by the various perpetrators of the civil war are all aimed at plunging the civilian population into crisis. Civilians are deliberately starved, oppressed or massacred, so that combatants might benefit from the logistical machine of humanitarian organisations and continue their fighting. The conflict continues to drag on with no settlement in sight. No-one really wants the Southern rebels to emerge victorious as this might endanger the whole country and have disastrous consequences in the sub-region. Humanitarian agencies are tired of being used by both the Sudanese regime and the international community for their own purposes. Action Against Hunger condemns the Realpolitik which is allowing civilians to be sacrificed to maintain the integrity of a Sudanese State.

Is everyone an accomplice, trying to profit from the Sudanese conflict? Such might well be the question to ask in view of the re-opening of old fault-lines between North and South, with nothing having been done to put an end to a civil war which has already claimed 1.5 million lives and forced another 5 million into exile.

Sudan might well be the first African country to have officially established an Islamic State and to manifest its intention to transfer its model of society to neighbouring regions. The Sudanese regime may well have long been suspected of fuelling international terrorism. Yet no-one appears to be interested in halting the never-ending conflict, a conflict that is needlessly forcing millions of people into deprivation in a country which has abundant resources.

The civil war has bankrupted the economy. The only ones to benefit from the 'turbaned New Liberalism' extolled by the regime to get rich quick

Sudan

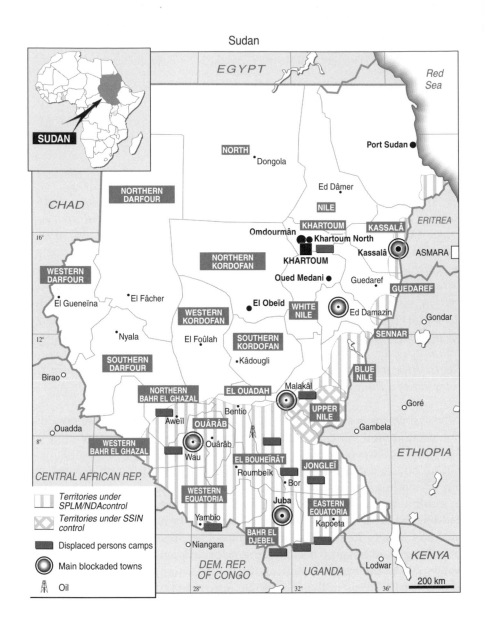

are the new business bourgeoisie.[1] Meanwhile, the misery of the majority of the 21 million Northern Sudanese (out of a total population of 27 million) increases every day. People no longer even have the means with which to buy food, not even the sorghum harvested nationally by farmers who no longer have the right to export. Indeed, indebted and poorly paid for their work, farmers no longer want to cultivate their fields, so making international humanitarian aid vital.

No-one any longer wants to go and fight in the dangerous outposts of the South, for here government forces hold just a few key towns and food aid has to be delivered by air, due to encirclement by Southern guerrillas. In June 1997, in order to swell the ranks, some 30,000 college graduates were forcibly recruited by the junta as 'fresh cannon fodder', just as they were coming to collect their results. During a peaceful demonstration calling for their return, 37 women lawyers were imprisoned, tried in the middle of the night and sentenced to beating.

Repression is the key to the strategy used by the Sudanese regime, the results of which have been denounced for more than five years by Gaspar Biro, the United Nations' Special Rapporteur in the country. Exactions include summary execution, disappearance and religious persecution, not to mention the slavery that has become institutionalised in the South and West of the country, where the Dinkas are regularly raided by militias backing the regime and the population in the Nuba Mountains has been reduced to forced labour.

Parked in the middle of the desert around Khartoum, in huge camps reminiscent of the 'homelands' of the *apartheid* era, more than one million displaced persons may be found, having lost all their belongings in the war. The Islamic junta does not permit these 'undesirable' residents to build their own non-collapsible houses in the camps or to settle in Khartoum should the capital be invaded and taken over by a non-Arab Muslim population. The shelters of these homeless, regarded as a breed somewhat apart, are regularly razed to the ground by bulldozers which rarely forget to pulverise non-Muslim places of worship in the process. Such destructive frenzy has even affected the buildings of humanitarian organisations. Only Islamic organisations are favoured by the regime, but their aid, annoyingly for those for whom it is intended – usually Christians or Animists – tends to be conditional on conversion to Islam.

1. Terminology employed by the Sudan Vigilance Committee which publishes a monthly report on the state of human rights in the country.

All this is part of the ambiguous nature of a regime which is perfectly happy to rely on foreign aid to prolong the war, yet condemns NGOs as organisations from the reviled 'Western' world. The charitable activity of non-Islamic organisations is only ever met with suspicion, attempts at control and efforts to intimidate. Journeys by Western fieldworkers within the country are subject to 'travel permits' from Sudanese civil security authorities who take advantage of any situation to carry out officious checks and cause endless delays. Should expatriates wish to travel to regions such as the Nuba Mountains where the government, for obvious reasons, does not like to tolerate any witnesses, so-called 'security reasons' are usefully employed to deny them access.

To the huge frustration of Westerners who would have liked to find an ally in the regime's opposition, the armed movements of the South are not, unfortunately, to be outdone. Like the junta of Khartoum, they unscrupulously seize thousands of children and force them to join their forces. Or else, in a fertile environment where ordinarily no-one should be starving, they orchestrate famines by depriving the population of their traditional access to food (through harvest and trading), only to attract foreign aid. In this, the SPLA guerrillas, under the leadership of John Garang, also forcibly recruit villagers to act as 'porters' to the armed forces, while simultaneously chasing civilians from their villages, only to pile them into displaced camps where their miserable situation is used as bait to attract foreign aid. These camps are always situated near the frontlines, so helping the soldiers of the SPLA to benefit from a pool of food, medicine and potential recruits, with the added bonus of good treatment by humanitarian workers.

NGOs are not oblivious to such manipulation. However, those who condemn these practices, or even start to question the actual destination of the aid provided, are immediately expelled, so having to abandon – against their will – a hostage population whose situation continues to deteriorate every year. Action Against Hunger recently suffered one such bitter experience.

Active in both North and South Sudan since 1989, and running large-scale emergency nutrition and rehabilitation programmes for both the displaced and those besieged by the rebels in towns such as Juba, Action Against Hunger was thrown out of South Sudan by the SPLA in September 1997. Once their food stocks and vehicles had been confiscated, the organisation's 21 fieldworkers were ordered to leave the country immediately, under the pretext that the security of the rebels was threatened by contacts maintained with Action Against Hunger teams working in Juba, on the Khartoum side. The reality appears somewhat different. It seems that the organisation became 'undesirable' from the moment it dared to conduct a nutritional survey to gain a better understanding of the persistence of malnutrition in the Labone camp despite massive aid. As for the 375,000 displaced persons benefiting from the programmes – most of whom were women and children – all signs would suggest that their tragic situation has little stirred those claiming to defend the freedom of people in the South against the government in Khartoum.

At the time, Action Against Hunger was intervening within the framework of a massive aid plan launched through an agreement signed in 1989 between, on the one hand, institutional donors for Sudan such as the European Union, USAID and UN agencies and, on the other hand, the Sudanese government for the North, in parallel with the SPLA for the South. The agreement, known as 'Operation Lifeline Sudan' (OLS), has led to permanent dependence on humanitarian aid.

OLS was initially conceived to facilitate access to populations in danger. It was to be a reference point for charitable intervention in Sudan and was made compulsory for NGOs wishing to assist victims of the civil war. Over the years, however, as it has grown in terms of both activity and finance, it has tended to become something of a huge 'charity business'. Propelled by Unicef in the South (and by UNDP in the North), OLS has today become a comfortable cloak with which to hide the manipulation and compromise of humanitarian aid in Sudan. It hides these from a world in which the misfortune of the Sudanese people has helped to generate an indispensable source of funds for a large number of humanitarian organisations.

First of all, aid is misused for religious reasons. The proselytisation of Islamic NGOs has been matched with that of Christianity by a number of NGOs in the South who have found fertile ground for their evangelism. The complete disorganisation of food distributions, meanwhile, does much to explain, despite the enormous quantities distributed, the seemingly undiminishable rate of malnutrition among groups at risk (children and their mothers). In this regard, little surprise should be shown at the suggestion that a significant proportion of aid and medicines goes straight to the soldiers.

Any NGO refusing to enter the game played between those responsible for OLS and the authorities, any NGO refusing to close its eyes to the real root of the Sudanese tragedy, will be told that it no longer has any reason to stay in the country. No-one dares to breathe a word for fear of being treated in the same way. The expelled becomes a leper, suspected of being at least partly responsible for the ostracism to which it has become victim. This is just one concrete example of the new age of humanitarianism, ushered in with the fall of the iron curtain. Humanitarian NGOs are a product greatly in demand, but disposable once used. They should go where told – and be silent. Otherwise they cannot go at all.

The major powers effectively tolerate the Sudanese tragedy, since none of them wishes to see the conflict exported, the ramifications of which might well reach beyond the Sudanese borders. Since the President of Sudan took the 'wrong' decision to favour Iraq during the Gulf war, the United States has decided to support the Southern guerrillas, even if, in private, they remain troubled by the 'Marxist' character of John Garang. France, however, has shown significant indulgence towards the government in Khartoum. This it has done for reasons linked to its well-known 'Arab policy', as well as, more importantly, due to fears of the potential impact that the country's explosion might have on the region. The opposition, having taken refuge in neighbouring countries (notably Asmara, in Eritrea), maintains little credibility since it is too divided and in any case lacks the logistical means with which to launch an attack on Khartoum (the war between Ethiopia and Eritrea having caused it to lose a good part of its equipment and finance). Meanwhile, in a region already traumatised by the Great Lakes conflict, the SPLA's calls for the creation of a 'New Sudan' have simply caused worry about the risk of contagion by secessionist claims. Control of the waters of the Nile, as much a preoccupation for Egypt as the exploitation of petrol resources in the South is for a number of American companies, would be difficult to accommodate amid regional explosion. Already, numerous Somali-like warlords, with support from Khartoum, are reducing the SPLA's sphere of influence.

Thus, as long as Sudan is wasting its energies on an internal conflict between North and South such that any hegemonic ambitions be contained within the Sudanese territory, few will have any motivation to become involved in what could, despite the spill-over into Uganda, still be considered an internal affair. Sending humanitarian organisations to Sudan, even if at the cost of their lives, has enabled the major powers to maintain a presence without getting directly involved.

However, the conflict appears to be at a standstill and can obviously not be resolved through arms. Neighbouring countries have become exasperated by the need to host huge refugee camps – which double as useful sanctuaries for the opposition. The recent example of Kivu, from where

Laurent Kabila's forces began their invasion of Zaïre, underlines the dangers. Since then, it has become clear that humanitarian intervention does not suffice, particularly once NGOs start to question their role as 'jack of all trades', manipulated by all parties present and suddenly undesirable once bold enough to go beyond their purely charitable role and question the ultimate aim of their work.

It is now time to put an end to the tragedy which has been played out in Sudan for 15 years. While the junta long preferred to destroy the South through famine rather than fail in its attempt to create an Islamic State, it now realises how utopic and unrealistic this is, and has begun to recognise the possibility of self-determination by the South's non-Muslim population. Divisions within the South together with waning government power in Khartoum have, therefore, made the prospect of a ceasefire – perhaps even a peace agreement – envisageable.

In July 1998, the various parties to the conflict agreed to cease fighting temporarily so as to allow for the delivery of humanitarian aid: the famine was taking on dramatic proportions, particularly in Bahr el Ghazal. As always, a good part of the assistance destined for victims was diverted by combatants from both the North and the South, with international agencies having neither the means nor the political mandate to stop such a scandalous exploitation of misery.

In this regard, one might wonder just how much longer 27 million Sudanese can survive on the infusion of humanitarian aid without the world realising the absurdity of the situation – a situation that is financially preposterous, politically pointless and, in particular, humanely unacceptable.

Somalia

A country adrift

JEAN-MARC JOUINEAU

Chronology

1969	Coup d'état and accession of General Mohamed Siad Barre to power.
1977–78	Ogaden war with Ethiopia and defeat of Somali army.
1981	Creation of country's first political opposition parties in the north.
1988	Formation of the Hawiye-dominated United Somali Congress (USC), including General Aideed and Ali Mahdi.
1990–91	Civil war and removal of Siad Barre by USC. Mahdi appointed interim President.
1991–92	Fighting in the south of the country between partisans of General Mahdi and General Aideed.
1992	Beginning of the great famine in the south. NGO arrival 'en masse'.
End of 1992	Operation Unosom, followed by Restore Hope under US command.
1993	Unosom II; violence and retaliation.
March 1995	End of operation Unosom II and departure of all foreign forces.
September 1995	Attack and siege of the prosperous Bay and Bakool regions by General Aideed, followed by continuous fighting ever since.
August 1996	Death of General Aideed during heavy fighting south of Mogadishu; replaced by his son Hussein.
December 1996	First official meeting in Nairobi; resumption of negotiations between Aideed, Mahdi and Ato.
November 1997	Disastrous floods in the south; aid becomes difficult due to fighting.

Somalia

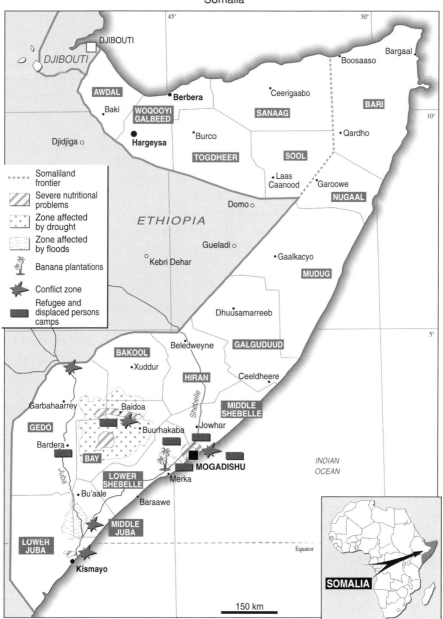

Legend:
- Somaliland frontier
- Severe nutritional problems
- Zone affected by drought
- Zone affected by floods
- Banana plantations
- Conflict zone
- Refugee and displaced persons camps

DJIBOUTI

DJIBOUTI

AWDAL

Baki

Berbera

WOQOOYI GALBEED

Hargeysa

Djidjiga

SANAAG

Ceerigaabo

Boosaaso

Bargaal

BARI

Burco

Qardho

TOGDHEER

SOOL

Laas Caanood

Garoowe

NUGAAL

ETHIOPIA

Domo

Gueladi

Kebri Dehar

Gaalkacyo

MUDUG

Dhuusamarreeb

Beledweyne

GALGUDUUD

BAKOOL

Xuddur

HIRAN

Ceeldheere

Garbahaarrey

Baidoa

MIDDLE SHEBELLE

GEDO

Buurhakaba

Jowhar

Bardera

BAY

Shebelle

MOGADISHU

INDIAN OCEAN

LOWER SHEBELLE

Merka

Bu'aale

Baraawe

Juba

MIDDLE JUBA

LOWER JUBA

Equator

Kismayo

150 km

SOMALIA

For a variety of completely unconnected reasons, Somalia regularly appears at the forefront of debate. None of the coverage on Somalia reveals any logical evolution: security incidents in the south, catastrophic floods, peace negotiations between the country's principal leaders, the kidnapping of humanitarian aid workers in Mogadishu, new political alliances. Such an imbroglio of events has already discouraged a number of foreign observers and caused the departure of the UN, together with a number of NGOs, from the field. Is this the result of a legitimate misunderstanding or of general error?

Has Somalia become a total mystery, far too dangerous for foreign actors, or is it in fact undergoing reconstruction based on patterns incomprehensible to the outsider? How can its population manage to survive amid such apparent chaos? To what degree can humanitarian aid bring real benefit without becoming embroiled in the conflict? All these questions remain unanswered. Perhaps only one conclusion might be reached: in a country now adrift, much of the population remains on the margins.

THE RATIONALE BEHIND ASSISTANCE

Orchestrated with a view to creating a greater Somalia,[1] Siad Barre's accession to power by force in 1969 exacerbated both clan and regional tensions, leading to an all-out civil war and his removal. The same problems always seem to have the same effects. Thus, the contested appointment of Ali Mahdi as the country's interim President simply fractured the winning clan, and launched a new and even more atrocious and fratricidal war – only a few months after Mahdi came to power. The confrontation still persists.

In 1992, the civil war, together with a disastrous drought, led to a terrible famine, provoking UN humanitarian intervention on a scale hitherto unknown. Despite the huge efforts made, no political solution was found, so leaving the country's 'warlords' responsible for the situation. The massive and rapid retreat of Unosom II's forces in March 1995 only strengthened the power of the faction leaders, still in place despite the

---

1. Greater Somalia is a fictitious entity comprising five geographical zones: north-west Somalia or Somaliland; Djibouti; the Ethiopian region or Ogaden; present Somalia; and northern Kenya or Jubaland. Each zone forms one of the points of the star shown on the Somali flag.

American price-tag on their heads. Once more, they could be found shuffling their cards in a game to reconstruct spheres of influence, already the fruit of past divisions.

PERPETUATION OF THE CLAN SYSTEM

To understand the conflict in Somalia, the first element that should be taken into consideration is that of the clan. Traditionally, the clan is the driving force around which Somali society is structured. It is a system which has developed out of the more or less direct descendency of individuals according to a highly complex genealogical tree going all the way back to its two original 'founders', Saab and Somaal. Belonging to a clan means being part of a system of solidarity and mutual protection that exists among members of the same clan and allows for the resolution of the various conflicts between individuals and groups through arbitration by the elders.[2] The system is based on tribal order and can be sub-divided all the way down to the smallest entity of kinship. As such, it helps to maintain stability among the different communities. It should also be mentioned that each clan traditionally possesses a recognised territory.

The different and successive systems of leadership in Somalia since independence in 1960 have inevitably had to take clan structure into account when forming alliances. Thus, Siad Barre – ironically the founder of Somali 'Scientific Socialism', a system that placed particular emphasis on a society that was to transcend clan entities – surrounded himself with a strong and homogeneous clan structure that controlled all key posts, the MOD alliance.[3] In this regard, he laid the foundations for the emergence of a clan-based opposition. In fact, created in the 1980s, the different political opposition parties of Somalia all have origins directly linked to clan or region, such as the SNM in Somaliland (Issak clan) or the SSDF in the north-east of the country (Majerteen clan). And all arose in response to clan abuse of power. Indeed, this party system remained intact after Siad Barre's removal, in fact fragmenting even further into a multiple of sub-entities symbolic of the country's total explosion along clan lines following the outbreak of civil war.

2. The elders are essentially the clan's wise men.
3. Marehan, Ogaden, Dolbahante: three sub-clans of the larger Darod clan. Siad Barre himself was from the Marehan clan.

The UN intervention leant very heavily on these newly created 'political entities', promoting them to the rank of international negotiator. In doing so, it consolidated the rise to power of their militaro-politico-clan leaders, the principal aim of whom was to provide wealth and employment to their particular clan. The strategy of top-down negotiations with non-representative clan leaders, or leaders of homogeneous geographical entities having more locally based economic interests, not only contributed to reinforcing imbalances but also ran counter to the initial objective of resuming the peace process.

Negotiations between the principal southern leaders have, to date, all been doomed to failure despite the signature of a number of agreements and the involvement of influential international mediators. In fact, these same reputed leaders have now become victims of their own lack of representativity at home in that their power has become exclusively tied to control over a parallel economic system and, therefore, to the military and economic agents dependent on it.

The clan entity, then, is being used as a means to an end, that of political mobilisation, given that it forms the only real system of reference still in existence. Such divergent interests will not be conducive to real progress in the peace process unless the true representatives of traditional Somali society, the elders of the different clans, are involved. However, these elders have lost much of their influence due to the civil war, massive population movement and, above all, the advent of the warlords.

AN ECONOMY IN TATTERS

The conflict aside, Somalia is a country with scarce natural resources, heavily dependent on external support for survival. Given semi-arid conditions, farming is possible only in the south of the country, notably in the regions between the Shebelle and Juba rivers. The principal resource, meanwhile, given a predominantly nomadic population, remains that of camel and goat-breeding, destined for export to countries in the Arabian peninsula. Export-oriented 'banana plantations' in the Lower Shebelle region to the south of Mogadishu, on the other hand, provide the country with Italian currency.

The country's resulting dependency on external aid has given rise to something of a 'welfare' culture, developed above all under the regime of former dictator Siad Barre, when all basic services were provided free to the population, education and health included. At the time, humanitarian aid had taken on such huge proportions, especially after the war with Ethiopia in 1977–78, that by the 1980s it came to represent more than half of Somalia's GDP! This humanitarian 'godsend' continued to provide a basic income until 1995, at which time most organisations left the country.

The consequences of the civil war were catastrophic: destruction of all existing infrastructure, monopoly over the country's few traditional resources by a few 'businessmen', control over trade routes by these same men and their newly formed militias, trafficking of all sorts of goods through Somali ports.... The list goes on.

After several months, the country was in a spiral of complete and utter disintegration, without a functioning State structure and thrown into disarray by permanent warlord conflict. While it is true that massive humanitarian intervention in 1992 made it possible to re-establish regular supplies, the revival of a degree of economic dynamism helped to sustain the pre-existing 'humanitarian welfare culture', although in a different form. This it did by creating an important number of jobs and by providing food, health care and medicine free-of-charge. The aid also gave rise to a parallel network of income opportunities, with militia groups under the control of the various militario-economic leaders misappropriating supplies destined for the most vulnerable populations. By unintentionally strengthening their power, humanitarian aid helped the respective armed forces of the different warlords to survive and to pursue the war effort.

The departure of Unosom II in 1995, as well as that of a number of humanitarian organisations discouraged by the insecurity and diversion of aid, significantly reduced the advantages of humanitarianism – and with it, the direct aid supplied in the form of salaries and other benefits to employees of governmental and non-governmental organisations. Such an abrupt loss led to an increase in banditry and the systematic looting of all resources, to the detriment primarily of those already the most vulnerable, given that they are the least protected. Particularly affected have been the agropastoralists living along the rivers and dependent on the harvests for their survival. The loss has also reinforced the parallel economy that transits through Somalia and, consequently, the power of local actors trying to counter the results of the international community's 'defection'.

A POPULATION HELD TO RANSOM

Within this complex and unstable situation, much of the civilian popula-tion has found itself with no direct access to resources that might otherwise ensure their survival. Admittedly, the present situation cannot be compared to that of the huge famine of 1992–93, which led to the death or forced displacement of several thousands. Nevertheless, present conditions have left Somalis on the verge of a similar tragedy – a tragedy that still looms over this fragmented country. Faced with this reality, a decreasing number of humanitarian organisations are trying, despite growing difficulties, to continue their work.

THE NUMEROUS REJECTED

The new power relationships established by the country's leaders have become reflected in the almost automatic politico-clan affiliated support of the vast majority of the population. Indeed, in the absence of any alternative source of income, not much room is left for any choice other than chronic civilian dependency. The passive support obtained, meanwhile, simply serves to strengthen the power of these same leaders and hence the logic dictating the war. This said, such a solution is only feasible for those who are members of a 'strong clan', one that controls the country's wealth and benefits from the latter's redistribution.

Others remain excluded from the informal economy, being made all the more vulnerable. Among these are:
– displaced persons who have fled fighting, poor harvests or flooding and have been reduced to living in a hostile environment. Mogadishu alone has a population of about 150,000 displaced persons, which corresponds to approximately 20% of the town's total population!
– Ethiopian refugees who have been living in various camps for almost 20 years and lack clan support;
– so-called 'inferior tribes' such as the Bantu. Despite being the country's first inhabitants, the latter survive on a daily basis from the gains to be had from fishing or seasonal labour. The decomposition of Somali society has rendered them entirely dependent on other clans, with no support from the rest of the population and, as a result, in an extremely precarious situation.

Moreover, in the south of the country where they live, the civilian population is always the first victim of the continual fighting among warlords. This is also the case in Mogadishu, where the population is sometimes forced to flee the town (as during fighting in Medina in 1996, for instance), although more often than not there tends to be an influx into the area, with populations fleeing highly tense areas such as the Bay region.

Such displaced persons have to leave their homes amidst disaster, in most cases also being forced to leave part of their families behind in order to protect the few belongings they may still have, in an attempt to avoid systematic pillaging by militia groups.

THE HUMANITARIAN IMPASSE

Over the years, the nature of humanitarian aid to Somalia has also changed. The period of abundance, corresponding to that of high media coverage of the spectacular UN intervention between 1992 and 1995, is over. Somalia has, instead, been left to pale into insignificance, as if classified a 'chronic and insoluble political problem'. In parallel, the financial resources that once came from the outside have whithered away for those organisations that have decided to continue activities. Numbers have fallen dramatically, a trend which is set to continue. As a result, humanitarian aid is having to become ever more targeted and better focused on the country's most vulnerable populations, while changing in nature as well. In this regard, the assistance of the early days is being progressively replaced by a more participatory approach, involving communities in both the implementation and the follow-up of defined objectives. While the trend may be inevitable, even from a 'technical' point of view, humanitarian needs still remain dire for a population deprived of everything and having little hope of an improvement in conditions in the near future. Here, the approach appears somewhat incomprehensible to both the local population and international NGOs' local partners, for whom humanitarian aid represents an integral part of traditional subsistence networks. As a result, those organisations still present in Somalia are under growing pressure to explain their new way of working.

Changes have also led to a marked deterioration in security conditions for those humanitarian actors still present in the field. First and foremost, such organisations have become a more and more restricted target, increasingly visible and exposed within the politico-clan context of the country's south. The kidnapping of International Red Cross and Somali Red Crescent personnel in Mogadishu in April 1998 illustrates the tenfold risk. Growing dangers have meant that the armed guards in charge of the protection of both people and goods have had to be kept, at a time when limited financial resources require a streamlining of personnel. The imperatives of security have further reduced the resources available for programme implementation (logistics, human resources and so on, all of which have a direct impact on the income of entire families, and open the door to incidents motivated by the sometimes violent reaction of those who see their source of income whithering away).

Another problem that has arisen from the current situation is the increasingly limited access to the most vulnerable, those for whom humanitarian programmes were initially conceived. Increasingly difficult security conditions make it physically impossible for humanitarian organisations to supervise their activities over long periods of time. Thus, the Therapeutic Feeding Centre opened by Action Against Hunger in February 1996, in the enclave of Medina in south Mogadishu, only became accessible to expatriates at the beginning of 1997, due both to continuous fighting in the area and to problems experienced in obtaining transit permits.

Such a set of circumstances has forced humanitarian organisations to adapt their interventions so as to reduce risk-taking as much as possible, while continuing to bring aid to those worst affected by the permanent insecurity. The only way to achieve this has been to give greater responsibility to local staff and local partners, in a better position to have permanent access to such sensitive areas.

Lastly, another difficulty for NGOs arises from their relative isolation in south Somalia where, following the departure of all UN expatriates, they currently represent the only international presence. Today, they form the final rampart for the population and the only ones capable of being witness to the situation. All these NGOs form part of a network called the Somali Aid Coordination Body (SACB), based in Nairobi. Including all those involved in the Somali conflict (UN, embassies and donors), the consortium aims to provide support and a framework of intervention for humanitarian aid, within a somewhat rudderless country. Initially, the SACB was to act as a mediator for humanitarian aid, but it has increasingly moved towards conditioning aid delivery (in reputed emergency areas) and incorporating significantly more political aspects. This is occurring to such an extent that NGOs and their local partners increasingly feel that they are being used as levers of action at a level different from their own objectives. For those NGOs in the field, such a balancing of humanitarian aid and non-humanitarian considerations represents an instrumentalisation of aid which they find difficult to accept given the urgent and dire needs of certain populations.

Thus, Somalia, one of the poorest countries in the world, is to be found in a situation from which there is apparently no way out, deprived of a government since the outbreak of civil war in 1991, and hostage to a few non-representative 'political leaders', with an international community weary of the latter's endless procrastinations and gradually losing interest. The absence of any kind of re-distributive system other than that based on the seizure of aid has led to the impoverishment of a large part of the population, excluded from informal subsistence networks and owing their survival to external aid, part of which is also siphoned off. Humanitarian aid, then, is caught in an impasse, forced to substitute a non-existent state in order to respond to the most basic needs of a population in despair. Neither does it have the means to tackle root causes – in itself not a particularly ingratiating role and one made all the more difficult in view of the growing threats to expatriate security, but most definitely an indispensable role if the country is to be prevented from falling into total oblivion.

Mogadishu, Somalia:
women in the fight against hunger

IESHA SINGH

Mogadishu today, once the heart of the Somali State as it was formed in 1960, lies riven into four clan and occupationally based enclaves. Each enclave has its own infrastructure linking the rural-metropolis nexus, and a corresponding array of checkpoints regulating flows of people and merchandise. All have been affected by damage sustained during the war, and influencing levels of economic activity and opportunity.

Yet, while once the sounds of rockets and bullets screaming overhead formed the backdrop of everyday life, today they are more sporadic. The conflict that burst onto the global stage at the beginning of the 1990s has become drawn out into a protracted crisis, characterised by stalemate and international disinterest. With the collapse of talks in Cairo and the indefinite postponement of the Bossasso Conference,[4] the capital appears to have fallen into an uneasy slumber, the ashes smouldering beneath.

As debates about the peace process persist, and rivalries over clan and resources continue, for the civilians of Mogadishu the first and foremost preoccupation is that of survival. It is a preoccupation that tends to be all the more acute for the refugees and displaced of the city, for it is they who have lost most of their belongings and social support networks in flight, and it is they who have had to make the greater effort in adapting to environmental change and a mis-match in skills and competence. Nevertheless, altogether the primary struggle is one against hunger.[5] And

4. The Bossasso Conference was destined to bring together representatives from all clans and all areas from both Somalia and Somaliland to discuss future peace arrangements. The Cairo talks were to act as a prelude to this.
5. An underlying assumption throughout this chapter is that hunger is seen to be a physical and mental state caused by lack of food (for whatever reasons), and one that can, in itself, go on to create significant vulnerability to malnutrition and ill-health, both of which can be further aggravated by inadequate hygiene and sanitation.

across the board, it is women who appear to be at the forefront of a spectrum of activities related to this fight, and associated issues of household food security, nutritional status, health and hygiene.

WOMEN ON THE FRONTLINE: ANOTHER KIND OF BATTLE

To secure food

Whether refugee, displaced or resident, women have tended to take up the relay not only in the quest to produce food where possible, but also in the pursuit of income to purchase any food available on the market. Following the death or departure of their husbands, or as the supportive capacities of men have declined in the wake of social disruption and market contraction, these women have reacted with strength and determination. In this, they have not always been alone, drawing upon the support and contribution of their children, their elders and where possible that of their husband, brother or uncle. For despite an often considerable incompatibility with market-skill requirements, significant numbers of men do manage to contribute in some measure to daily food security, most often as construction workers or market and dock-side porters, or through begging.[6] This said, they have not, arguably, revealed quite the same initiative and versatility – and in many instances, visibility – as women.[7]

In itself, female involvement in income generation is not as singular as an initial glance might suggest, even though Somalia is a patriarchal society where providing for the family has traditionally been considered part of the male preserve. Among the urbanised residents, the current emphasis on productive activities may well be reminiscent of the inflationary experiences of the 1980s. In an attempt to supplement their husbands' sharply eroding incomes, large numbers of women were compelled to find employment, much of this in the informal sector (with small stalls for fruit, vegetables and clothes, for example). However, unlike the present situation, the imperative for women to work outside the home proved relatively short-lived.

6. The notion of food security as used here is a little peculiar, characterised by the short-term, due to the general insecurity in Mogadishu.
7. Men have also more generally been charged with wiling away their time 'politicking' and chewing *khat*, a natural stimulant.

For those of an agropastoral heritage (the majority of refugees and displaced),[8] life within the household unit was always characterised by a strong division of labour organised around principles of gender and age. In this regard, women's activities stretched across a whole gamut of activities, from those that took place within the ambit of the household, such as the milking of cattle, goats and sheep, to those that took place around the household, on the farm or the grasslands, such as sowing, ploughing and harvesting, and those that took place in the local market, including the sale of small amounts of milk, butter, meat and crops from the farm.

Today, in a bid to improve the availability of, and direct access to, food, women among the poorer socio-economic strata in particular may be seen cultivating small plots of maize, sorghum and beans, or rearing sheep and goats in and around their homes (camps included). To improve indirect access to food, on the other hand, they may be found preparing peanuts or ropes for subsequent sale by their children; tailoring for their friends and neighbours; selling clothes, fruit and vegetables, or various handicrafts in the streets or markets of Mogadishu; or offering their services as cleaners and launders to those households of more middling socio-economic status.[9] Women among these latter households, meanwhile, may be involved in the NGO sector or, relatively less formally, in the *khat* and gold trades. Across the socio-economic division, there is also some evidence of prostitution as a means of income generation, particularly among the female-headed households (FHHs).[10]

Women are also prominent in the search for, and provision of, external assistance. In the first instance, women from among the more deprived households, especially FHHs, can be regularly discovered entreating distant relatives, friends or strangers for support. In itself, this activity is not completely new, although it has gained substantial importance with the conflict and tends to be clan-based. In the second instance, women from the diaspora in North America and Western Europe have been active in sending remittances to family members left at home. For those who fled Somalia after the coup of Siad Barre in 1969, this too, has historical antecedents.

---

8. Pastoralism is a mode of production based on livestock (in this context, camels, cattle, sheep and goats), but depending on natural forage – and in arid regions, on constant or periodic movement in search of pasture. Agropastoralism is a more semi-sedentarised form of pastoralism, supplemented by agricultural activities. Markakis, J. (ed); 1993.
9. Handicrafts might include mats, baskets, small fans and bags made from palm leaves, and so on.
10. Power-Stevens, T.; 1995.

To ensure family well-being

For those women remaining in Mogadishu, this already highly charged agenda is aggravated by household maintenance and reproductive work. Activities here might include housework (cleaning, tidying, laundry), water and fuel collection, and food procurement, preparation and service, with childcare and care of the elderly and sick being further, integral components of all of these. As families are extended and may comprise as many as nine persons, the responsibilities tend to be onerous and complex. These women are to be all things to all people, such that neglect of any one responsibility is sure to have negative repercussions elsewhere.

Accordingly, women may be regularly observed ferrying water from the nearest well, gathering fuel from the bush, grinding maize in the nearest clearing, bending over an open fire to prepare the family meal, sweeping in and around the house, accompanying a malnourished child to the nearest traditional healer or Supplementary Feeding Centre, walking to the market to buy food, and so on. It is women who have the primary responsibility for ensuring that diets are balanced and that food is properly cooked; and it is women who, among a host of other activities, are called upon to determine whether a child is ill and then seek help.

For those from the poorer socio-economic strata, assistance in fulfilling these roles may be obtained through the family and clan. Hence, younger children may contribute to collecting water from the nearest well or gathering twigs and sticks from the street, while girls and elderly women, in particular, will often undertake child care and housework. For those who are more affluent, help in fulfilling these roles may be more forthcoming through hired labour and the ability to pay for certain services such as water and fuel delivery, as well as through family and clan.

Whatever the conditions, in war-torn Mogadishu it appears to be women who hold the roles of most significance in the struggle against hunger and all that this involves. Moreover, in a context where divorce is, and widowhood has become, somewhat endemic, such a situation is becoming more common given growing numbers of FHHs.[11] Thus, it might be said that in the fight against hunger, as the elderly, the men and the

---

11. Somali society is essentially a polygamous one, where a man may effectively divorce his wife by pronouncing the full Islamic divorce formula 'I divorce thee' three times, in the presence of witnesses, thereby dissolving the marriage. Lewis, I.M.; 1994; p. 62. It may at least be partly for this reason that divorce may be said to be endemic. Widowhood, meanwhile, is obviously more a direct result of the current state of war.

children bring up the rear, the women are resolutely launching a civil offensive and, as the principal combatants, are besieged from all sides.

ACTORS AND STRUCTURES: THE PROTAGONISTS IN THE BATTLE

Although multi-faceted in nature, the obstacles faced by women can essentially be conceived as embedded in patterns of social organisation, as expressed through cultural and politico-economic relationships. These relationships are dynamic and constantly undergoing change, whether gradual or accelerated, transient or permanent. They are, therefore, specific to time and place, contingent upon historical conditions. In this respect, the violent conflict that swept across Somalia at the beginning of the decade has been (and continues to be) an important catalyst in stimulating and precipitating transformation, obviously interacting with existing relationships as it does so.

Cultural underpinnings, their reproduction and reinforcement

At the more immediate ground level, the conflict has witnessed a multiplication in some cases or an intensification in virtually all cases of the hunger-related roles and responsibilities of women in Mogadishu. Although activities relating to family health and nutritional well-being have traditionally dominated women's lives, in the current context of conflict-induced and climatic insecurity these activities have – in becoming almost Herculean in stature – taken on renewed importance. In a similar way, the stakes for those involved in activities to improve food security have also risen; even where this may not be a particularly new phenomenon, the challenges entailed have nevertheless increased. Women's roles might be said to have become more visible and more heavily weighted.

At the same time, these changes have been more generally both constrained *and* augmented by certain norms and values informing social practice, and ultimately forming part of the opposition with which women, consciously or otherwise, have to engage. Of relevance might be the 'time factor', and the 'last and least principle'.[12]

---

12. The list is not exhaustive and makes no mention either of concerns about levels of education for females in general or of periodic problems of infection arising from the practice of female infibulation in an often unhygienic environment.

The 'time factor' essentially relates to the amount of time women can spend on any one activity (with or without the assistance of other family members), given the numerous tasks for which they are ultimately responsible. Thus, fuel and water collection, housework and food preparation all whittle away at the amount of time women can specifically assign to income generation and/or child care, to the detriment of both. For example, while men might be able to devote as many as nine or ten hours to productive activities, women on the other hand, being subject to a fuller and more diverse day, tend to be restricted to an average of four to seven. This automatically reduces the amount that can be earned in any one day.[13] At the same time, the primacy of subsistence detracts from that of family care. Indeed, the Somali proverb *nin baahan dab kama bayro* puts it quite well: *a hungry stomach has no ears*.

These phenomena further add to the pressures to which women and their families are subjected, with the result that even more stress is placed on family cohesion. Yet, where relief might come in the form of collective endeavours involving men and boys in activities such as housework and child care, beliefs and norms regulating gender divisions are such that this is limited, most notably among the poorer socio-economic strata where the need is all the greater.

The 'last and least principle', meanwhile, can be taken to refer to the customary distribution of food within the household. According to this principle, women tend to eat last and least, so that others may benefit from any given amount of food. In the current situation of scarcity, use of this method of distribution as a coping mechanism appears all the more salient, but as one that has become part of *normality*: a constant in these women's lives (again, especially among the poorer socio-economic strata, and particularly the displaced). Somewhat paradoxically, however, this could be having negative effects on the health and nutrition status of women. Despite the cardinal roles women play in the fight against hunger and the strength demanded for this, women, in eating last and least, are perhaps among the most vulnerable sectors of the population. The situation is further compounded when consideration is taken of the amount of time women spend in pregnancy and breast-feeding, and the greater energy and protein levels required for these, combined with an

13. It is not known to what extent there are differentials in the perceived value of each type of work according to gender, although it can be assumed that these perceptions do affect earnings to some extent.

increasing general propensity to eat fewer meals per day (relative to the pre-war situation) and a switch to cheaper, often less nutritious foods (particularly carbohydrates).[14]

In part, these changes are obviously a function of the wider and more general food production and distribution system in Somalia. Interestingly enough though, it tends to be the women themselves who make any conscious decision regarding food distribution within the household, often claiming that 'a woman has to be tolerant and understand that as a woman, she has to be last. If she learns otherwise, she will forget her place, her husband and her children.' Men, on the other hand, tend to note that such a distribution finds both its cause and its rationale in a tradition that has spanned the generations. In a time of flux and instability, this tradition must no doubt represent a pillar of certainty to which many people cling.

Together, then, the 'time factor' and the 'last and least principle' make the struggle of women in Mogadishu all the more difficult – an ever steeper gradient in an already up-hill struggle. The system of beliefs, norms and values which govern Somali society and effectively give men a privileged position relative to that of women form a common denominator for both. While men tend to be looked upon as rational and intelligent, women tend to be perceived as emotional and irrational, such that their counsel and work are, by implication, defective and hence secondary.[15] From here, perhaps, arises the proverb *naag ama u samir ama ka samir*, meaning *you must be patient with women or forget them entirely*.

Following this logic, the roles and responsibilities of men would appear relatively more appropriate in the public and more visible sphere of life outside the household, while their overall authority in matters regulating private life within the household would need to be definitive. Hence, it is men who dominate virtually all explicit decision-making, and it is men who, in the last instance, tend to control family earnings. Indeed, these are considered to belong to the husband or father, who then 'devolves' power to

14. Before the war, a gender division in the type of meat served could also be discerned, with females in general being given meat considered of inferior quality, usually the intestines. Today, however, by virtue of circumstance, everyone tends to receive the same food (among the poorer socio-economic strata, at least).

15. Women's emotional irrationality is said to be the result of their biological nature, symbolised by three elements related to the female productive role: the menstrual blood, child birth and breast-feeding. CODEP; 1996; *The Gender Dynamic: Analysis and Policy*; Oxford Brookes University, UK.

the female adult, giving her a specific amount of money for household purchases.[16]

Women, by contrast, would need to be discrete and their ultimate control over resources be regulated, for which reasons they might be said to be better placed to work in and around the home, in the private, more invisible sphere. As a result, their position is relatively inferior. Such an explanation contributes to an understanding of why time remains an important constraint for women, with men effectively unable to alleviate the burden, despite the dilemmas that the present circumstances might raise. It also contributes to a better understanding of why women eat last and least.[17]

The values and beliefs underpinning these two phenomena effectively form a structure and a principle of organisation within which women struggle in the fight against hunger, although it is a structure which is essentially intangible and of which few are arguably conscious. Indeed, its very assumptions have been largely internalised by Somali society, with both men and women being instrumental in perpetuating and reproducing the culture evident today. Both continually look to it as they go about their lives. This said, given a patriarchal society where the position of the male is predominant, the balance between the two actors, men and women, may actually lie with men: men may well be those more active in upholding this culture. Although there might exist a greater respect for women's workload and the constraints they face, this would not appear to have provoked accommodation and concrete change.

The dynamics of the political economy and those who nurture it

At a somewhat different, although nonetheless inter-related level, the Somali conflict has been host to the development of a war-oriented political economy, straddling administrative and geographical boundaries. The balkanisation of the country into restricted clan-dominated regions and

16. Somewhat confusingly, the wife or mother may be entrusted with the safe-keeping of any surplus money, something perhaps indicative of trust and an element of rationality? However, in the current circumstances, where virtually all the family budget is given to the wife, this devolution tends to be dictated more by pragmatism and poverty, than by patriarchal structures.
17. While suggesting a degree of perceived inferiority, the importance of women's roles as peacemakers is not refuted, although it is arguable that this role of mediation is one that elevates their political status. For an explanation, see: Power-Stevens, T.; 1995; p. 101.

zones has limited 'internal' movements of people and business, such that 'external' movements are flourishing. With few authoritative and systematic controls, each pocket of the economy has become increasingly globalised and outward-oriented through labour export, remittances, trade and investment.[18] Moreover, in side-stepping internal instabilities and diminished purchasing power, this is helping to sustain the various factions and therefore the conflict.

Each pocket of the economy could be said to work along the principles of an unhindered liberal capitalist market economy,[19] where concomitantly only those with sufficient purchasing power and/or political clout can exploit it and make an effective bid in the market place. Thus, the conflict has witnessed two mutually interdependent tendencies, whereby some members of the Somali community have stood to gain (a minority), while others have substantially lost (the majority).

In this respect, the conflict has involved an acceleration of asset-transfers (already begun under the Barre regime) and more particularly of those relating to land resources. The importance of this cannot be understated, given the grounding of the Somali economy in the primary sector, that is, in agriculture and livestock. In 1990, for instance, agriculture alone was thought to represent some 65% of the GDP.[20] Prominent in calculations, then, has been control over the fertile inter-riverine areas, today largely occupied by the Hawiye clan group. The latter, mainly through the Habr Gedr sub-clan grouping, has consequently been able to wield control over the vast banana plantations which produce the country's most important export crop.[21] This has been done in collaboration with two (competing) trans-national corporations, the American company, Dole, and the Italian subsidiary, Somalfruit – and has also been to the exclusion of other clan groupings.

It is somewhat ironic that while the majority of Somalis are confronted with a food deficit, a minority (hand-in-hand with global agribusiness) act as net exporters of food. Conditions of marginalisation and deprivation of the majority are therefore significantly locked into the dynamics of a larger political economy.

18. Prendergast, J.; 1996.
19. Despite the bottlenecks and impediments caused by the inadequate and damaged transport and communications infrastructure. Sabrie, A.M.; 1997.
20. Economist Intelligence Unit; 1996; *Somalia Country Report*; Third Quarter; EIU.
21. Cassannelli, C.V.; 1997; *Somali Land Resources in Historical Perspective*; in Markakis, J. (ed); pp. 68–73.

Aggravating these conditions have been the consistent looting and destruction of economic assets – homes, crops, livestock and water sources included. In some cases, this has been done to deter the enemy, to gain advantage against an opposing clan, or due to affiliation with the 'wrong' (especially minority) clan; in others, it has been done to create a compliant, dependent population or simply to gain materially, whether in Bay, Bakool, Mogadishu or elsewhere. This further impedes any meaningful production and trade, causing ever greater impoverishment and threats to survival.

Both asset transfer and destruction have been crucial triggers to destitution, displacement and family breakdown, with those fleeing attacks on their homes and property often subject to additional military action en route or at their destination. The result in Mogadishu has been a disempowered majority that can neither voice an effective demand in the market place, nor easily gather the resources needed to enter the market as an effective supplier (assuming any necessary skills and training).

The situation is further exacerbated by the increasing fragility of the productive base for staple goods outside Mogadishu. On the one hand, any investments made tend to be directed towards cash crops for export, *khat* for immediate consumption, and arms and weapons.[22] On the other hand, agricultural activity has itself diminished due to fears among many of the displaced to return to their lands, with large amounts of agricultural land returning to bush as a result. In parallel, the gradual curtailment of spontaneous movement and subsequent increase in concentration of pastoralists can only be heightening environmental degradation and simultaneously reducing pastoralist productivity.[23] In a setting where very little of the pastoralists' output is for sale in the market anyway, supplies of goods to Mogadishu would be further reduced. Both availability of and access to food have been adversely affected.

Thus, much of the insecurity that pervades the fight against hunger in terms of food finds its roots in the current political war economy – in the market structure that it has spawned and in the clan factions and their leaders who violently uphold it. With roles and responsibilities that take them out of the private household domain, women are very much caught up within this. Their struggles to feed their families are inherently conditioned by the structure of the Somali political economy and the public actions of its principal players. At the same time, the immensity of these

22. Waldo, M.A.; 1997.
23. Markakis, J. (ed); 1993; Intro.

struggles is made all the greater by the demanding roles and responsibilities of the household domain (that is, of family well-being), conditioned as these are by the norms and values of Somali society. However, beyond an inner circle of family and clan support (although even here, subject to certain constraints), there are few upon whom these women can call for assistance. Indeed, in many ways, they are acting in something of a vacuum.

ASSISTANCE IN PERSPECTIVE: RIGHTS AND DUTIES ASSESSED

Looking more closely at the fight for food (given its overriding importance to the inhabitants of Mogadishu), ordinarily the international legal system should provide some support. It is, after all, supposed to be a weapon of the relatively weaker against the stronger, a means to improve their position. In this, although there exists no specific and recognised right to food *per se*, there do exist several related instruments, found principally in International Human Rights Law (IHRL) and International Humanitarian Law (IHL).[24] In the case of a country such as Somalia, wracked as it is by internal conflict, the most important among these laws might be presumed to be: the two International Covenants of 1966, on Economic, Social and Cultural Rights and on Civil and Political Rights (part of IHRL); and Common Article 3 of the four Geneva Conventions of 1949, together with Additional Protocol II of 1977 (part of IHL).[25] In fact, however, none of the

24. While IHRL finds its principal field of application in times of peace, some of its standards are said to be non-derogable (that is, they cannot be suspended or limited), no matter what the situation. In such instances, IHL, being designed to protect individuals in times of war and violent conflict, might be said to act as a reinforcement. In certain instances where IHRL is derogable (in times of public emergency threatening the life of the State), however, IHL might be said to act as something of a poultice to an open wound. However, there does not yet appear to be any consensus as to what exactly constitutes a hard core, non-derogable right. Moreover, even when taken together, the two legal regimes essentially represent more of a 'patchwork' of rights and duties, rather than a coherent ensemble, each contingent upon the nature of the prevailing circumstances. Darcy, J.; 1997; p. 10; and Tomasevski, K.; 1995; p. 74.

25. The former State of Somalia was never a signatory to the Additional Protocols (Personal Communication; Department of IHL, British Red Cross; 06/05/98), although it did sign the two Covenants in 1990 (Personal Communication; UN Information Centre; 06/05/98). This notwithstanding, both the Covenants and the Geneva Conventions, together with the Additional Protocols, are generally considered to form part of customary law, given increasing usage across the international stage and a majority of States actually being party to them. Thus, they are said to be 'binding' (Detter, I.; 1994; pp. 15–18). However, it should be noted that international laws are binding only to the extent that States party to them are willing and able to enforce their application. Due to the primacy of sovereignty, the international legal system is devoid of any central legislature, executive or courts to enforce their application. The UN has simply been invested with a mandate to act on behalf of these States, as opposed to acting in its own right.

rights stipulated has, in the Somali case, been effectively translated into corollary duties and assistance to the women of Mogadishu and their families.

As enshrined in international law, Somalis, like everyone else, are holders of the right to life. Thus, Article 6 of the International Covenant on Civil and Political Rights stipulates that: *'Every human being has an inherent right to life.... No one shall be arbitrarily deprived of his life.'* It is a right commonly said to be held against everyone else, there being a general duty to respect it.[26] In a similar vein, but in relation to civilians specifically, Common Article 3 to the four Geneva Conventions declares that: *'All persons taking no active part in the hostilities shall in all circumstances be treated humanely'*, also prohibiting a series of acts such as *'violence to life and person'*. This is further extended by Article 14 of Additional Protocol II, such that: *'Starvation of civilians as a method of combat is prohibited. It is therefore prohibited to attack, destroy, remove or render useless, for that purpose, objects indispensable to the survival of the civilian population, such as foodstuffs, crops, livestock, drinking water installations and supplies and irrigation works.'*

While the Geneva Conventions essentially bind States, Additional Protocol II not only binds the official authorities, but any dissident armed forces within their ambit (that is, the State itself, along with its critics, including those who may take up, or have already taken up, arms against the government).[27] However, in the case of Somalia not only has there been blatant disregard of these rights (with the destruction of the means of subsistence and the killing of innocent civilians in crossfire, for instance), but neither is there any legitimate entity willing and able to ensure respect for them. Although many bodies exist with ostensible governmental functions throughout the Somali territory, none has been recognised, either internationally or, in many instances, nationally. None has a legitimate monopoly over coercion nor a desire to safeguard the 'public interest'. Thus, the search 'within' Somalia for responsible governmental authorities to fulfil obligations to protect against threats to life, for instance, is rendered somewhat null and void. Partially contingent on this is also the inability to monitor the behaviour of the armed factions in Somalia.

The provisions so far mentioned can be interpreted as being largely negative, involving the right not to be arbitrarily deprived of one's life, as

26. Vincent, R.J.; 1986.
27. Richieri, F.; 1997.

opposed to entailing positive steps to preserve life. In this respect, Article 11 of the International Covenant on Economic, Social and Cultural Rights can be seen as going some way in responding to the deficit. It delineates the right of everyone *'to an adequate standard of living'*, as well as *'to be free from hunger'* (where the intention of the latter does not appear to constrict the former).[28] It also sets forth a number of corresponding obligations. These comprise improvements to methods of production, conservation and distribution of food, as well as ensuring an equitable distribution of world food supplies in relation to needs.

In achieving the full materialisation of these rights, Article 11 also establishes duties that go beyond those of States in respect of their domestic duties (obviously not applicable in the current scenario). Thus, it further distinguishes States in respect of their external duties, individuals (to other individuals and their community, as written in the Preamble of the Covenant) and the international community.[29] Each of these, in turn, is generally said to have three correlative duties: duties to *avoid* depriving, duties to *protect* from deprivation and duties to *aid* the deprived.[30]

However, 'outside' Somalia, the will and commitment of States and the international community to take up these duties might also be called into question. At one level, food tends to be perceived as a trade commodity rather than a right,[31] where trade is to take place in, and be promoted by, an open global market or political economy *with minimal regulations*. Hence, the activities of companies such as Somalfruit and Dole are to be seen in more of a positive than a negative light.[32] In this sense, the international community, by omission (that is, by refraining from the regulation of global economic activity), may be party to the continuing prevalence of hunger in Mogadishu, given the external flows of food over which these companies – and those clans implicated – preside.

At another level, the debacle of UNOSOM and the final departure of the UN troops in March 1995[33] has resulted in the physical retreat (although

---

28. Carles, I.; 1997.
29. Carles, I.; 1997.
30. Carles, I.; 1997.
31. Tomasevski, K.; 1997, in Zwi, A. and Macrae, J. (eds).
32. Some guidelines do exist for the regulation of the international trade system, such as the OECD principles of 1976 for TNCs (Singh, I.; 1996; *Concepts Related to the Fight Against Hunger in International Law*; AAH). However, their relevance to the present context is debatable.
33. Under the aegis of the UN, a series of peace initiatives was attempted, each one resulting in failure and accusations of preferential treatment towards certain politico-military factions – and away from General Aideed. The UN period concluded in ignominious withdrawal.

an arms embargo is still in force)[34] of most of the international community from Mogadishu. Those organisations remaining tend to be located in the relative calm of Somaliland. With the end of the Cold War and the proliferation of intra-State conflict, the situation has been further compounded by more general donor fatigue and withdrawal from international relief assistance, such that even contracts to NGOs are relatively limited.[35] This in an environment where sub-contracting to NGOs has gained significant importance over the past few years. As a result, the implementation of the duties to avoid depriving, protect from deprivation and aid the deprived is substantially thwarted, despite an ability to identify the holders of these duties.

It is recognised that any sustainable resolution of the Somali conflict and the fight against hunger ultimately resides with the Somalis themselves. Nevertheless, upholding some of the rights mentioned above would make an important contribution to security and predictability, and thus to the fight against hunger of those in Mogadishu (as elsewhere). However, the result so far visible has been that the women of Mogadishu, together with their families, have taken up the burden of the responsibility in the realisation of any right to food. This they have done in contradiction to legal provisions that tend to classify them as passive 'objects' of the law and 'victims' of disaster. It is 'we', rather than the women and communities of Mogadishu, who might be said to watch from the sides.

CONCLUDING COMMENTS

It is not known what the future holds for Somalia. In the immediate term, if peace is not around the corner, dilemmas will keep tearing at Somali society. These will gradually weaken and disenfranchise ever greater numbers of Somalis (although some may be able to break through the

---

34. Personal communication; Somali Desk, BBC Worldservice; 06/05/98.
35. Here, it might be noted that Article 18(2) of Additional Protocol II provides for the possibility of humanitarian assistance. Thus: *'If the civilian population is suffering undue hardship owing to lack of the supplies essential for its survival, such as foodstuffs and medical supplies, relief actions for the civilian population which are of an exclusively humanitarian and impartial nature and which are conducted without any adverse distinction shall be undertaken subject to the consent of the High Contracting Party concerned.'* Although no 'duty' appears discernible here, humanitarian agencies are accorded a 'right' to provide relief, subject to the consent of (and by implication, potential manipulation by) the legal government (on the assumption that one exists). The *'droit d'ingerence'*, or right to interfere and/or intervene, however, attempts to circumvent this, although its status is very much open to dispute (Tomasevski, K.; 1995; in Macrae, J. and Zwi, A. [eds]).

barriers and challenge this) and simultaneously push the visibility of women even further (particularly in the struggle to find food).

If and when peace does arrive, questions of resource distribution and employment creation will all come to the fore. Entangled among these will be the changes that have occurred in gender roles and responsibilities, together with the future discourse of the incoming government. In order to avoid marginalisation and/or resentment of one or other group, and of one or other gender, a fine and informed balance would need to be struck. The gauntlet has been thrown down. When will it be taken up? By whom and with what support?

Bibliography

Broudic, C.; 1997; *Etude Socio-Economique Realisée a Mogadiscio*; Action Contre la Faim.

Carles, I.; 1997; 'The Right to Food'; LLM Dissertation submitted to University College London.

Darcy, J.; 1997; *Human Rights and International Legal Standards: What do Relief Workers Need to Know?* RRN Network Paper No.19.

Detter, I.; 1994; *The International Legal Order*; Dartmouth Publications.

Lewis, I.; 1994; *Blood and Bone: the Call of Kinship in Somalia*; Red Sea Press.

Macrae, J. and Zwi, A. (eds); 1995; *War and Hunger – International Responses to Complex Emergencies*; Zed Press (particularly chapters by Duffield, M. and Tomasevski, K.).

Markakis, J. (ed); 1993; *Conflict and the Decline of Pastoralism in the Horn of Africa*; Institute of Social Studies/Hague (particularly chapters by Cassanelli, C.V. and Markakis, J.).

Power-Stevens, T.; 1995; *Somalia – a Case Study*; in *Gender, Conflict and Development*; Baden, S. (eds); BRIDGE/IDS.

Prendergast, J.; 1996; *Frontline Diplomacy: Humanitarian Aid and Conflict in Africa*; Lynne Rienner Publications.

Richieri, F.; 1997; 'Starvation under International Humanitarian Law'; LLM Dissertation submitted to University College London.

Sabrie, A.M.; 1997; *The Performance and Constraints of the Civil War Private Sector in Southern Somalia with Particular Reference to Mogadishu*; Position Paper for the Workshop 'Toward a Unified Strategy for Development in Somalia'.

Singh, I.; 1997; *Gender Pilot Study in Mogadishu, Somalia*; Action Against Hunger.

Vincent, R.J.; 1986; *International Relations and Human Rights*; Cambridge University Press.

Waldo, M.A.; 1997; *The Somali Private Sector Development: the Economy of North-East Somalia: an Assessment Report*.

Afghanistan

A silent failure

THOMAS GONNET

Chronology

April 1978	Coup d'état and overthrow of the Daoud government. The 'Communist Revolution' leads to the disappearance of more than 50,000 people, mostly intellectuals, religious leaders or former government members.
December 1979	Soviet invasion of Afghanistan.
February 1989	Withdrawal of Soviet troops. The toll is heavy, with one million dead, two million injured and nearly five million refugees.
April 1992	Fall of the Communist regime; Najibullah is overthrown. In Kabul, Rabbani takes power, provoking combat with Uzbek, Hazara and Pashtun factions for nearly three years. As a result 70% of the city is destroyed. Appearance of the essentially Pashtun Taliban movement in Kandahar. These 'religious students' gradually take control of the country's south-east.
September 1995	Taliban offensive continues. Overthrow of Ismael Khan, governor of Herat, and capture of the city which constitutes a Tajik stronghold in the west of the country. The crossroads between Pakistan and Central Asia is established, thus opening the door to the commercial projects of Pakistan and its allies.
September 1996	Capture of Kabul by the Taliban and withdrawal of Rabbani's government and his commander Ahmad Shah Massoud to the Panshir valley. Formation of an anti-Taliban coalition, grouping together Tajiks, Uzbeks and Hazaras. The *Shari'a* law is imposed over the two-thirds of the country under Taliban control.

May 1997	Taliban offensive in the north of the country, due to support from the Uzbek, General Malek. Concern in Russia. Some of the humanitarian programmes in the region are suspended.
September 1997	Taliban offensive on Mazar-i Sharif leads to pillaging and bombing of the town. After pushing the Taliban back, Uzbek and Hazara factions turn on each other in a fight to control the city. In Kabul, tightening of the *Shari'a* and ban on women affects access to hospitals. After condemnation by international humanitarian agencies, the Taliban revoke the decision.
February 1998	The embargo imposed by the Taliban for more than one year on the Hazarajat threatens the civilian population. After three months of respite, there is a renewed upsurge of fighting in the country's north and around Kabul.
February and June 1998	Strong earthquakes in the Takhar and Badakhshan provinces cause 3,000 and 5,000 deaths respectively, and make more than 50,000 people homeless.
20 July 1998	Expulsion of 30 Western NGOs from Kabul by the Taliban.
August 1998	Taliban forces advance towards the north-east of Afghanistan, until then held by the opposition.

Throughout its history, Afghanistan has experienced numerous periods of political, economic and cultural prosperity. Located at the crossroads between East and West, rich in ethnic diversity, traditional craftsmanship, literature and art, the country has made significant contributions to the expansion of trade and the burgeoning of Islam. Although politically and geographically isolated, it has defended its independence with tenacity, skilfully exploiting its position as a buffer State vis-à-vis imperialists, preserving its neutrality and resisting all attempts at annexation. Having developed a system of government by the Rule of Law, Afghanistan was able to overcome ethnic and religious divisions and lay the foundations for a nation propitious for development.

By the end of the 1970s, however, Afghanistan's economic situation gave cause for concern, to say the least. The country's agricultural production was barely enough to maintain self-sufficiency, although 80% of the population was dependent on agriculture. Reasons for the extent of the country's under-development were to be found in its rural poverty, its illiteracy and infant and maternal mortality rates – among the highest in the world – and in a life expectancy of only 44 years. Agriculture was

Afghanistan

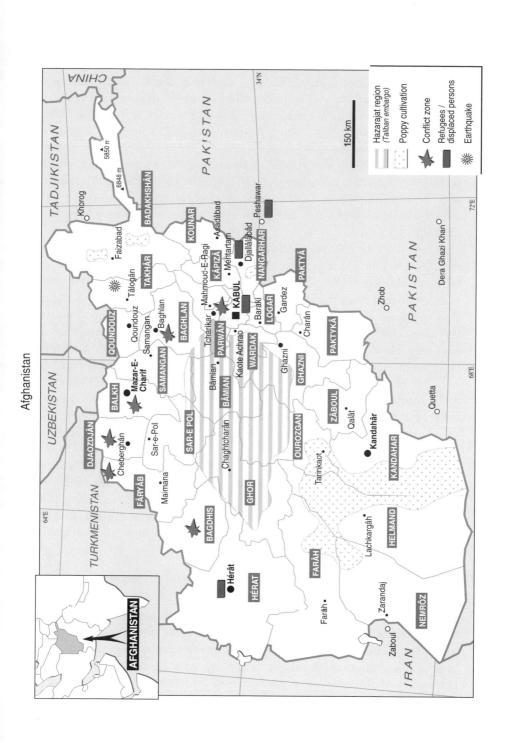

UZBEKISTAN
TADJIKISTAN
CHINA
TURKMENISTAN
PAKISTAN
IRAN

AFGHANISTAN

Khorog
Faizabad
BADAKHSHÂN
5850 m
6848 m
TAKHÂR
Tâloqân
KOUNAR
Asadâbad
Mahmoud-E-Ragi
KÂPIZÂ
Mehtarlam
Djallâlâbad
NANGARHÂR
Peshawar
Qoundouz
Samangan
Baghlan
BAGHLAN
QOUNDOUZ
Tchârikar
KABUL
PARWAN
Baraki
LOGAR
Gardez
Charân
PAKTYÂ
Mazar-E-Charif
BALKH
SAMANGAN
Kaole Achraô
WARDAK
Bâmian
BÂMIAN
Ghazni
GHAZNI
PAKTYKÂ
Cheberghân
DJAOZDJÂN
Sar-e-Pol
SAR-E-POL
OUROZGAN
Qalât
ZÂBOUL
Zhob
Quetta
PAKISTAN
Dera Ghazi Khan
34°N
Maimana
FÂRYÂB
Chaghtcharân
GHOR
Tarinkaot
Kandahâr
KANDAHAR
BAGDHIS
Lachkargâh
HELMAND
Hérât
HÉRAT
FARÂH
Farâh
Zarandaj
NEMRÔZ
Zaboul

64°E   68°E   72°E

150 km

Hazarajat region
(Taliban embargo)

Poppy cultivation

Conflict zone

Refugees /
displaced persons

Earthquake

characterised by inadequate road infrastructures, irrigation systems and trade networks, by the absence of any system of credit, by the fragmentation of land ownership and by low-quality inputs that were further lacking in quantity, all of which combined to make productivity low. Only 13% of the land was cultivated. Today, Afghanistan ranks seventh among the world's poorest countries.

The responsibility for this disastrous situation essentially lay with the turbulent succession of regimes which, since the foundation of Afghanistan in 1747, alternated policies of development with those of repression, all of which aimed to serve the interests of an elite, an ethnic group or an ideology.

Then, with the collapse of the State in 1978 and the Soviet invasion, the country was plunged into a war that brought about its social, economic and cultural disintegration. Having survived the atrocities inflicted on the country during more than 10 years of Communist rule, the civilian population now finds itself subject to the corruption and manipulation of warring factions, one of the major concerns of whom is to maintain the war economy. However, this 'instrumentalisation' of the conflict by Afghan belligerents also serves the interests of a number of other important and neighbouring States, so further fuelling the conflict (explained below).

Tyrants in search of power have always used hunger as a weapon, making considerable efforts to sustain hunger, increasing constraints and incessantly inventing new means of repression, and inhibiting all desire for emancipation.

Today, against a background of increasing impoverishment, political instability – associated with the increasingly ethnic character of the civil war – has given rise to banditry, corruption and the disintegration of the social fabric that once made up Afghanistan. Traditional Afghan solidarity and the values that once made Afghanistan a nation have all been eroded.

THE SHATTERING OF THE AFGHAN CONSTITUTION

Having managed to federate the traditionally autonomous, feudal and bellicose tribal structures, in part by guaranteeing protection from foreign attack and the defence of Islam, Afghan monarchs gradually came to endow the country with all the trappings of a State, such that by the beginning of the century a constitution had been established and the foundations for a modern nation laid. However, the Rule of Law often had to yield ground to a system that served the interests of an ethnic group, an urban elite or an ideology – all to the detriment of other minority groups.

POWER IN THE NAME OF THE PASHTUNS

Although all Afghan ethnic groups have been strongly influenced by *pashtunwali*, the traditional Pashtun code of values, the Pashtuns have always tended to seize and monopolise power in something of a tribalo-imperialistic structure. Other ethnic minorities were always relegated to the lower end of the social hierarchy, or even subjected to slavery, as were the Hazaras until the 1920s. Pashtun feelings of superiority over other groups have been reflected several times in policies of marginalisation – in terms of access to education facilities, appointments to official posts and the promotion of the Pashtun language at the expense of other languages spoken in the country, particularly Persian.

While the various regimes never systematically refused to strengthen and modernise the State, developments essentially profited the dominant ethnic group. As a result, the regions of Hazarajat and Badakhshan, for example, which were difficult to access and largely unurbanised, remained under-developed, deprived of the infrastructures and public services that were necessary for effective national integration. Today, they remain Afghanistan's poorest regions.

POWER IN THE NAME OF AN URBAN ELITE

Modernisation of the Afghan State also led to exploitation of the country's wealth to the advantage of an urban elite, completely cut off from the rural population and the middle classes. The education system, moreover, while rudimentary in the interior of the country, was for a long time only accessible to the upper bourgeoisie of Kabul.

By the turn of the century, the regime had gradually become consumed by a corruption that came to oil the wheels of State. The peasant classes were sometimes forced into exile in order to avoid an ever increasing tax burden, while State actors and clan members, through reinforcing the feudal system, became rich. The gap simply grew between, on the one hand, the Royal Court who lived in pomp and luxury and, on the other, the ordinary population.

In the 1960s, when the government decided to develop the country's road infrastructure, no economic impact study on local handicraft production was undertaken. Thus, when foreign-manufactured products began to pour into the country, the government remained indifferent to the concomitant destruction of thousands of traditional jobs.

Finally, in 1971–72, with the announcement of famine in the country's interior (due to bad harvests related to drought, followed by an extremely harsh winter), the regime refused to provide even minimal assistance to its population, indulging instead in the diversion of food aid received from the international community. This was sold to the disaster-stricken communities at eight times the price, while thousands of people died from hunger.

POWER IN THE NAME OF AN IDEOLOGY

The coup d'état of 1978 aimed to establish a Marxist-Leninist regime in Afghanistan. The new government soon tried to impose its conception of society through massive reforms in the domains of education, industry, agriculture and so on. However, ideological upheaval, together with the physical elimination of all opponents to the regime, provoked popular resistance. Not even the invasion of the country by Soviet troops and recourse to the most cruel behaviour repressed it. In order to deprive the Mujahideen of their food sources, the Soviets forced the rural population into displacement by destroying crops and irrigation networks, massacring domestic farm animals, bombing villages and mining valleys intensely. Today, 177 sq. km of agricultural land, together with 3 sq. km of irrigation networks, are still mined. The production deficit has been estimated at around 23,000 tons of wheat – an amount which would ordinarily be sufficient for 15,000 people. According to the United Nations, Afghanistan will not be mine-free until at least the year 2009. Between 1979 and 1989, nearly one million Afghans went into exile, with five million finding refuge in Pakistan and Iran.

Throughout the country's history, the influence of the religious clergy over most of rural Afghanistan and the clergy's attachment to ancestral tradition, together with their opposition to modernisation and urbanisation perceived as the imposition of a Western system, have caused significant disruption to the Rule of Law and a return to more tribally oriented conceptions. Thus, justice would become linked to the *Shari'a*, and political power dominated by religious leaders.

One such regime, with support from the anti-Soviet resistance, was consolidated during the 1980s through the *Jihaad* or Holy War. The ideology of Communism was supplanted by that of Islamic fundamentalism. However, the new Islamic parties soon sank into an internal struggle for power and when, in 1992, they attempted to establish an Islamic State, their coalition disintegrated into civil war. In Afghanistan, the Islamic State became characterised by violence used to subdue other ethnic groups and to subjugate minorities.

The ideological battle reached its apogee in 1995 with the advent of the Taliban movement, defending the principle of the anti-State, denying all democratic principles and making a mockery of human rights. A product of the Qu'ranic Schools and lacking membership of the rural elite, this movement of 'theology students' has no administrative competence whatsoever, referring only to Islam and Pashtun traditions for government. The implacability of their political decisions is justified by the extent of the chaos they wish to combat. However, such an interpretation of Islam, together with the bans being imposed by the new 'Ministry for the Prohibition of Vice and the Promotion of Virtue', is no longer done in unanimity, even among the Pashtuns themselves.

'INSTRUMENTALISATION' OF THE WAR

A war economy sustained

The Afghan resistance was long-sustained by rural populations who fed, sheltered and helped the Mujahideen in their fight against the Soviets. The fall of the Communist regime should rightfully have led to the announcement of the end of the *Jihaad* and the dismantling of militia groups. However, for a large number of combatants, the war economy that had developed over 10 years of Communist rule had enabled them to exert considerable power, a power which they were loathe to surrender. Justifying pursuit of the war by the need to defend the interests of the ethnic groups each one represented, the militia groups continued to survive at the expense of the civilian population, imposing taxes, pillaging markets and terrorising those who resisted.

Such banditry was to be found throughout the country, regardless of ethnic affiliation. It was particularly evident in Kabul between 1992 and 1996, during which time the Mujahideen under Commander Massoud behaved in a somewhat barbaric manner, particularly with regard to women, who were continuously subject to kidnapping and rape. As a result, Massoud's militias not only managed to lose all credibility, but also managed to stir up feelings of revulsion among the urban population, despite the fact that this was mainly Tajik.

The pillaging, rape and kidnapping suffered by the communities of Charikar when captured by the Uzbeks in July 1997, together with those experienced more recently during fighting between Hazaras and Uzbeks to control the town of Mazar-i Sharif, are further illustrations of the war's tribal characteristics. In each case, the first reflex of all those involved is to loot the civilians of another ethnic group.

In their sweep across the south and west of the country, the Taliban, on the other hand, managed to disband and disarm a large number of militia groups, so bringing security to the predominantly Pashtun communities of the region. This subsequently facilitated the return of one million refugees, further encouraged by the return of land by local authorities.

The development of mafia systems

Far from devising a political strategy, the search for compromise with the combatants has given rise to increasingly corrupt behaviour, notably through pay-offs to the latter. Thus, the 'siege' of a valley usually takes place by 'buying off' the commander controlling it, rather than through the outbreak of hostilities. Hence, the unexpected fall of Herat to the Taliban in September 1995 can be explained by the dishonourable behaviour of Ismael Khan, respected Governor of the province and close ally of Commander Massoud.

Such corruption subsequently spread to trade in vehicles and other manufactured products, organised clandestinely between Pakistan, Iran and Turkmenistan, with the Taliban regime taking advantage by levying import tariffs.

Lastly, the rapid expansion in opium production (reaching a figure of 2,800 tons in 1997, of which some 96% comes from Taliban-controlled regions) has meant that Afghanistan now ranks among the world's leading narcotics producers. Through the imposition of a 12% tax on poppy production, the Taliban reap substantial profits from these activities, estimated at around US$95 million, before refinement in Afghan, Pakistani, Irani or Central Asian laboratories. Other taxes are imposed on its transport and exportation. The Taliban authorities' policy of 'wait and see' with regard to the increases in land area made available for poppy cultivation has led to a concomitant decline in that available for wheat production. Over the past few years this has caused severe cereal shortages in the relevant regions, necessitating recourse to costly imports, essentially from Pakistan.

A *civilian population held to ransom*

Over the past few months, large numbers of combatants have become disillusioned by both the stalemate in the conflict and the appalling treatment of prisoners of war, such that commanders have been forced to adopt a policy of forced conscription of young recruits. However, the massacre of 2,000 Taliban prisoners by Uzbeks in September 1997 triggered popular revolt near Kandahar when, in January 1998, the 'students of theology' were trying to enrol similarly young men. In this, peasant communities have shown themselves unwilling to sacrifice their labour force, a labour force which is indispensable for the country's reconstruction.

In Kabul, both the Hazaras and, to a lesser extent, the Tajiks have been the object of Taliban raids attempting to recoup numbers lost to opposition troops. Having become prisoners, a number of these men were then sent to the frontlines to fight for the Taliban. Here, a triple objective tended to be achieved: the sacrifice of these men to almost certain death, the impoverishment of their families by depriving them of vital labour power and the limiting of the risk of civilian revolt in Kabul, with the pressures exerted on the various ethnic minorities such that many choose to go into exile.

In central Afghanistan, the Taliban have been further accused of committing several massacres of elderly Hazaras, women and children as a form of revenge after war losses. Mutual allegations of killings by various factions have thus spiralled, further poisoning relations between the Afghan communities and reinforcing tensions among civilians as a result.

Certain factions have also overtly used hunger as a weapon, by directly imposing embargoes on civilians. Thus, throughout the winter of 1996 the Taliban managed to maintain a total blockade of Kabul city, already under siege for several months. The city's inhabitants were soon confronted by a shortage of staple foods and a rate of inflation that was so high that any food still available on the market became unaffordable. In April 1997, the Taliban set fire to numerous wheatfields on the Chamali plain to the north of the city, so wreaking revenge on a number of farmers whose sons had rallied around Commander Massoud.

Taken together, the eight provinces of northern Afghanistan alone represent some 40% of irrigable land and 53% of cultivable land. In normal times, this is a surplus region. However, military activity and the increasing scarcity of labour power due to population displacement have meant that while part of all harvests become trampled underfoot, another part cannot be collected.

Moreover, since spring 1997 the Taliban have been imposing an almost total embargo on the Hazarajat region, levying heavy taxes on the few imports authorised and monopolising the purchase of wood exports such that these are bought at 'rock-bottom prices'. Bamian Valley was also bombed to impede the delivery of humanitarian aid, while in the central region the WFP estimated that some 160,000 people were under the threat of famine – with 10,000 tons of food being required to alleviate the situation. In May 1998, negotiations led by the UN to obtain a lifting of the embargo witnessed unprecedented blackmail by the Taliban, who made delivery of a limited amount of this aid conditional upon 20% of it going to a region under their control.

The behaviour of Khalili, the Hazara leader, was not without some Machiavellism either. Although it would have been possible from March 1998 to deliver this aid through the north, Khalili refused, allowing the nutritional status of his people to deteriorate. He was, no doubt, waiting for the right time to condemn, on the one hand, the policies of his adversaries with regard to civilian Hazaras and, on the other, the failure of humanitarian organisations to take action – all the while exploiting the compassion of the international community so as to call for massive supplies of humanitarian aid.

Maintaining the population in a state of under-development

Implementation of the Taliban doctrine regarding employment restrictions, free movement, education and access to health care for women is inevitably leading to a further deterioration in the general sanitary conditions of a country already surviving on humanitarian aid, as well as to the impoverishment of the general populace.

From an economic point of view, widows, who constitute 13% of household heads in Kabul, are no longer able to meet household needs and have now to depend on humanitarian agencies. Meanwhile, incomes gained from handicrafts made at home, such as the spinning of wool, knitting, sewing and embroidery, and the making of quilts, have tended to be cut by half due to the need for an intermediary to procure raw materials and subsequently sell the finished product. Their work has, therefore, significantly depreciated in value.

The directives enacted by the Ministry of Health since September 1997 not only represent a step backwards, but are deadly for both women and their children. A direct correlation is known to exist between the amount of education obtained by mothers and the mortality rate and nutritional status of any children they bring into the world. Ignorance of elementary principles of hygiene and family planning, the poor diets of pregnant women in relation to mineral and vitamin content, and the absence of medical care during birth all contribute to the disastrous mortality rates in Afghanistan. According to Unicef, the country ranks second among those affected by this scourge: 17 out of every 1,000 women die during labour. The latest surveys conducted by Action Against Hunger reveal that the nutritional status of under-5-year-olds has been deteriorating since 1995, with some 50% of these suffering from problems of retarded growth and weight. Levels of acute malnutrition are getting worse.

Political instability is the cause of an inflationary and largely unproductive economy which is gradually gnawing away at the purchasing power of numerous Kabulis. It is the irregularity of incomes and the resulting precariousness, rather than socio-economic conditions in general, that are at the root of the malnutrition to be found among young children. Considering only monetised income, less than one-third of families affected are found to be above the poverty-line!

With daily work becoming ever more scarce, particularly in winter, families are forced to sell off their assets in return for food or fuel, or sometimes to purchase medicines or pay their rent. Once their possessions of value have been exhausted, families are then forced to borrow. And when there are significant price rises, as was the case for wheat flour in March 1998, most families reduce their level of consumption.

Animal products such as meat, eggs and dairy products, or red beans, for instance, are now consumed only sporadically, perhaps once or twice a month, on the occasion of a surplus or a special social event. Fruits are considered a luxury, unaffordable for most households.

Poverty, then, is becoming increasingly visible in the streets of Kabul, with rising levels of begging and crime, notably among young children.

Interference from neighbouring countries

Over the past few years, nearly 30% of the country's food needs have had to be met by imports, mainly from Pakistan and Iran, with most going to urban areas. Kabul is now dependent on the outside to the tune of 80% for flour, 100% for ghee (oil made from animal fat), 100% for sugar and 70% for rice – compared to 20%, 60%, 90% and 30%, respectively, 20 years ago. The costs of transportation and import tariffs levied by the Taliban simply add to the costs of external procurement.

At the border, Pakistani authorities also demand payment for the right of passage, the actual sum varying according to tacit agreements made between the supplier and the customs officer. For a known merchant, this may be anything from 20% to 30% of the purchase price of any goods being transported, while for those less well known, the figure may reach as much as 50%. In May 1998, following the official closure of the Pakistan-Afghan border, Kabuli suppliers estimated the flow of imports to have been reduced to one-third of what it should have been. Furthermore, taken together, both factors – the blockade and the corruption of certain adminis-trative services of the Pakistani customs authorities (leading to a reduction in supplies, together with an increase in the charges to be paid) – have led to goods being sold at a price 30% higher than their purchase price. Opening the border would obviously permit three times as much food to be imported – most importantly, at lower prices.

Dependent on imports, Afghanistan has also found itself in the position of an exporter. Thus, when Pakistan was faced with wheat shortages in February 1997, and had banned exports to Afghanistan, the resulting price rises made the export of a number of Afghan stocks attractive. Moreover, 150,000 tons of surplus wheat from Afghanistan's northern provinces were exported to Tajikistan, Turkmenistan and Uzbekistan, usually after having been requisitioned by the army and resold for hard currency. Hence, despite a good harvest in 1997, the country's total cereal deficit was found to be 710,000 tons.

Rather than promoting exchange between surplus and deficit areas, the conflict has encouraged the forging of closer links with 'allied' countries more inclined to maintain the war economy and exploit Afghanistan's poor resources.

Pakistan, furthermore, aims to use Afghanistan as a weakened ally in order to counter Indian hegemonic designs in the region, whilst also furthering Pakistani interests in relation to its border with Afghanistan and the North-West Frontier Province. The Taliban, as a result, enjoy significant military support from the latter, although no effort whatsoever is made by Pakistan to provide the Taliban with even the most rudimentary of administrative management skills which might otherwise help restore the Rule of Law.

CONCLUSION

Afghanistan's situation is all the more pernicious given that all the visible signs of alarm that might ordinarily provoke international opinion are either absent or little seen. There are no spectacular concentration camps, no famines afflicting young children or epidemics decimating the population. As a result, media infatuation with the Afghan crisis, so prevalent during the 1980s, has gradually dwindled, now appearing only as news flashes induced by earthquakes or floods.

And yet, human rights are systematically violated, ethnic persecution has multiplied and the majority of the population is being increasingly impoverished. Power has been monopolised for the sake of an ideology and to the advantage of petty chiefs, almost as if the latter wanted to seek revenge for History, demonstrating total aversion to the slightest hint of democracy, equality, progress and any modern concept of society.

Pakistan, India, Iran, Turkmenistan, Uzbekistan and Tajikistan, not to mention Saudi Arabia, the United States and Russia, have all found in Afghanistan scope for the defence of their geo-strategic, political and economic interests, often using the country as a theatre to stage a proxy war.

Will the recent public awareness campaign on the situation of Afghan women be enough to end instrumentalisation of the conflict? How many years will it take before Afghanistan, one of the first countries to join the Non-Aligned Movement, manages to liberate itself from foreign influence and restore a Rule of Law, favourable to the development of all its ethnic groups?

Kabul, Afghanistan: the tragic segregation of women

ANNIE BLAISE

THE DEVASTATING CONSEQUENCES OF THE SEGREGATIONIST POLICY IMPOSED BY THE TALIBAN IN AFGHANISTAN

During the night of 26–27 September 1996, Taliban militia groups captured Kabul, capital of Afghanistan. This they did almost without fighting. Four years of a fratricidal war among Mujahideen resistance fighters, from 1992 to 1996, had paved the way for these now famous Taliban, these 'seekers of knowledge' in Arabic, or 'students of theology' as they are more commonly known. Being mostly Sunni Pashtun in origin, they now hold more than two-thirds of the country, on which they have imposed an Islamic order the orthodoxy of which is almost unparalleled in the Arab-Muslim world.

Women have been the first victims of this Islam of a bygone age. Their very existence denied, they have no choice but to submit to the regime. Their segregation has been decreed by law, like that between Blacks and Whites under South African law. The restrictions being imposed on them continue to increase every day, further reducing their freedom of movement to the point where their chances of survival have been put into jeopardy.

Today, the tragedy experienced by Afghan women goes well beyond the simple obligation to wear the *chadri*, or veil. It also goes beyond the mere religious or cultural. The policy of segregation is having real and disastrous consequences. Being threatened by death due to a lack of health care is not a question of culture. Life and death are universal values. The question is no longer one of human rights, but one of the right to life. Beyond any judgement of Pashtun culture and Afghan tradition, our indignation is justified because it is the very lives of Afghan women and their children which are at stake.

The Taliban and their fear of women

As Muslim fundamentalists, the Taliban movement made its advent into Afghan politics in 1994. The Taliban are originally students of theology schools, known as *Madrasseh*, found in the rural areas. Students of such schools follow an extremely conservative teaching, based upon study of the Qu'ran and texts from the 7th to the 10th centuries, no doubt remote from modern realities.

Their suspicion of women is inculcated very early on, later turning into a fear of women, stimulated by total ignorance of all that concerns a sector of the population considered impure. Hence, the Deputy Director of the religious police in Kandahar was able to state that: *'Women are inferior to men. Their brains are lighter, they are weaker, and they are sometimes impure. Thus, the testimony of a man is worth that of two women. Women must be protected by their fathers, then by their husbands.'*

Single, and leading a life similar to a seminarist, the young Taliban must avoid talking to women, even thinking about them, so as not to be distracted from their religious studies. These studies are extremely long: an average of eight years for junior Taliban, 13 years if they want to become a *mullah*, and 16 years to become a *Mawlawi*. The effect of the war, however, has been such that, as soon as they enter puberty, students are to alternate six months at the front with six months of studies.

Frightened by women, about whom they know almost nothing at all, the Taliban were also somewhat disconcerted by discovery of the 'town'.

FROM COUNTRYSIDE TO CAPITAL: A CULTURAL SHOCK

Determined to overcome their poverty-stricken past, the Taliban were originally poor peasants who came from some of the more isolated mountainous areas of Afghanistan (the Qu'ranic schools which they attended being free; that is, with free provision of board and lodging, and sometimes clothes as well). As such, they came from a highly conservative milieu, unpenetrated by modernist ideas from the city.

Having first arrived in, and conquered, Kandahar, capital of 'Talibestan' (although equally 'royal' city and fiefdom of partisans of the former king, Zahir Shah, himself Pashtun, and to whom the Taliban, although revolutionary, often refer), these poor peasants soon found themselves little kings. Arrival in Kabul in 1996 caused an even greater shock. After having been locked away in their seminaries for so many years, and completely cut off from city life (and not just that of the capital), these young students were soon confronted by a reality for which they were by no means prepared: that of a large somewhat modern and relatively developed capital. Given that Kabul had evolved in a manner somewhat different from that of the rest of the country, the shock was all the greater. As a symbol of corruption and vice, having been subjected to Soviet power and influenced by the West, Kabul was considered by the Taliban as having 'erred'. During the war, moreover, the capital's inhabitants had eventually come to accommodate Soviet domination, something that the Taliban, veterans of the Russian resistance who had sometimes been injured in combat or forced into exile, could not forgive. Urban and rural dwellers showed open disdain for each other.

Besides the effect of Soviet influence *per se*, which had been at the origin of much of Kabuli women's liberation, the war (as is the case in all wars) also played a significant role in reinforcing the trend by giving responsibilities and employment to women that had, hitherto, been confined to their husbands now on the frontlines. As factory workers, judges and teachers, the women of Kabul soon became accustomed to a certain amount of freedom. Even before this evolution, during the 1930s King Amanullah (like Atatürk in Turkey) had begun reforms to change women's status; thus, the obligation to wear the veil, for example, was abolished. Later, under the reign of King Zahir, the Prime Minister had even adapted the constitution to give women the same right to vote as men. By the 1970s, women – some of whom had attended university – had acquired a certain amount of power. However, as of 1992, following the departure of the Communists, the various resistance movements, despite being less fundamentalist than the Taliban, began to impose a considerably more strict form of Islam. Nevertheless, such transformations essentially affected only the capital.

Throughout this time, little change was brought to bear on the position of women in the rural areas. Before the Taliban, for instance, although it was not compulsory to wear the *chadri*, it was nevertheless common practice (except for Hazara women and the nomads). Women from the countryside, moreover, tend to wear it with pride when they go into town. The *chadri,* like a uniform, cloaks social distinctions.

Nevertheless, even if the rural areas were more traditional than the urban, one huge difference with the present situation is that a woman who did not wear the *chadri* when this was common did not run the risk of a public beating, as is the case today in Kabul. The issue is not whether the *chadri* is worn or not, but rather that non-compliance is punished by beating. The practice, followed due to tradition and not imposed by force or violence, would no doubt have changed over time. And if women in the countryside lacked access to health care or education, it was not because this had been banned by the authorities, but rather because the country was too poor to provide such services.

Thus, even if the countryside (because it is more traditional) has been subject to fewer upheavals due to Taliban policies and violence, relative to Kabul, the present situation can still be considered as one of the worst setbacks for the position of women in the history of mankind.

DIFFERENT INTERPRETATIONS OF THE TALIBAN'S SEGREGATIONIST POLICY

Ever since the Taliban took control of Kabul in September 1996, the city's new authorities have adopted an impressive list of rules denying the fundamental rights of half of Kabul's population, around 600,000 women. This they have done with the intention of imposing an unequal relationship derived from a literal reading of the Qu'ran.

First to be introduced, on pain of being stoned, was the compulsory wearing of the *chadri*, followed by a ban on working, then on studying. Schools and universities closed their doors to young girls (once they are nine years old) and to young women, so legally depriving them of education.

Women are not allowed to go out on their own. Any work is subject to the presence of a male member of the family. Women are forbidden to talk in public, to laugh, to sing, to address a man, to talk to a stranger and even to directly receive humanitarian aid. Excluded from public life, deprived of employment, education and health care, they have only one purpose left to them: reproduction, in conditions that are often extremely difficult. They have only one right: that of obedience – while they hide.

This radical Islamic regime draws upon the support of a whip-wielding police force whose very name is evocative of its duty: 'Police for the Prevention of Vice and the Promotion of Virtue'. Any breach of the regime's strict rules is punished by traumatising and humiliating physical harassment, both for women and for any men seen as responsible for them. The women of Kabul are continually haunted by the fear of being caught, threatened and insulted.

Men, too, are also subject to whipping by such monks-cum-soldiers. Their rights are violated, the length of their beards subject to strict control, long hair cursed as a hide-away for Satan, and so on. Neither should the ethnic character of the conflict go without mention, for whether male or female, it is better to speak Pashtun on arrest. It is, moreover, *pashtun-wali,* the code that regulates the life and honour of Pashtun men, that is significantly more visible than precepts from the Qu'ran.

In terms of education, the closure of universities to female students who had in 1987 comprised some 40% of the student population in Kabul (and even more in 1996) has been traumatic. The closure of schools to girls, meanwhile, has witnessed a distinction between those in the countryside and those in the cities. The reform policies imposed by the first Afghan Communist governments after 1978 gained little acceptance in the countryside. The construction of schools, often the only solid buildings in villages, as well as the arrival of a city teacher 'in exile', frequently not even speaking the same language as the villagers, were little appreciated by peasants, in revolt against the city. In the countryside, when a child is sent to school, the family loses labour power for the fields. Moreover, in order for several villages to benefit from the schools, these schools were not built in one particular village, but tended to be placed at the intersection of several villages, forcing children to walk four or five kilometres in order to get there. In this regard, it was seen as more prudent for young girls to stay at home, especially once they had entered adolescence.

Whatever the case, even if hardly any village girls attended school after the age of nine, the ban imposed by the Taliban has been perceived as an attack upon the Afghan people, particularly Kabulis who are aware of the importance of education for future mothers. Proof of this is to be witnessed in the risks run to hold clandestine classes and ensure that girls receive at least a minimum education.

The measures taken by the Taliban have, no doubt, been the most radical and severe in regard to the health care system. On 6 September 1997, the Ministry of Health banned women from going to Kabul's 22 hospitals and 26 clinics in order to prevent 'mixing' with males. Instead, women requiring care were left with only one clinic, having only 45 beds, without running water and without any operating theatre. Women were violently expelled from the capital's public hospitals, some just when they were due to give birth. However, two months later in November, faced with the outcry of NGOs firmly opposed to the institutionalisation of an inequality between men and women in terms of health care access and going as far as to cause the death of some of them, the Taliban revoked the order. Instead, women were to be allowed to seek treatment in hospitals provided that a strict separation between men and women was observed and that women were treated only by female medical personnel. Yet the situation has far from been resolved. The fear of leaving their homes, the lack of female health care staff (nurses and female doctors are no longer allowed training) inhibits most women from being properly treated.

In a country already economically poor, torn apart and partially destroyed by the war, such prohibitions threaten the very survival of women, particularly by affecting their food and nutritional status.

FOOD PROBLEMS AND CHILD MALNUTRITION

According to the classical indicators for human development defined by the UN, Afghanistan now ranks 170 out of 174 countries and is one of the poorest countries in the world.

As a result of the civil war which has devastated the country since 1978, Afghanistan's food situation has become very precarious. Trade and the transport of goods have been disrupted by the fighting. Road closures regularly threaten supplies to the capital. Agricultural production has been badly affected by the deterioration in irrigation networks, by landmines and by disruption of distribution channels. Insecurity and population movement have further limited production. Thus, although self-sufficient in the 1970s, the country is now dependent on imports, with 30% of food requirements being imported.

Unemployment remains high (one working person usually has to look after five other persons) and inflation continues to spiral, so reducing incomes and limiting household access to food (around 32% of households lack readily available food stocks).

Although food security has improved due to better security conditions in the south since 1995 and to an increase in agricultural production, Taliban policies (refusing women an income) have simply aggravated the decline in household purchasing power, depriving them of access to food.

KABUL NO LONGER PLAYS THE ROLE OF A CAPITAL

It is crucial to bear in mind that the Taliban are, above all, peasants, visibly more gifted in work in the fields than in the administration of a capital. Today, the Afghan countryside can no longer feed its capital, due to an inefficient administration. Typically, it is the capital that stimulates the surrounding countryside and that is subsequently supplied by the latter. A capital can only exist and play a role as such if there is a State, an administrative system to levy taxes, pay civil servants, establish a network of markets and facilitate trade links. The Taliban, however, have proved unable to impose such a structure. Kabul has sunk into poverty: taxes are no longer to be obtained, customs duties are no longer levied and the State no longer has the resources to pay its bureaucrats. Kabul has become unproductive. With neither factories nor industry (except those oriented towards the war effort), the capital can no longer govern, it can no longer administer the country.

The peasant population of south Afghanistan had more or less established a tacit contract with the Taliban. In exchange for non-contestation of their power and once peace had been established, villagers expected the Taliban to reconstruct the country, to rebuild the roads and to pay civil servants and teachers. Yet not only is fighting continuing in the north of the country (where the Taliban are immersed in a war against the Tajiks under Massoud, the Uzbeks under Dostum and armed groups of Hazaras), nothing at all that was destroyed in the war has been rebuilt.

The peculiar situation of Kabul is at least in part responsible for the food insecurity suffered by Afghans today, not to mention the rates of child malnutrition.

The nutritional surveillance system put in place by Action Against Hunger has, through nutritional surveys conducted every six months since 1995, allowed data to be collected showing the development of chronic and severe malnutrition in children between six months and five years old in Kabul. The observations are frightening. While the overall malnutrition rate appears to have stabilised around 7.5%, some 76.5% of children were found, for a given height, to weigh less than the normal median weight. Although they might not now be considered malnourished, these children run the risk of becoming malnourished with the smallest of infections, such as respiratory diseases or diarrhoea. By December 1997, mortality rates were already estimated at around 2.17 out of every 10,000 children of less than five years old *per day*. This is far beyond the threshold for alarm. In terms of chronic malnutrition, 35% of children were found to suffer from stunted growth, this having sometimes begun while the foetus was still in the uterus. Pregnant women's poor diets, then, are weakening the foetus and affecting growth.

Such malnutrition (not directly linked to the advent of the Taliban) can be partly explained by parental poverty, poor living conditions (including the cold), the lack of hygiene (with polluted water), unbalanced diets (essentially cereal and rice based, and thus deficient in vitamins and minerals), and the lack of maternal knowledge about food, health and hygiene.

The policies established by the Taliban vis-à-vis women, including restrictions on information diffusion and the crippling of household incomes, only exacerbates these problems.

THE IMPACT OF THE TALIBAN'S SEGREGATIONIST POLICY ON FOOD INSECURITY AND CHILD MALNUTRITION

The most dramatic impact witnessed due to the measures imposed has been that caused by the ban on women working. Families no longer able to count on an income from men have obviously been the most affected. The subsequent reduction in income has meant that these families, already poor, can no longer afford to eat properly. The position of widows gives particular cause for concern. Relatively numerous (almost 45,000 or 13% of households in Kabul are headed by women who have lost their husbands due to the war), these widows are no longer able to meet family needs. Instead, they are constrained to remain indoors and forbidden to work. Here, too, the situation is much more harsh in the cities than in the rural areas where women, once they marry, go to live with their husband and the husband's family. Should the husband die, the woman is automatically taken in charge by her in-laws. This is not the case in Kabul where hundreds of widows can be seen wandering the streets, begging in front of the mosques or in the markets. Their children, of course, were the first to receive treatment in Action Against Hunger's feeding centres – that is, until the organisation was expelled from the country in July 1998.

Obstacles to women's employment have had a similarly disastrous impact in the area of health. Involved in the treatment of 10,000 malnourished Kabuli children through three hospitals, 15 day centres and 25 feeding centres, Action Against Hunger, like other NGOs in the same domain, was directly affected by the measure. Given that children inevitably tend to be accompanied by their mother, treatment must be dispensed by female personnel, something not to the taste of the Lords of Kabul. Similarly, home-visitors interviewing and educating mothers at home have also to be women. We had obtained a derogation allowing 70 women to be involved in such work. However, the reality proved less positive, due in particular to constraints on women's movements, such that the pressure on these women and the risks they ran were enormous. At every checkpoint, the documents authorising them to work were continually questioned.

The impact of measures prohibiting female access to health care is just as disastrous. In the short term, female mortality rates are set to increase (due to a lack of available beds, often fatal journeys to be made in the search for a hospital, and so on). In the medium term, the reduction in female medical personnel being trained will lead (if it has not already led) to a decline in mother-and-child health care services. Even in their roles as mothers (the only roles left to them), Afghan women are not much better protected. Seventeen women out of every 1,000 die in labour, 30 times more than in Europe. Thus, measures implemented by the Taliban only reinforce existing inadequacies in pre- and post-natal care.

Lastly, if the new generation of Afghan women does not have access to higher education, particularly medical education, then who is going to pass on such knowledge? Tomorrow, who is going to be able to take care of ailing Afghan women? Who is going to be able to instruct mothers about the elementary principles of hygiene, health and nutrition necessary for the survival of their children? The link between the level of maternal education and rates of child malnutrition has been established. Ignorance has never been conducive to progress.

Our role, as a humanitarian organisation, is neither to interfere nor to judge the culture or religions of the countries in which we work. The respectful, patient and open attitudes of teams in Afghanistan have been indicative of this. But our role also consists of condemning the deadly edicts of a semi-paralysed regime when these threaten the lives of women, men and children. As one of our female staff told us: 'I am a believing Muslim, but I don't think that this is what Allah wanted.'

Such condemnation led to our expulsion from Kabul in July 1998, together with that of 30 other international NGOs. The tragic fate of Afghan women is surrounded by silence, and will continue to be so until the Taliban finally realise that humanitarian aid is the only lifeline for the most vulnerable of the country's population.

Bibliography

Michael Barry; 1984; *Le Royaume de l'Insolence: La Résistance Afghane, du Grand Moghol à l'Invasion Soviétique;* Flammarion.

Christian Hell, Amin Tarzi, Kacem Fazelly and Étienne Gille: *Les Nouvelles d'Afghanistan,* no. 79/80, AFRANE.

UNDPC Annual Report; 1997; Afghanistan, Opium Poppy Survey.

FAO/WFP special report; August 1997; *Crop and Food Supply Assessment of Afghanistan.*

The Amazon and north-eastern Brazil: useful droughts (for some)

SYLVIE BRUNEL

The year 1998 was marked by major nutritional problems in both the Amazon and north-eastern Brazil, the climatic conditions of which are fundamentally different – the one being extremely humid and the other semi-arid – although demographically the regions are relatively similar. As in Sahelian Niger, Central America and South-East Asia (notably Kalimantan, Irian Jaya, Papua New Guinea and also the Philippines), such difficulties have been attributed to El Niño, the universal scapegoat for the difficulties of numerous peoples, brought together by their vulnerability – a vulnerability that lies above all in their neglect by national policies.

Every population suffering from under-development and chronic poverty, with all the daily insecurity that these entail, is susceptible to becoming a victim of El Niño...or of any other disaster, natural or man-made (particularly civil unrest or economic crisis). Landless peasants, livestock breeders with lifestyles seen as incompatible with a technology-based civilisation, political minorities, and extremely poor regions marginalised within the national economy will always and everywhere be the first victims not only of natural disasters but, more importantly, of man-made ones.

In north-eastern Brazil as in the Amazon, drought is a 'blessing' for the powers that be, each one serving to strengthen the power of already influential landowners. As the Brazilian President, Fernando Henrique, declared during his electoral campaign in 1995: 'Brazil is not a poor country; it is an unjust country.' Once in power, however, this same world-renowned sociologist, supposed to be sensitive to social issues, acted in just the same way as his predecessors. Did he really have much of a choice faced with the heavy-weights of Brazilian society, with its feudalistic system of land ownership and the denigration of those who were poorest?

'DROUGHT AS AN INDUSTRY' IN NORTH-EASTERN BRAZIL

In north-eastern Brazil the climatic crisis has, as always (given that for the past two centuries the region has been regularly plagued by drought and floods), brought home the inadequacy of agricultural structures, the fragility of the economic bases of the *sertaõ* and the growing distinction between a coastline which is undergoing rapid modernisation and a hinterland left behind in archaic feudalism.

Characterised by strong economic interdependence between the semi-arid interior, the *sertaõ*, which is based on extensive cattle-raising within large land-holdings (*fazendas*) and a humid, densely populated coastline based on sugar-cane monoculture, north-eastern Brazil has been a region in decline since the 17th century. The depreciation of sugar prices on the world market has led to both the irreversible disintegration of a province which had hitherto been Brazil's economic engine, as well as a gradual shift in the country's centre of gravity towards the more 'useful triangle' of the south, during a series of 'successive cycles' (coffee, gold, tobacco, soya, etc.).

On average, droughts occur every 12–13 years, with the last one taking place in 1985. Although each drought (as with each flood) is announced in advance, thanks to meteorological satellite observations, each one seems to catch the region off-guard, requiring the release of emergency funds (a large part of which never arrive at their destination), the sending of food sacks (much of which is diverted) and the hasty implementation of 'work fronts' with a view to employing the peasant population – suddenly deprived of all means of subsistence – in so-called public works (which, in fact, usually only benefit a few), in return for money or for food.

Yet, a national policy to fight against droughts has existed in north-eastern Brazil for more than one century.[1] Based on the construction of dams and reservoirs (groundwater in the north-east is proof that the semi-arid climate is not without remedy), then on the somewhat over-ambitious industrial development of the coastal areas, with the support of financial incentives and tax exemptions, this policy should have strengthened local capacities to resist recurrent natural disasters. Little has ever come of it: despite the huge sums of money that have been spent by both SUDENE and

---

1. The largest drought recorded in the history of the north-east dates back to 1877 when, according to the historian Cunniff (*The Great Drought of Northeast Brazil*; University of Texas, Austin), 250,000 persons died and present-day institutions were established.

DNOCS,[2] thousands of *flagelados* are thrown onto the streets with each and every drought. Starving and having lost all their possessions, they are forced to join the 'work fronts' in the interior in order to eat, to swell the numbers of the urban proletariat along the coast or to migrate towards Amazonia.

1998 has by no means been an exception to the rule. Announced by the National Institute of Spatial Research (INPE), as of October 1997, and duly attributed to El Niño, this year's drought wreaked havoc as usual, arousing the indignation of the national press as it 'discovered' the tragedy in the north-east. And yet, the pattern of food crises in north-eastern Brazil is always the same: the flight of families having lost their harvests, child malnutrition, consumption of wild plants, roots and animals,[3] and the misery of thousands of *flagelados* thrown onto the streets with just a small bundle of clothes.

The only thing which was new was the revolt organised by the *moradores*, the landless peasants who until then had tended to accept their fate despite attempts at organisation by the Church (based on Liberation Theology and grassroots church communities), together with peasant union groups. This year the Landless Peasants' Movement (MST), the principal opposition group to President Cardoso, orchestrated the pillaging of granaries and aid convoys, as well as the looting of urban supermarkets. Brazil's political class and in particular the 150 Parliament members of the relevant states (themselves wary of warning about a catastrophe already publicised) immediately accused the MST of 'trying to capitalise on the misery' engendered.

In fact, the movement had simply adopted a method already well known to the large landlords of the north-east who, disliking anyone else taking political advantage, have themselves for more than one and a half centuries capitalised on this same misery. If the efforts of such landowners have to date remained somewhat fruitless, this is neither a coincidence nor a misfortune in that each drought reinforces the socio-economic power of the *fazendeiros*. By co-ordinating regional aid, by distributing federal food assistance (for how else to reach the peasants employed on their huge

---

2. SUDENE: treasury for the Development of the North-East, founded in 1958 and based in Recife. DNOCS: National Department for Works Against Drought, in existence since 1909 and based in Fortaleza.

3. It should be noted in this context that the peasants of the north-east are not, in times of need, above eating lizards, varanus and other reptiles.

estates?), the latter appear as benefactors to the unfortunate and over-whelmed people, and so manage to buy votes for the subsequent general elections.

A good number of the 70,000 reservoirs built by DNOCS in the north-east are even constructed within the territory of these *fazendas*. Not only do these large landowners directly benefit from the implementation of 'work fronts', but their huge herds of cattle continue to have access to water, while the crops of the peasants whither away. While there exist a number of irrigated greenbelts created under the aegis of several organisa-tions (most prominent amongst them, DNOCS and the authority in charge of developing the Rio Sao Francisco), their success remains somewhat limited. Totally dependent on collective regulation, the peasants are now no longer under the yoke of the *fazendeiros*, but under that of the engineers. 'The drought industry', as Jorge Coelho has described it, goes some way to explaining the influence of large landowners in the Brazilian Parliament, landowners who have blocked any serious attempt at land reform for more than a century.

Hence, the *moradores* have only one solution: migration towards the big cities along the coast, towards the sugar-cane plantations, towards the south or towards the Amazon.

IN THE AMAZON: EXPECTED DEFORESTATION

At the beginning of the 1970s, after the failure of policies intended to transform the north-eastern interior, the government launched its 'National Integration Project'. In this, the response to climatic difficulties in the north-east and the problem of 'land shortage' linked to patterns of land ownership, was to encourage migration to the Amazon, 'a land with-out people for a people without land', as so famously put by the General-President, Emilio Medici, in a speech in Recife in 1970.[4] For the Brazilian military, in power since 1964, it was important that organising the settle-ment of this 'green desert' of over 5 million sq. km occur within the context of a particular strategy. This was a strategy whereby the poor migrants from the north-east were to be a tool to be used to open up the Amazon so as to integrate it into national territory and to stake out the Brazilian

4. Quite an inconsiderate statement when one thinks of the Indian communities who had long lived in the Amazon.

claim vis-à-vis the other riverine States. Hence, investments had to be made, and the land occupied. In the same year, the Brazilian Institute for Agrarian Reform (IBRA), symbolically enough became known as the National Institute for Colonisation and Agrarian Reform, with the first Trans-Amazon link being launched across a distance of some 3,000 km.

However, the final third of the route was never completed, being abandoned in 1980. The dream of the Promised Land soon became a nightmare for a good number of candidates participating in the Amazonian adventure. Brutally transplanted into an environment so fundamentally different from that of their origins, they were confronted with over-whelming difficulties, resulting from their isolation in an extremely humid and unhealthy climate (something previously unknown) and with problems of planting and selling their crops. Thus, malnutrition and mortality rates among these uprooted peasants began to escalate, with a large number consequently abandoning the land they had so painstakingly cleared after a cheap sale. While a number returned to their original regions, the vast majority ended up in cities either in the Amazon region – to the delight of local politicians able to benefit from a Federal aid propor-tional to State population – or in the south, the traditional destination of north-east migrants (of the 1.8 million who left the region between 1970 and 1980, three-quarters headed to the big cities of the south, rather than submit themselves to the Amazon).

Others became *garempeiros*, gold-diggers involved in the destruction of the forest, its rivers and its peoples, all in the pursuit of an illusory eldorado. Between 1987 and 1990, some 40,000 people invaded the territory of the Yanomani Indians, polluting the water with the mercury used in their gold panning activities, devastating the forest, killing game and causing epidemics and the spread of venereal diseases. In 1990, under international pressure, the Federal government decided to expel the diggers and created a reserve of about 10,000 sq. km for the Yanomanis, but this has surreptitiously been eroded through land colonisation as large numbers of *garempeiros* stayed on clandestinely.

Small-scale colonisers who had remained on the land, believing themselves to be the rightful owners, were confronted by the *fazendeiros* who attempted to expropriate this land. The latter claimed retroactive property rights (actually acquired through *backchich*[5]), and did not

5. Bribery money.

hesitate to chase the colonisers out using militia groups or by violent intimidation.

In one decade 40,000 sq. km have been gradually converted into extensive cattle ranches either by large landowners or large companies, often foreign (and here one should be careful not to underestimate the role of Asian forestry companies). The State has given its support to them, granting tax reductions, loans, subsidies and so on: its aim is to abolish the internal border and to exploit fully what Brazilian authorities consider, with some justification, to be a huge reservoir of natural resources. Consequently, colonisation of the Amazon is being pursued 'beneath the hooves of cattle'.

Both small-scale colonisers and native Indian tribes are being dispossessed of their land, becoming insecure occupiers and being treated like slaves. These *caboclos* find themselves in hostile territory – land which is not even that of their ancestors – and in the same miserable and humiliating situation which had caused them to migrate in the first place. Their environment continues to deteriorate, forcing them to clear more and more new land so they might feed themselves. There is nothing less adapted to the Amazonian environment than the slash-and-burn methods used by the colonisers, whether large companies or individual peasants: exposed and fragile, the land is worn out quickly, with the layer of topsoil being eroded away by rain and leaching. As a result, ever more new plots of land have to be cleared, so pushing mineral exploitation deeper and deeper into the forest. Indeed, the colonisers have little alternative: grants from INCRA are allocated to cleared land (the value of which, in the Roraima, for instance, is 10 times higher than that of forested land). The large landowners, having the political power and in collusion with the BTP enterprises, are the first to benefit, while the small-scale colonisers are left with what remains. While they do all the hard work, others reap the benefits.

In this context, forest fires are simply a method for opening-up the Amazon. This year, due to fires used to clear the land and to drought, the area of land destroyed has been immense, to the detriment of both small-scale colonisers, whose plots of land have simply disappeared up in smoke, and Indians, who have been forced to flee their ancestral homes. Today, the 20,000 Yanomanis (of whom half live in Brazil) find themselves under threat from all sides. Their land area has diminished, the duration of the drought has caused food reserves to become exhausted, with future harvests having also been compromised, the game they once chased have been killed off and the rivers have dried up, reducing access to drinking

water and further provoking the proliferation of malaria-carrying mosqui-
toes in areas of stagnant water. Parasitic and intestinal diseases are more
widespread than ever.

The fires are fatal for the most vulnerable, but nevertheless serve the
interests not only of the *fazendeiros*, allowing them to extend their control
over land and their economic wealth through enormous cattle ranches
(which, as in the north-east, allow for control of political power), but also of
the Brazilian government itself, which gains by reinforcing its grip over
the Amazon.

In this respect, one should not forget the difficulties successive
Brazilian leaders have had in overcoming international criticism of their
management of the Amazon. Confronted in the 1990s with deforestation of
the area, the question was even posed as to whether the area should be
designated part of the common heritage of mankind by placing it, as with
Antarctica, under international surveillance. It was thus imperative that
the Brazilian government take control of the situation and re-affirm its
sovereignty over the Amazon. In May 1997, therefore, the Amazon Alert
System (SIVAM) was established and placed under the direct and exclusive
control of the army, not even on the pretext, as Jean-Jacques Sevilla
emphasises, of dedicating it to ecological surveillance of the forest or the
struggle against what has been called a 'flourishing Amazonian narco-
traffic'.[6] In 1998, while fires were raging and causing peasants to starve,
the Brazilian General co-ordinating operations to quench the fires declared
to NGOs that 'international assistance was totally useless'. The fight lay
instead with a ban on slash-and-burn techniques during January,
ironically just at the time when the rains were due and despite the fact
that these techniques would have permitted these small farmers to
prepare their fields, so compromising future harvests.

But just how much influence can a handful of *seringueiros*,[7] native
Indians and *caboclos* wield against such powerful vested interests for
whom droughts and forest fires are beneficial? Hence, the bloody suppression of their uprisings and revolts, amidst the indifference of both legal
and political authorities, despite a number of short-lived declarations of
intent.

6. 'L'Amazonie sous le feu des militaires'; *Le Monde*, 5 June 1998 (see also the articles in *Le Monde*, 6 April).
7. Itinerant latex collectors in the Amazon forest. Their leader, Chico Mendes, was assassinated in 1988 on the initiative of large landowners, then benefiting from police protection.

The recurring droughts of the sertaõ

The north-east of Brazil has a land area about three times that of France (1,660,000 sq. km). It is subdivided into three zones: the *mata*, a humid region characterised by sugar cane plantations, the *agreste*, a climatically intermediate zone where both small and medium-sized landholders can be found breeding cattle to supply cities in the coastal areas, and the *sertaõ*, covering an area of 850,000 sq. km and dedicated to extensive cattle-rearing due to what has been considered a semi-arid climate, despite rainfall of 400–800 mm per year.

In fact, the problem has not been so much the lack of rainfall, but rather its irregularity, varying not just between years, but also within the same year. There is not a shortage of water, as signified by the 70,000 dams and reservoirs built over the past century, hence the enormous underground water tables, wadis and rivers, some of which are as large as the Jabuaribe, the Parnaiba, the Piranhas and, above all, the huge Rio Sao Francisco river.

Since droughts have been regularly monitored (from the beginning of the 18th century), the periodicity of droughts which can be predicted a month ahead due to the introduction of satellite observations and to the 'early warning system' occur regularly enough:
– 18th century: 1710–11, 1721, 1723–27, 1744–45, 1754, 1760, 1772, 1777–78, 1790, 1793;
– 19th century: 1804, 1809–10, 1816–17, 1824–25, 1833, 1844–45, 1877, 1879 (the 'great drought'), 1888–89, 1891, 1898–1900;
– 20th century: 1903, 1915, 1919, 1931–32, 1942, 1951, 1953, 1958, 1970, 1976, 1979, 1985, 1988.

In 1936, a 'pattern of droughts' was discerned, together with identification of those communities prioritised for financial aid from the Federal government. Needless to say, the definition of relevant communities has since been enlarged several times, as being a member of it guarantees subsidies for a local community. Today, then, it encompasses a little less than three quarters of the north-east.

In 1998, according to the FAO early warning system, the drought (which affects 10 states) threatens 10 million people and is expected to last at least until the end of the year. The production of cereals and legumes (maize, rice, beans, cassava and soya), which in 'normal' years reaches almost 4.5 million tons for grain and 10.5 million for cassava, is expected to be reduced by half.

According to SUDENE, in May 1998, 4.8 million out of the 10 million people in the 1,233 communities concerned were reported to be 'threatened by famine'.

Agrarian feudalism in the north-east

Some 23% of the land in the north-east is owned by 779 concerns (approximately 0.07% of the total number of landholdings). Each of them has an area of more than 10,000 hectares. At the other end of the scale, 68% of farms are less than 10 hectares and occupy a mere 5% of the total cultivable surface. What better illustration could there be of the unequal distribution of land in north-eastern Brazil?

This is due to history: the first region to be discovered by the Portuguese was the north-east – the cradle of Brazil – which saw the development of its humid coastal areas from as early as the 17th century, with sugar-cane plantations cultivated by black slaves imported from Africa and by native Indians. The interior, meanwhile, was subject to pioneer colonisation, with huge concessions of more than 10,000 hectares each being awarded by the King of Portugal to his 'valorous conquerors'.

Economically complementary to the *mata*, which it supplied with meat, leather and draught animals (notably to run the sugar mills), the *sertaõ* was developed early on for cattle raising and occupied by *vaqueiros* on horseback, guardians of the enormous herds of zebus (on average, there are approximately 10 hectares of land for every animal) and by the *moradores*, precarious occupiers giving four-fifths of their yield to large absentee landowners.

Social structures have developed very little since the 17th century. The large landowners continue to reign as masters over the region, sequestering land left fallow and monopolising political power, something that allows them to resist any attempt at agrarian reform, and monopolising the Federal subsidies allocated for more than a century to the fight against drought and the development of the north-east. The *sertanejos*, Indians, whether native or mixed race, have no choice other than to submit or disappear. Armed militias are charged with subduing any recalcitrants trying to 'change' the situation, rather than choosing the worst option and migrating to the south or the Amazon.

Bibliography

Josué de Castro; 1965; *Une Zone Explosive, le Nordeste du Brésil*; Seuil-Espri
  − 1965; *Géopolitique de la Faim*, Editions Ouvrières.
Amazonie: Nordeste, Sahel Politiques d'Aménagement en Milieux Fragiles (a collective work), Harmattan-Unesco, 1991.
Hervé Théry; 1995; *Le Brésil*; Masson. 1997; *Environnement et Développement en Amazonie Brésilienne*; Belin.
  − 1996; *Pouvoir et Territoire au Brésil: de l'Archipel au Continent*; MSH.
Bernard Bret; 1991; *Les Hommes Face aux Sécheresses: Nordeste brésilien, Sahel africain*; EST.
Bernard Bret, Hervé Théry; 1996; *Le Brésil: de la Croissance au Développement?* Documentation française.
Martine Droulers; 1995; *L'Amazonie*; Nathan.
Sudene, *Aspectos do Quadro Social du Nordeste*.
Manuel Correia de Andrade; 1985; *A Seca, Realidade e Mito*; ASA.
  − 1980; *Land and People in Northeast Brazil*; University of New Mexico Press.
Sylvie Brunel; 1986; *Le Nordeste Brésilien, les Véritables Enjeux*; LSF.

North Korea: a real famine?

SYLVIE BRUNEL

Chronology

1948   Creation of North Korea, the former Korean State having been divided between the Communist North and the pro-American South.

1949   Beginning of the Korean War, provoked by North Korean invasion of South Korea. The United States, mandated by the UN, drives the North Korean forces beyond the 38th parallel.

1953   The Pan-Mum-Jon Agreements confirm the division of the Korean peninsula; 35,000 American soldiers continue to be deployed in South Korea along the border with North Korea. Both countries have lived with the fear of invasion for 35 years.

1994   Death of the 'Great Leader' Kim-Il Sung, replaced after three years' official mourning by his son, Kim-Jong-Il, the 'Great Ruler'.

1995   First call for international aid after floods destroy harvest.

Has North Korea really been afflicted by famine? Or are the authorities of this decaying country trying to stage the 'bluff' of the century: to recover with the help of humanitarian aid? This is the question that charitable organisations have been posing since 1995, when the country first called for international aid.

AUTHORITIES LITTLE INCLINED TOWARDS TRANSPARENCY

In September 1997, the American NGO, World Vision, condemned a famine that had made 3 million victims (out of an estimated total population of 23 million!). At the same time, in a small booklet[1] critical of the international community, Beijing-based journalist Jasper Becker accused World Vision of non-assistance to a country being transformed into one huge extermination camp.

Yet for the NGOs that followed into the field, MSF among them (present, in fact, since 1995), finding the all too well-known signs of famine – such as those witnessed in Biafra in 1968, in Ethiopia in 1984 or in Somalia in 1992 – has been a little difficult. Whereas accounts from refugees in China or South Korea tell of apocalyptic scenes of cannibalism, abandoned children, and entire families being reduced to living off roots, the scenes presented by the country's authorities would appear otherwise. In the crèches and hospitals shown, subject to constant escort by interpreters and civil servants, the children may well have lost weight and there may well be cases of acute malnutrition, but it would be difficult to talk about a famine in the real sense of the word, that is, the dramatic denutrition of entire populations. However, even when faced with simple or inoffensive questions, such as the hour and composition of children's meals, personnel become uneasy and leave 'officials' to reply on their behalf.

When hoping to proceed with their own analysis of the food situation, NGOs invariably meet with refusal by local authorities. Free movement is totally out of the question. While humanitarian aid may be welcome, and medicine and food accepted with open arms, programmes remain under strict government control. The government defines areas of intervention and terms of distribution. Indeed, the ideal situation for the government would be one in which NGOs content themselves with playing the role of basic-need food suppliers, and do not interfere with the exact destination.

The country's authorities host delegations from all over the world to whom they show exactly what they want and these are almost always the same crèches in the same provinces, crèches that have become real 'showrooms' obviously staged to arouse the international community's compassion. The government seems to oscillate continually between significant reluctance at revealing the population's misery, which would be an admission of failure, and the need to convince the international community of the urgency and magnitude of needs, which pushes them to 'exhibit' scenes of malnutrition. At the end of the day, however, the strategy adopted by Pyongyang seems to have paid off: since 1995, North Korea has received the largest amounts of food ever delivered in the world. Indeed, a

---

1. *Famine en Corée du Nord, 1998: un peuple meurt*, l'Esprit frappeur.

number of United Nations agencies, such as the World Food Programme (WFP) and Unicef, continue to exhort the international community not to abandon North Korea's hostage population.

A COUNTRY GONE BANKRUPT

So what is the food situation really like in North Korea? Since the question places the lives of millions of human beings in the balance, errors cannot be made. A number of NGOs present in the country, such as Action Against Hunger or Médecins Sans Frontières, are convinced that a real and dramatic famine has afflicted the country and still persists in certain regions. Given that a number of provinces remain off-limits, aid organisations suspect the government of implementing a 'selective' policy, that is, of using a real famine to attract aid while deliberately depriving affected regions considered as 'secondary' of the same aid. This is done with a view to concentrating relief in areas strategic to the regime, notably the west of the country, the capital Pyongyang and the port of Nampo that supplies it. Indeed, at the end of April 1996, North Korean dictator Kim Jong-Il reputedly declared that he would rather see 70% of the population die so that the remaining 30% might be able to reconstruct the country anew.

Such comments bring back sinister memories reminiscent of Mao and the tragic 'Great Leap Forward' of 1958–62, during which 30 million people died of hunger following a catastrophic economic experiment in which millions of peasants were forced to abandon their fields only to launch themselves into disastrous mini-steelworks in their villages. The appalling precedent that this set endures in the minds of those who refuse to abandon North Korea, given that the regime remains one of the last bastions of the most totalitarian form of Stalinism. In a country transformed into one huge military barracks, a multitude of restrictions on the population – including rationing, terror, excessive propaganda, total control over both society and economy, provincial isolation, prohibitions on citizen movement, brutal repression and so on – have all been legitimised by this notion of the 'external threat'.

However, at the beginning of the 1990s the massive amounts of Chinese and former Soviet Union aid which once helped the regime to hold its own despite patent economic failure disappeared. Wheat from China, for instance, once covered one third of the country's food needs. Since 1995, the North Korean regime has been invoking successive meteorological disasters to account for its setbacks, particularly floods, but also droughts and typhoons, etc. Yet, were such climatic vagaries and the damage they were supposed to cause to crops actually real, then their impact has no doubt been significantly aggravated by the fact that after four decades of autarky and disastrous economic decision-making, the economy has now run out of steam and peasants have been discouraged from cultivating their fields. The country has become totally paralysed. According to the UN, agricultural production fell by 75% in four years! Calling for international aid by invoking an emergency situation has no doubt helped to mask the country's economic disintegration.

'EXTORTION DIPLOMACY'

In 1995, the United States, Japan and South Korea all responded to North Korea's call for help, but made their assistance conditional on the resumption of talks with the South, the relaxation of tensions and the opening-up of the country. Despite being influenced by 'reformers', for whom the death of the 'Great Leader' in 1994 (see chronology) opened up new possibilities, the regime was not quite ready for such a revolution. One of the crew members of a South Korean boat having just delivered 150,000 tons of rice, for instance, was arrested on charges of espionage, while the rice was seized by the army (at 1.1 million men, the army absorbs one quarter of the country's resources), subsequently the first to benefit from it. In February 1996, refusing to be subject to the steel grip of its sworn enemies, the North Korean government decided to renounce humanitarian aid altogether.

However, without humanitarian aid, the economy soon revealed itself unable to survive. It seems, in fact, that the North Korean government reserves its food stocks, already taken from peasants by government order, primarily for the army and the nomenklatura. Hence, the reduction in crops has hit the ordinary peasant hardest. Unable to benefit from privileged access to food supplies, a significant part of the population lives under the greatest of food insecurity, without necessarily being accessible to humanitarian agencies. Aid does not reach the poorest populations unless priority areas and/or sectors of the population have already had their fill.

The fate of North Koreans, then, is once more to be found in the hands of international aid. By taking its population hostage, the regime practises what Jean-Luc Domenach calls 'extortion diplomacy'.[2] Thus, humanitarian NGOs have been asked to supply food and medicine, for both structural and circumstantial reasons, in order to avoid the death of millions of human beings, especially children. To reach the potential mass of people affected by food insecurity, NGOs currently working in North Korea have found it difficult to understand how the regime functions.

THE STRATEGY OF LIMITED AID

Indeed, NGOs refusing to abide by the constraints imposed by the regime have no other choice than to pack up and go. In any case, supply is more than demand: others that are less demanding would be more than willing to take their place and benefit from the comfortable budgets allocated to NGOs working in North Korea. It appears, in fact, that the United States, the European Union, Japan and South Korea have chosen to keep North Korea alive through humanitarian aid and so avoid the country's implosion. Pushed into bankruptcy meanwhile, the regime prefers to launch itself into a suicidal confrontation with the South rather than face the humiliation of admitting failure. For the moment, the possibility of reunification has been ruled out, due to the economic crisis afflicting South Korea, in as much as the precedent set by Germany has underlined the astronomical costs of such an operation. Using a strategy that involves giving aid little by little, the status quo is thus being maintained.

As long as charitable organisations – perceived by North Korea as being directly government-emanated (something admittedly true for a number of American NGOs) rather than independent associations – do not adopt a common line of conduct by refusing to play the regime's game, the regime will play off rivalries, rivalries between NGOs and donors alike, so as to continue to receive aid, despite the often obscure use of food and medicine from the international community.

It is thus the will, whether real or pretext, to help North Korea's population (a population which is first and foremost a victim of a political regime that has been criminal in its blindness and incompetence) which paradoxically makes it possible for the regime to be maintained, and hence for the perpetuation of the misery of North Korea's people. And such a strategy may very well be deliberate.

2. Domenach, J.L.; 1998; *L'Asie en Danger*, Fayard.

Burma[1]: under-development as an instrument of political control

JEAN-FABRICE PIETRI

Chronology

March 1962	General Ne Win comes to power after a coup d'état.
1978	Arbitrary arrests and pressure exerted by the army cause 200,000 Rohingyas from Arakan to flee to Bangladesh.
1979–80	Return of some 180,000 to Arakan.
1982	Amendment to the law on citizenship. The law does not grant citizenship to the Rohingyas.
1988	Series of pro-democracy demonstrations; brutal force by the army is reported to have killed 3,000–5,000 civilians. Creation of the State Law and Order Restoration Council (SLORC); proclamation of martial law in Burma.
1989	Elections organised by SLORC lead to the victory of the National League for Democracy (NLD) under Aung San Suu Kyi, with 82% of the vote; Aung San Suu Kyi is placed under house arrest.
1991	Aung San Suu Kyi is awarded the Nobel Peace Prize.
1991–92	250,000 Rohingyas flee Rakhine to take refuge in Bangladesh.
April 1992	Bilateral agreement between the governments of Bangladesh and Burma on the repatriation of Rohingya refugees; 5,000 are repatriated under the agreement.
November 1993	UNHCR concludes an agreement with the SLORC for the repatriation and re-integration of the Rohingyas.
July 1995	Conditional and very relative 'freedom' of Aung San Suu Kyi.
July 1997	Burma joins ASEAN.
August 1997	230,000 refugees repatriated, and repatriation process officially completed but 20,000 refugees remain in camps in Bangladesh.

1. In 1988 Burma was renamed Myanmar by the authorities in power.

November 1997   The SLORC is dissolved by the junta and replaced with the State
                 Peace and Development Council (SPDC).

Summer 1998   On the 10th anniversary of the massacres of 1988, tensions
                 between the government and the opposition in Burma intensify.

Burma is characterised by an economy exploited by a ruling class which
reaps practically all the benefits to be had. The ruling power is adept at
using economic measures to reinforce its political domination over regions
or ethnic groups. Thus, the economy has become a systematic instrument
of political control. The human cost of Burmese-style 'development' has
been heavy, based upon the age-old authoritarian strategy of population
manipulation with no compensating mechanism of redistribution. Given
the underlying tone of political control, the government's economic policy
stands in sharp contrast to any notion of social development.

THE EFFECTS OF A DEVELOPMENT POLICY IMPOSED FROM ABOVE

Since 1988, Burma has gradually been introduced to a market economy.
The authorities have tried to stimulate foreign investment, particularly in
the energy and tourist industries. The form that economic liberalisation
has taken, however, is indicative of the government's desire to ensure
significant control over the economy, in both urban and rural areas, with
the presence of senior military officers or even family members of those
close to power on almost all the supervisory boards of consortiums and
other joint ventures, helping to ensure continuity between the political and
the economic. Thus, the most important business affairs remain under the
control of the military or their confidants. Such economic development,
imposed over the past 10 years, has failed to produce the expected results,
while continuing to be detrimental to the most vulnerable.

Expectations held by the former SLORC[2] with regards to the economy
were essentially founded on the country's entry into ASEAN and the
resulting anticipated flow of investment. Diplomatically speaking, the

2. The State Law and Order Restoration Council (SLORC) was the name the country's military
    leaders gave themselves in 1988; on 15 November 1997 the name was changed to the State Peace
    and Development Council (SPDC).

Burma

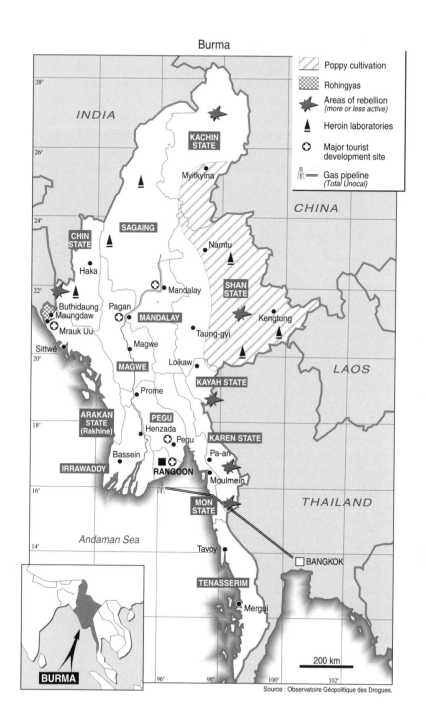

Legend:
- Poppy cultivation
- Rohingyas
- Areas of rebellion (more or less active)
- Heroin laboratories
- Major tourist development site
- Gas pipeline (Total Unocal)

INDIA

28°

26°

24°

22°

20°

18°

16°

14°

KACHIN STATE

Myitkyina

CHINA

SAGAING

CHIN STATE

Haka

Namtu

SHAN STATE

Buthidaung
Maungdaw
Mrauk Uu

Pagan

MANDALAY

Mandalay

Kengtung

Sittwé

Taung-gyi

LAOS

Magwe

Loikaw

MAGWE

KAYAH STATE

Prome

ARAKAN STATE (Rakhine)

PEGU

Henzada

Pegu

KAREN STATE

Bassein

Pa-an

IRRAWADDY

RANGOON

Moulmein

MON STATE

THAILAND

Andaman Sea

Tavoy

BANGKOK

TENASSERIM

Mergui

200 km

BURMA

96°   98°   100°   102°

Source : Observatoire Géopolitique des Drogues.

country's integration into ASEAN was a success, despite certain Western attempts to defer the event. The political support of countries within Asia, admittedly at the cost of certain adjustments, proved unfailing. However, the recent financial crisis afflicting South-East Asia has significantly compromised any potentially major investments, at least in the short term. Thailand, Burma's main trading partner, and Indonesia and South Korea, also long-standing trade partners, are no longer able to free-up the necessary capital. Having exhausted the capital on which the SPDC had based most of its strategy, the South-East Asian crisis has strangled a country unable to absorb the resulting shock and in search of funds.

With development of the country's infrastructure being minimal, the economy's avaricious appetite is instead being satisfied through the exploitation of natural resources that can be immediately and lucratively exported. Rather than strengthening the economy, this only weakens it. The exploitation of precious woods, of natural gas and of precious stones – not to mention the other illicit activities – not only does nothing to promote the development of productive economic networks, but also makes Burma extremely sensitive to regional economic downturns. The accumulation of wealth as well as the rapid acquisition of foreign exchange (often reinvested outside the country) is increasingly becoming the most visible feature of the regime's economic policy.

While present economic failures may well partly result from external factors, the fact remains that the regime's practice in terms of economic policy has left many perplexed. The pettiness and incompetence of an unwieldy bureaucracy has managed to discourage businesses that might otherwise have attempted to resist currently unfavourable conditions. Corruption, the absence of established rules and the age-old reflex of bureaucratic harassment are causing foreign investors, once enticed by the Burmese mirage, to withdraw. The regime has found itself with a bureaucracy left only with the pursuit of social control – no doubt politically effective, but economically disastrous. Due to inadequate development and revenue, financial reserves are falling dangerously, with the State possessing no more than 100 million dollars! The need to finance the mass of civil servants and military officers, two essential pillars of the regime, has caused the authorities to rely upon the smallest of economic flow, with the result that these will probably dry up prematurely.

The desire to develop Burma's significant tourist potential is indicative of a method of development which barely considers the general population's conditions and which is not, in any case, intended to benefit them. The bid to develop mass tourism in Burma, the result of a policy implemented in the early 1990s which was to culminate in the year 1996 (baptised 'the year of tourism'), has been a failure. Boycotting by a number of Western countries (with the notable exception of France) no doubt contributed to this. Condemnation of the human costs of developing infrastructures for tourism has probably had its effects as well.

Burma's incumbent regime has in fact been developing a concept of tourism that aims to target a more 'up-market' clientele, something which, in the eyes of the authorities, means that all signs of deprivation and poverty must be eliminated from potential tourist sites. This has been translated into the physical eradication of poverty through the displacement 'manu militari' of whole living quarters to the periphery, the original site being pulverised to the ground so as to make way for new infrastructures. The city of Rangoon has already undergone such 'cleansing'. So too have the ancient historical sites of Pagan and Mandalay: communities that once lived with and between the monuments have now been driven back to the edge of the 'tourist area'. As a result, huge suburbs now surround the capital. Lacking adequate sanitary structures, these are more similar to shanty rather than 'new' towns, housing the poorest among the displaced. The same phenomenon is underway for the sites of Mrauk Uu in Rakhine state, where entire areas of the town are being forced to relocate to areas outside. Interestingly enough, the town's only hospital unfortunately finds itself near the archaeological sites in question, as a result of which it has been condemned to demolition, without any compensation to help relocate and reconstruct. Whatever the case, the communities affected have been largely excluded from the economic circuit induced by a tourism controlled entirely by the ruling class. Not only are they deprived of the economic repercussions of such activities, but they are also forced to pay an immediate price through a deterioration in their living standards.

FORCED LABOUR, A NEW FORM OF SLAVERY

At the same time, such communities cannot be said to be neglected, often being forced to provide their labour power for the rehabilitation of tourist sites. 'Development' methods imposed by the SPDC are based largely on two criteria: massive foreign investment and a particularly cheap (since not paid) labour force. Known officially as 'community work', the practice of forced labour throughout Burma allows the country's authorities to recruit a mass of 'voluntary' workers whose conditions are often close to those of slavery.

The subjection of hundreds of thousands of people (either Burmese in origin or of an ethnic minority) to forced labour has transformed the country into one huge prison camp for:
– the construction and maintenance of civil infrastructures (roads, bridges, dikes and railroads);
– national works and the construction and maintenance of military camps;
– the development of tourist projects.

They are also used for military operations.

Since the launch of operation 'Visit Myanmar Year 1996', the use of forced labour for the development of tourist infrastructures has obviously increased considerably for the construction of pagodas, the rehabilitation of temples, airports, access roads to sites and so on.

Although the entire population has been subject to such forced labour, this forced labour is particularly widespread among ethnic minorities in rural areas where even children and the elderly have been included. Such physical effort, however, often exceed their capacities. Moreover, forced labourers have to bring their own food and do not benefit from any medical care. Cases of ill-treatment are also regularly reported.

The type of forced labour varies from region to region in terms of the number of working days, the nature of the work, the number of persons affected (which depends on the needs of the authorities in the relevant area) and the 'development' ambitions of the relevant authorities.

Another form of forced labour is portering. Here, labour power is made available to the army to ensure logistics during military operations. Portering is normally carried out by men, but where there may not be enough men present, then women and children may replace them. Sometimes, the family itself decides to send one of its children so as to relieve the man whose income-generating activities are essential to household survival. Forced portering is considered to be harder than forced labour, since porters are forced to leave their homes for indefinite periods of time and be subject to captivity and surveillance by soldiers in the barracks. Ill-treatment during forced portering is commonplace.

Forced labour has a disastrous impact on the population for a number of related reasons:
– first, psychologically, since the person can be commandeered at any moment, day or night, with or without warning and for an unspecified

number of days. The onus of enforced and constant availability almost amounts to slavery;

- second, the effects on the household's economy. A household with financial resources can be exempted from forced labour through payment, while others take their place. The poorest families, however, are unable to escape and are therefore regularly called to contribute their labour force, which obviously has a direct impact on their ability to undertake income-generating activities (both due to the time needed for these and the inability to plan them). Moreover, the smaller the family the more those members who support the household economy are likely to be diverted from carrying out the vital household activities and sent into forced labour. As a result, the family may be trapped into a circle of constant vulnerability. For casual workers, one day of unpaid work can mean one day of fasting for the whole family. Moreover, although a rotation system is supposed to exist, in practice it is not systematically applied, such that the same family might well be called to work more often than it should be.

FORCED POPULATION DISPLACEMENT OF MINORITY GROUPS

This said, Burma has ratified Convention No. 29 of the International Labour Organisation (ILO) on the prohibition of forced labour. The ILO has been calling on the country to comply with this convention for 30 years, but with little success.

Forced population displacement is also a widespread practice in Burma, with the authorities again making considerable use of this for the development of the tourist industry. However, other motives for displacement also exist, based on the ethnic affiliation or the political conviction of those displaced. These tend to include:

- the resettlement of members of an ethnic minority so that the regime might better exert control over them;
- the desire to remove any potential village support (whether voluntary or otherwise) to a group of insurgents;
- the development of an area into a tourist zone;
- the construction of military infrastructures, including the appropriation of surrounding lands.

Population displacement is accompanied by a variety of threats, intimidatory behaviour and ill-treatment, as well as other tried and tested means of persuasion.

Such forced displacement is in contradiction to the standards set by international law (displacement for the protection and security of civilians or for imperative military reasons) and takes place without any accompanying measures to ensure shelter, hygiene, health, food and security. The emotional disruption, the loss of possessions (homes and lands, etc.) suffered by the displaced are exacerbated by exposure to increasingly precarious living conditions, with families being relocated to areas often lacking in elementary infrastructures: access to drinking water, latrines, health centres and so on. Access to land tends not to be guaranteed and assistance in the construction of a new home is very rare. While such displacement is common throughout the country, it is particularly noticeable in the states of Rakhine, Kayin, Kayah and Shan.

The exploitation of the country's natural energy resources is characteristic of this 'development from above', one that defies all logic of social redistribution. In February 1995 a contract was signed between Burma, Thailand, the French company Total and the US company Unocal for the exploitation of the Yadana gas deposits (estimated at 160 billion cubic metres and reputedly one of the largest deposits in the world), together with the transport of the gas to Thailand. The project, worth an initial investment estimated at 5 billion dollars, is expected to provide the SPDC with an annual income of some 400 million dollars.

According to the management of Total, the project is allegedly being carried out with the greatest respect for local populations, so firmly ruling out any ideas of forced labour. Instead, direct dialogue with local communities, a high-wage policy, a support programme for neighbouring villages (construction of schools, an animal breeding centre, training for doctors, etc.) are all on the agenda.[3] It should be noted that all the international NGOs approached by Total at a local level for involvement in this 'social plan' (Action Against Hunger included) have categorically refused to support the project through their activities.

Indeed, the echoes coming from human rights organisations are of quite a different nature: expulsions, rape, looting and summary execution among them.[4] While the use of forced labour appears absent within the boundaries of the worksite, the implementation of infrastructures around

---

3. Based on declarations made by Joseph Daniel, Total's Director of Institutional Relations, in the *Nouvel Observateur*; 5–11 June 1997.
4. International Federation of Human Rights; October 1996; *Burma, Total and Human Rights: Dissection of a Work-Site*.

it (roads, railways, bridges, etc.) to promote access, surveillance and exploitation of the site has mobilised a massive 'voluntary' labour force, using the methods described above, throughout the country. The location of the project in a geographically sensitive area (where Mon and Karen guerrillas are active) has also led to the omnipresence of the Burmese army (and its methods), together with an objective correspondence of interests between the SPDC and Total/Unocal for the project's smooth realisation and exploitation. Such a unification of interests appears to have provoked significant confusion in terms of type and collaboration of resources, given that the 'security advisors' employed by Total/Unocal have few scruples about being associated with the military operations of Tatmadaw.[5]

Such operations for economic development, then, have led both directly and indirectly not only to an increase in the number of violations perpetrated against the local population (who, moreover, gain nothing from the project), but also to further political, financial and military support for the ruling power.

UNDER-DEVELOPMENT AS AN INSTRUMENT OF POLITICAL
DOMINANCE: THE CASE OF THE ROHINGYAS

The policy of 'development from above', together with its disastrous humanitarian effects, can in other regions be contrasted with a kind of 'under-development from above'. Using the same methods (forced labour, displacement, taxation, etc.), the authorities have been forcing certain regions into economic impoverishment with a view to exerting greater social and political control over communities.

Such is the case of the Rohingyas, a pressurised minority group subject to a slow but effective policy of repression. Action Against Hunger has been operating in the region for four years and has witnessed the use of 'hunger as a weapon' in a very concrete manner.

The Rohingyas are Muslims of Indian origin, the majority of whom live in the north in the state of Arakan, on the border with Bangladesh. They account for more than 90% of the local population in the Maungdaw and Buthidaung districts where Action Against Hunger works. Settlement of

5. Name of the Burmese army. For more details about this collaboration, the reader might refer to the report written by the International Federation for Human Rights.

the Rohingya community, now more than one million strong, took place in two main phases. The first one occurred from the 8th to the 10th centuries; the second and substantially larger one during British colonisation. Integration within the Arakan community was relatively smooth until the Second World War, at which time confrontation between the Muslim and Buddhist populations surfaced, each wanting to affirm its own political and cultural identity.

Looking at the present situation, the Muslim minority has essentially been subject to two different types of pressure. First, they are victims of governmental non-recognition as citizens, the result of a policy of ethnic segregation. One of the four social objectives specified within the government's official programme is 'the promotion of national integrity and prestige both while protecting and preserving the nation's cultural heritage and identity'. In this, a policy of protection of 'races' recognised as 'national' (Burmese, Kachins, Shans, Kahyas, Chins, Mons and Arakanese) is being promoted to the exclusion of all others. Refused recognition, the Rohingyas have been denied Burmese citizenship. As a result, they have no legal rights. The main reason for Muslim non-recognition stems from their being regarded as illegal immigrants from Bangladesh who have settled in Burma illegally. Their exclusion was institutionalised in the 1982 law on citizenship.

Muslims are also victim to regional hostility from the Buddhist Arakanese population in search of past splendours and hegemony. The Arakanese accepted submission to Rangoon with difficulty, such that resentment is widespread and often expressed at the expense of the Rohingyas, easy targets for scapegoating. The authorities have tended to take advantage of the antagonism between the two, inciting the one against the other in a manner as provocative as it is artificial. Hence, the authorities have brutally encouraged the resettlement of Arakanese villages on traditional Rohingya lands, the latter receiving no compensation for surrendering their 'paddy fields' and often being forced to contribute their labour to the construction of the new village! One can just imagine the feelings engendered between the two communities.

In 1992, subject to such pressures, some 250,000 Rohingyas took refuge in Bangladesh, fleeing abuses by the Burmese authorities. The movement in population alerted the international community to the issue and also created diplomatic tension between Burma and Bangladesh, a country already faced with overpopulation and a difficult economic situation and therefore refusing to integrate such a huge population influx.

Testimonies:
bringing a child back to life

Each of the following testimonies was written by one of Action Against Hunger's volunteers, whether a doctor, nurse or nutritionist. Together, the testimonies were published in the French daily newspaper, *La Nouvelle République du Centre-Ouest*, between 22 December 1997 and 2 January 1998. As Chief Editor Dominique Gerbaud wrote:

'We don't want to fall into the habit of decrying such misery, but instead we want to highlight the anonymous work that goes on, on the other side of the world. For once, the victims of hunger will be given a name and a face. For once, we will not bemoan the fate of children suffering from hunger – and perhaps, even dying from it. What we have wanted to do is shed a different light on their distress – not to ignore it. We felt that the mere fact of talking about it and of underlining the work of a humanitarian organisation whose sole objective is to fight world hunger would be enough to emphasise the latter's existence in the dozens of countries where people are still dying from malnutrition.

For a few days, we would like to invite our readers to follow those who help to bring a child back to life; who help to revive their taste for life and sow a few seeds of hope. These volunteers have agreed to give up their anonymity and to speak, often personally, sometimes intimately, about one child among many. A child they admired and saved.'

Since this report aims to be more than just a clinical and horrifying observation of what hunger as a weapon represents today, we found it important to include these short portraits. They explain in a way far better than any long speech why the use of hunger as a weapon is intolerable, and why certain people have chosen to commit themselves to humanitarian work and to struggle, in their own way, against such outrages. For they know that even if their work will not change the face of the world, they will at least save lives. Each one of these lives is for each of them a name, a face and a story whose destiny, in the midst of a history of violence, they did not want to see sink into oblivion, into a mass of statistics.

© Action Against Hunger

*Sylvie Bernard, a 31-year-old nurse
working in Bardera, Somalia*

Ambuyo: the struggle

SYLVIE BERNARD

Why is it that some children will be better remembered than others? It's hard to tell. Ambuyo is one of those children whom I'll never forget and who has now become part of my life. Famine had struck and Action Against Hunger had been in Bardera, Somalia, for two months. Although the situation was less dramatic than during the first few days, numerous children continued to flock to our feeding centres. Each one weighed less than 70% of the normal weight-to-height ratio.

She came with her father and her brother, Mohammed, her mother having recently died. Ambuyo, at almost 12 months, was prostrate and listless. She had lost her hair, she wouldn't try to walk or talk and, inevitably, she was severely malnourished. What attracted me to her was probably the way her father cared for her. He was always so thoughtful and we could see that he would do anything to save his daughter. His will to fight encouraged us, for so many parents seemed to be overwhelmed and to have accepted their awful fate.

In our centres, we saved many children and adults, but this also required their co-operation, something not always easy when people lose all hope.

After one month, Ambuyo had almost reached a normal weight. She was then transferred to a centre for children in the process of recovery, where she received two portions of porridge every day. Little by little, we saw her smile again, then walk and begin to talk. Sometimes, I would carry her on my back, just like Somali mothers do. We were so attached to each other and I would always be filled with wonder at seeing her so well after having been so ill.

Then I had to leave Bardera for Mogadishu. But I returned six months later and I wanted to see Ambuyo. She was well, walking and talking. Although she didn't recognise me, I was happy.

I have now been back in France for a year and a half. Somalia was five years ago. Sometimes I take care of the children in the clinic where I now work. I smile at them; they seem so beautiful and so happy.

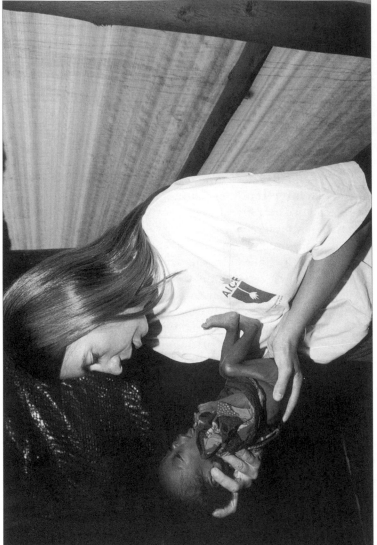

Christel Braconnot, a 30-year-old nurse working in a nutritional centre in north Burundi in 1994–95

© Anne Nosten

Jeremy: the shock

CHRISTEL BRACANNOT

Little Jeremy arrived at the centre in his mother's arms. You could hardly see him, rolled up in his cloth. He was three months old and skeletal; his face was all wrinkled, his eyes seemed enormous. He had the head of a 'little old man', the symptom of severe malnutrition.

He was the first malnourished child I had ever seen at such a young age. We had between 100 and 150 children in the centre, so I was used to seeing malnourished children, but this one was so small, it was a real shock.

We took him in immediately, adapting the treatment for his age. Later we had other very young children, so we made a special room for them which we used to call the room for 'shrimps'. The children used to weigh between 1.5 and 2 kg (3.3 lbs and 4.4 lbs) on arrival.

I was so surprised, but an improvement was visible from the very first days. Jeremy was crying less and drinking his milk greedily. Once he started smiling, we knew that he had been saved. Jeremy stayed at the centre for a long time, not because he was recovering slowly – on the contrary, he put on weight rapidly and soon regained the lovely chubby cheeks of a well-fed infant – but because his mother was a great help to us.

She trusted us right from the start and followed the treatment with extraordinary patience. Once her child was out of the critical phase and she had more time, she naturally looked after the other mothers who had difficulties feeding their infants as she had had with hers. She would explain the treatment and the importance of following it. Above all, she would comfort those mothers who were afraid of losing their children: she would tell them that we could save them and would show little Jeremy, by then a beautiful little boy who was full of life.

Once they left the centre, they both continued to visit us regularly, just for the pleasure of talking to us and showing us that they were both well.

Jeremy is proof that with a little milk, care and love, we can save lives even if, at the beginning, the situation seems hopeless.

The daily struggle of an old woman who no longer wants those closest to her to risk their lives

© Hermine

Nino, the grandmother

MARIELLE BERNARD

A 35-year-old social worker working in Zugdidi, Georgia

In the administration's building of the gas-pipe factory in Zugdidi, every available space had been taken over by families of Georgian origin who had fled the Abkhazi region.

In one of the offices that simultaneously served as lounge, kitchen, bedroom and bathroom for six sat Nino the grandmother – silently. As a sign of mourning, like almost all the other women, she was dressed all in black.

During the day, Nino regularly disappeared from their common room. When night fell, she would leave the house, leaning on her stick, her pockets full of plastic bags and secretly walk the 30 kilometres which took her to the family house in the neighbouring district of Gali, on the other side of the newly erected border.

Danger! She had to cross the river. The only bridge was under strict surveillance. She had to follow a well-trodden path to avoid the landmines, and she had to turn off her lamp to hide from militia groups on patrol.

Once at home, she stayed crouched in the shadows so as to remain invisible and give the impression that the house was uninhabited. When evening came, she would fill her pockets and plastic bags with food before retracing her footsteps. She would take away as much as she could carry of the potatoes and nuts that had been left there, and some clothes and some pretty crockery to exchange in the market.

Nino was a widow. Two of her sons had been killed in the conflict and she did not want any more of her family to put their lives at risk in order to support the family while in exile. Thus, with the authority of women of her age, she would not let anyone else participate in these nocturnal escapades – the only way of improving their daily life.

Manna, her 20-year-old grand-daughter, told me that Nino was going less and less often on these nightly journeys now that Action Against Hunger had opened its canteen in the factory rechristened 'Community Centre'.

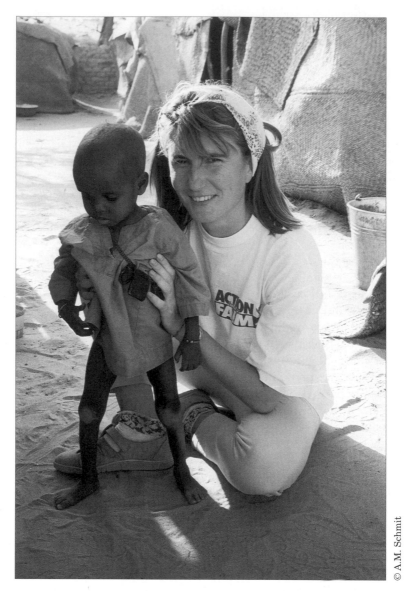

© A.M. Schmit

*Muriel Dupuy, a 28-year-old nurse
working in Mondo, a small village in the Kanem, Chad*

Abdoulaye, 'the dying one'

MURIEL DUPUY

Once I had seen Abdoulaye, two weeks after my arrival in Chad, I understood exactly why I had come to Africa. Abdoulaye, 5.5 kg at three years old, weighed the same as a four-month-old child in France and looked the image of death.

That day, I was on a regular visit to the therapeutic feeding centre (TFC). The children were making progress. The team was efficient, the TFC was working well and the children were sitting with their mothers…a routine visit.

But no: it turned out to be a day unlike any other for Abdoulaye arrived.

His mother had her back to us, so I only saw how thin he was: his emaciated feet hung lifelessly towards the ground. His head, too weak to be held straight, fell wearily and heavily backwards.

I will never forget my first impression of Abdoulaye. I could see all his bones. A real lesson in anatomy. His arms, too long, just hung beside his body. You had to guess where his elbow might be. What I found most amazing was his bottom: you could see craters. You could even imagine the head of his femur to be in his hip. Eating his meal seemed like torture to him. He swallowed the therapeutic milk that his mother would leave so patiently at the back of his throat, with great difficulty. Sometimes, it would take him an hour to finish it. His forehead would be all wrinkled with pain. You would have thought it was the face of a little old man, a face with no trace of youth.

Abdoulaye did not have any major problems, apart from persistent diarrhoea. He soon began to recover. One week after his arrival, he could be found sitting among the other children, moaning because the milk did not come quickly enough.

By the second week, he was pushing his hungry mouth towards the plastic cup full of milk that he now drank greedily and with pleasure.

By the third week, Abdoulaye had become a child like all others. One month after his admission, he was full of the joy of life. Who would ever have recognised the same dying child in this laughing one?

Abdoulaye is learning to walk again on his shaky legs. They are still too weak to support him properly. But this child has chosen to recover and to live.

His mother is also smiling again. When I told her that her child was beautiful now that he had put on weight, she replied that, even as a skeleton, he had still been beautiful!

What more is needed than a little milk and love in order to want to recover and to live?

The love of a father

EMMANUELLE PIETRI
A 31-year-old doctor working in Kabul, Afghanistan

It was before the first Eid. That is, before the celebrations following the end of Ramadan and lasting four days in Afghanistan. The mother appeared to be around 25 years old, and the father about 65 years but must no doubt have been 20 years younger. In the harsh climate, the war and deprivation had had a physical impact. They brought their child to the paediatric hospital in Kabul where Action Against Hunger had established an intensive therapeutic feeding centre in 1995.

It was already night, in the middle of an Afghan winter. The snow that covered the city hid the ruins and the rubbish, the grime and the misery. This baby was minuscule, one month old according to the mother, and weighing 1.7 kg. A little wreck all wrapped up in rags. It was a boy and he was breathing with difficulty.

Looking at his height of 46 cm, one might have thought that he had been born prematurely, but his mother didn't know his exact date of birth, nor the date at which she should have given birth.

The father was amazing. It was exceptional in Afghanistan to see the fathers of sick children. Perhaps this was due to a sense of modesty, a sense of detachment from 'women's occupations', a lack of feelings of responsibility or shame when faced with the illness and malnutrition of their child? It was probably a little of all of these. This man, then, had already struck me by his mere presence.

He was tall for an Afghan, with a wrinkled face and pale blue eyes. It was he, not his wife, who beseeched us with his look as he handed over to us the little pile of rags that was his son, his first born. The intensity of his look filled the whole room, a room already saturated with suffering and fear. It was the feeding centre's 'first room', the room where all the worst cases were placed. The room where many would die.

The two had arrived with their child that morning. My assistant – an Afghan doctor who was exceptionally motivated in a world where everything seemed to be collapsing – and I had gone to the hospital in

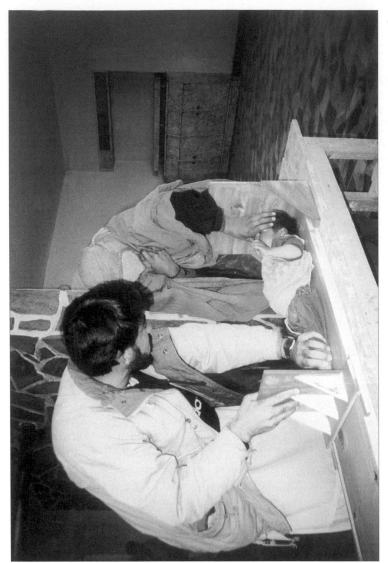

In Kabul's paediatric hospital where a child is being measured, the erratic presence of the doctors, even if inexcusable, can be explained – they haven't been paid for months

© M. Bernard

the evening, shortly before the curfew, to check that there was enough food for the mothers and enough medicine and milk for the children.

Upon seeing the child's state, we checked the prescriptions that had been made out that morning by the hospital doctor. Only a laboratory test had been prescribed, due to the child's diarrhoea, but no treatment beyond that!

Such a prescription would have condemned the child to death within a few hours. That day, in violation of rules stipulating that prescriptions made by Afghan doctors should never be directly changed, I decided to take things into my own hands.

I spent the four days of the holiday visiting the hospital three or four times each day because I was worried that there might not be a doctor there and because I didn't want this child to die. This must seem incredibly pretentious, but it's the kind of act over which you have little control. However accustomed you are to seeing children die, although you obviously want to save all of them, sometimes you end up irrationally attached to one particular child, refusing to let it die.

The second day, despite treatment, the child was in an awful state. His father was still there. Suddenly, he knelt down before me, his eyes shining and launched into a long speech in Persian, none of which I understood. I felt embarrassed, imagining that he was pleading with me, a European doctor, to save his child.

Far from it! He was simply telling me that he knew his child was going to die, and was asking me for authorisation to take the child home, so that he would not die in hospital. In this case, the hospital's Director would charge money for the corpse to be handed over, money that the father did not have, and if he could not pay, he would not be able to take the body home.

I asked him to give me some time. Nothing worked. In the end, I told him that I would pay the costs myself, in the unfortunate case that this be necessary.

The next day, the baby was less pale, had an almost normal respiratory pattern and was losing less liquid. Three days later he was almost pink. The battle had been won.

Nearly two months later, the child left the hospital, weighing 2.7 kg. His father was there, smiling with his clear blue eyes.

Joëlle Levine, a 30-year-old nurse working in Bo,
the second largest town in Sierra Leone

© Burger/Phanie

Letter to Menda

JOËLLE LEVINE

Dear Menda. You arrived at the therapeutic feeding centre in Bo one evening with your mother: exhausted, with no more energy, no longer even able to cry. Insecurity permeated the country. Terror had been reigning for months. Your physical state gave rise to the worst fears.

You had walked for three days in the bush, avoiding uncertain roads with a fear that was written all over your face. You had lost your daddy and your elder brother, both killed in the village during the fighting. The day after your arrival, your mother left again, by foot, to look for your younger brother, left behind with sympathetic friends.

Menda, at the age of six years, you were already contemplating the tragedy of the situation, with little complaint.

An intense current coursed between us. You came to put your hand in mine discretely, remaining there for long moments at a time, in silence, with a serenity that contrasted with the violence you had known all these months.

When your mother returned with your younger brother, you came to look for me, and only by looking at your shining eyes I understood that what remained of your family had finally been reunited.

Your condition improved, but slowly. Your medical treatment was quite intense and your small appetite made each meal a trial of strength.

You remained like this for six weeks in the therapeutic centre and moved later to the supplementary feeding centre where you would come to collect your two hot meals every day. So our meetings became more and more rare. Your recovery seemed imminent and each day the hope of seeing you healthy again grew stronger.

You know, Menda, our meetings had a special meaning for me. I'm not afraid to admit that the type of relationship we had between us helped me to overcome the physical and psychological difficulties inherent in such hard humanitarian missions.

I left Sierra Leone after one year. Do you remember, little Menda, the day of my departure? It was so hard to leave this violent country, but most of all to distance myself from all the children who had been my main concern for so many months.

What joy you gave me when, at the airport, I saw you arrive by bike, with a nurse from the centre. You hugged me tight, without a word, and our silence was filled with emotion, tenderness and hope.

Today, in a country where the situation is still precarious, I still think of you, Menda, and of all the children, and I wonder if you are safe somewhere and still ready to fight for your life. To live or to survive, is that the question? If it is to survive, for what future? Life, much more than death, has a future that shines through Menda's eyes.

I will never forget you, Menda.

However, Burma, immured in an autarchic system for 30 years and then subject to boycott by a number of Western countries since the beginning of the 1990s, has been searching for a way to break out of the political and economic isolation into which it has been sinking for some time. Hence, a change in foreign policy. This change in foreign policy was first expressed through normalisation of economic relations with the country's more immediate neighbours, Bangladesh and Thailand. Burma's agreement to repatriate the Rohingyas became part of this policy, also reinforcing its application to join ASEAN. Nevertheless, Rohingya persecution and exodus did give rise to some protest and indignation within ASEAN, given the strength of Islam in Indonesia and Malaysia.

As a result, a repatriation programme was initiated, first within the framework of a bilateral agreement between Bangladesh and Burma, subsequently under pressure from the international community and with UNHCR supervision and international NGO assistance, Action Against Hunger included. Involvement of the international community in the resettlement process has been seen as a gesture of goodwill on behalf of the Burmese authorities.

However, since the effective integration of Burma into ASEAN in July 1997, the willingness to make concessions has come to an end. The situation in the state of Arkan, then, particularly for the 200,000 or so Rohingyas repatriated, has hardly improved. The policy of population repression continues, under the eyes of the United Nations.

The government has found itself in a delicate position, having to consider the interests of several parties. Confronted by international opinion and ASEAN's Muslim countries, it cannot afford another massive exodus of Muslims, but at the same time it obstinately refuses to really integrate them either politically (denial of citizenship status) or economically. In the districts of Maungdaw and Buthidaung where Action Against Hunger works, this status quo has been manifest in a policy of economic non-development, population exploitation and the creation of an ethnic ghetto under high military surveillance.

Beyond a few short-term projects for export products already entirely controlled by the local authorities (who alone reap the profits), the government has not drawn up a single economic plan for the region. This in a region traditionally subject to rice deficits (the production deficit for the 1997–78 season was estimated by the UN to be 17,500 tons). One of the priorities for agricultural policy in the area should have been the expansion of cultivable land, since at present only 19% of the land is

cultivated (89% of which is used for rice). Still more resolutely, a political desire to maintain the region in a state of under-development has been manifest by:
– a total lack of structural investment;
– control by local authorities (mainly the armed forces and border police) over the most profitable sectors, including the brick industry and shrimp farming;
– denial of access to land for Muslim communities.

In fact, the majority of Rohingyas lack access to land, since it is also impossible for them to buy or even rent this (according to a decree issued in April 1997, Arakanese landowners are prohibited from renting their lands to Muslims). Thus, in 1995, the percentage of persons without land was estimated to be around 52%. If, however, only those repatriated from Bangladesh are considered, the figure rises to as much as 90%. Moreover, plot size is limited: 94% have less than five acres and 75% less than three acres. Legally, since 1953, the government has been the sole landowner, with the right to determine land utilisation.

The Rohingyas, then, have had no other choice but to work as casual labourers, subject to production calendars and seasonal variations. Confiscation of Muslim land for the benefit of the military (essentially for the creation of military camps) or for that of Buddhist communities forcibly relocated to the region (each family automatically receiving three acres of land) simply exacerbates the situation.

Reduced to dependence on uncertain daily work, Muslims (together with a number of Arakanese) are subject to severe restrictions on their freedom of movement – a considerable handicap in their search for employment. Having already been constrained to stay within the state of Arakan (it is almost impossible for a Rohingya to travel to Rangoon unless huge sums of money are paid to various Burmese civil servants), Muslims are now hardly ever able to leave even their own district. The government refuses to grant them the authorisation necessary to travel within the state of Arakan. Travel permits must be requested for travel between villages, with registration with the relevant authorities being compulsory every time. Such restrictions on the freedom of movement are a visible constraint to trade and commerce possibilities and, more generally, to employment opportunities.

A series of 'officious' measures may be added to the list of more official measures that weigh heavily on the population. Wielded by the civil and military authorities, these tend to be arbitrary and uncontrolled. Most

important among them are the ad hoc (in addition to the formal) taxes levied. Whether in the form of money, rice or anything else, they contribute to undermining any hope of development. These are essentially the result of two factors:
- an administrative system which encourages corruption and all that is arbitrary. Civil servants are given very low salaries by the government, or in some cases no salary at all, particularly at the village council level. To this is added the venality of charges, such that civil servants survive and grow wealthy by tapping into those they serve;
- a strong military and police presence in evidence in the border zones (that is, the army, the border police [Nasaka], military intelligence and the ordinary police). Under-paid soldiers (receiving only three to eight dollars a month) and officers transferred for several years gain only from their impunity to get as rich as possible.

Such informal taxes have been accumulating, leading to asset depletion and the impoverishment of both Muslim and Arakanese households. They permanently thwart any desire for development.

The policy to maintain the region in a state of under-development is due to several governmental objectives. First among them is the desire to prevent the region's population from mixing with that of the rest of the country. Over-militarisation and restrictions on the freedom of movement are used to keep control over what has become an ethnic ghetto. Two systems operate to ensure this. One is based on the police and military, with troops having been deployed to encircle the area. The other is based on an administrative system that combines both Burmese and Muslims collaborating with a view to escaping oppression while getting rich.

Another objective lies in the desire to maintain pressure on the population such that daily survival becomes the order of the day and structured protest impeded. The search for food has become the main concern, over and above concerns about identity, cultural recognition, justice or even citizenship. Burma's authorities intend to prevent the population from becoming rich and to prevent any possible emergence of a cultured elite capable of contesting its legitimacy. Hence, also, the colonisation of the area through both forced relocation of Arakanese communities from other regions, the construction of a number of structures symbolic of Buddhism (pagodas and meditation centres, for instance) and land confiscation.

In the same way, the government would also very much like to see the gradual and discrete disappearance of the Muslim population, while preventing any mass exodus that might provoke an international reaction.

As a result, encouragement is given to a limited but regular number of people wishing to leave the country who, as a result, will be unable to benefit from the status of political refugee and will be perceived as economic migrants instead (a term already taken up by the UNHCR in Bangladesh).

For those who work in the region on a daily basis, the main effects of this policy have been more than evident. A large sector of the population is to be found in a situation of food insecurity. Employment opportunities are limited due to the lack of employment creation measures. The opportunities for families still having some capital to improve their lot is similarly limited by their inability to invest this. For the majority of the population, there is little hope of improvement. Even departure for Bangladesh means the loss of the few possessions they may still have, although for those who no longer have anything this is seen as the only solution left to them.

The system of control and informant networks has caused the Muslim community to fragment: distrust is now often stronger than any sense of belonging to a larger community. We are now faced with a community that no longer trusts itself and that only rarely shows some sign of collective solidarity. In the larger context, one might expect conflict between the Arakanese and Muslims to break out, with the former also subject to national and local economic degradation, and increasingly using the Muslims as a scapegoat. Divisions are maintained and fostered by the government. As economic depression takes an ever greater hold over the country, tensions are increasing.

PART 2

HOW TO FACE THE HANGMAN?

Pharaoh's Dream

AHMEDOU OULD ABDALLAH

When Pharaoh awoke from the dream in which he had seen seven fat cows and seven thin cows, he called Joseph to interpret what had become a real nightmare. For all those familiar with the Bible or the Qu'ran, this story is well known. Joseph's verdict is equally familiar: for seven years Egypt would enjoy prosperity and excellent harvests, followed by another seven years of severe drought which would induce terrible famine. To avoid the famine, the Pharaoh was advised to store the surplus from the seven good years in order to redistribute it during the years of shortage.

Today, thanks to technical progress, the kind of successful preventive policy implemented by the Pharaoh would put an end to famine. Modern pharaohs, however, use hunger as a political weapon, deliberately starving their people. They do not need anyone to interpret their dreams or predict the future: they fully understand the precariousness of the economic situation and they are perfectly well informed as to the risks of famine for their people. Whether in Afghanistan, Sierra Leone, Iraq or Congo, political leaders or warlords hold innocent people hostage, starving them in order to attain their political objectives.

It is high time that hunger ceased to be a tiresome subject evoking either abject misery or commiseration and charitable consolation. It is also imperative that famines no longer be associated with technical incapacities or the inability of certain countries to be self-sufficient or manage their agricultural resources appropriately. While it might be true that there are regions with relatively unfavourable environmental and climatic conditions for agriculture, and others – or sometimes the same ones – in which movement of produce between areas of surplus and those where there are consumers or shortages is constrained due to poor infrastructure, this does not make it any less scandalous that severe famines continue to occur, and are even prolonged.

Interestingly enough, the most deadly famines have tended to strike countries with the environmental and climatic conditions that actually promote the production of cereals, such as southern Sudan or the former Zaire. In reality, it has been local pharaohs or their opponents who have caused hunger. Their supporters and other soldiers provoke violence and combat, causing insecurity and leading to the flight of peasants and livestock breeders, the destruction of crops, the burning of cereal stocks and the slaughter of animals. Behind every refugee or displaced persons camp lies a tale of political conduct that is sometimes unintentionally bad, but is often deliberately harmful, by one or more modern-day pharaohs.

Rural populations that are taken hostage and pursued no longer have the ability to feed themselves, still less to provide for the overpopulated towns which depend so heavily on the countryside. Hunger is a weapon – a weapon all the more formidable in the irresponsible hands of those who should be responsible for its prevention. Inefficient governments, bankrupt by their own corruption, facing populations sceptical of their political wisdom, and fearing elites who might eclipse them, attempt to subdue their subjects by starving them, destroying traditional systems and burning harvests. Those subject to such treatment take refuge beyond the borders, putting heavy strains on an already unstable environment. Opposing forces, meanwhile, in their fight against governments, may force entire communities to flee the land of their ancestors and take refuge in camps supported by international humanitarian assistance. In sum, then, climate and geography often play marginal roles in major famines – it is man who starves man.

How, then, can the victims of famines resulting from political misconduct, civil or inter-State wars be protected? International opinion and major powers only act once a crisis has already taken place, with more preventive action appearing difficult to implement, all the more so as governments invoke the notion of national sovereignty to block any kind of 'interference'.

A consensus which integrates governments, international organisations, civil society and influential people must be reached. This consensus should reaffirm the right to food and condemn all those who deliberately force their people into starvation.

The workers in humanitarian organisations are today's Josephs. However, their mission is not to interpret the dreams of pharaohs, but rather to explain a number of sad truths to them, so that they might stop using hunger as a weapon against unarmed peoples.

Against the use of hunger as a weapon – legal instruments providing an objective obligation to take action

MARIE-JOSÉE DOMESTICI-MET

In a world engulfed in civil wars of the third and fourth generations,[1] where it is civilians rather than combatants who are being targeted and killed, sophisticated weapons are not always necessary. Although private trading in kalashnikovs may well have put the latter into the hands of those least experienced, such as the young boys of Liberia, the kind of carnage that the machete might wreak has also been more than visible. And yet the proposition is even simpler than that: in this context, hunger has become a weapon, a weapon that is formidable in efficiency when used in situations already characterised by a certain vulnerability – that inflicted by under-development.

Hunger is a significant weapon even in an age of nuclear proliferation. We know that in the mid-1980s, Mengistu invented the use of food stocks as bait to trigger mass deportations. Today, we have seen how the regime in Burundi cares little about the food insecurity of those fleeing the hills, as they become herded into resettlement villages. In Sudan, the regime in Khartoum unscrupulously uses hunger as a weapon to promote Islam, while the guerrilla forces of the SPLA have turned malnutrition into the

---

1. The first generation corresponded to 'political' civil wars in which adversaries confronted each other in the name of different conceptions of the State and/or society (the Wars of Secession, Sunderbund and Spain, for instance). The second generation corresponded to wars of national liberation, while the third was indicative of 'peripheral' conflicts, which transported the confrontation between East and West to the Third World, in the competition for empire. Civil wars of the fourth generation are those which have developed since the fall of the Berlin Wall, which lack the clear division characterising the bipolarised world and which therefore often lack the support of a Great Power. There are two consequences. First, the search for new identification criteria – in this case, endogenous ones given the disqualification of 'proletarian internationalism' and the loss of meaning in the term 'the free world'. Hence, the idea of ethnic purity. Second, the absence of any 'overarching leader'. This said, the targeting of civilians had already begun in previous phases.

norm rather than the exception. One might even go as far as to say that restrictions on the delivery of humanitarian aid to refugees are a good way to promote a more rapid and 'voluntary' repatriation. Even worse, hunger is a weapon that can kill simply by abstinence, or by a combination of malicious intent and a general abstention to actively stop its use as a weapon.

Such was the case during the winter of 1996–97, when the international community resorted to spy satellite myopia as a pretext to declare the loss of hundreds of thousands of people in the forests of Kivu, the survival of whom would have further complicated the political scene in the Great Lakes.[2] While those who used the pretext might not have chosen hunger as a weapon, they allowed it to take its course – with regret, but nevertheless consciously.

Such an observation challenges the progress that we had believed accomplished during the first half of this decade. Its gravity is without possible comparison to the criticism made of other operations.[3] The issue here is no longer that of aspects related to humanitarian aid, but rather the total absence of such aid. Similarly, it is no longer the audacity of the law in endorsing aid which has caused such a scandal (as at the time of the debate about 'the right to interfere') but rather the lack of courage of those who could have decided on such an operation, but preferred either to impede or abandon it. The reality today, unfortunately, is not one of interference in defiance of refusal by the territorial power, but one of abstinence despite the agreement of the territorial power, as in Zaire in 1996. In the latter case, the international community renounced intervening to rescue the 300,000 Rwandan refugees in the forests of Kivu in the belief that the problem had already been resolved since a large number of Rwandans from the camps had returned to their country. And the fact remains that the democratic benefits expected from such unhumanitarian abstinence have yet to materialise.[4]

2. See chapter on the Great Lakes.
3. Witness Bosnia, for their far too humanitarian nature, Somalia for their shortcomings, or Rwanda in 1994 where the political leader of State is said to have been involved in dubious personal relationships before providing effective assistance, with this also being delayed by the United Nations.
4. Some thought that a rescue operation of fugitives from Kivu would strengthen Mobutu and so resigned themselves to the death of hundreds of thousands of people in the hope that a regime under Kabila might bring about democratic progress. Exactly one year after the capture of Kinshasa by Kabila's forces, this was to prove a bitter memory (*Le Monde*, 17 May 1998).

It is now thought that the failure to intervene in Sudan could be even more serious. While events might not seem to be as intensely dramatic as those in Kivu, this is because they do not share the same characteristics in terms of unity of time and place, nor in terms of media coverage for that matter. However, just as much in this case, it has been obvious (and might one even say regrettable?) that those who could have intervened preferred to let events take their course.[5]

Humanity itself is being put in danger by a silence and inaction which is indirectly killing the most vulnerable among us. The humanitarian world which would have liked to take action despite the refusals, the obstacles and the dangers is in search of a reason, a foundation from which to demonstrate the legal impossibility of 'leaving people to die'. Little by little, the ardent quest for a legal reason to act 'regardless' is taking hold.

In view of the problems raised by the concept of 'interference' – a concept that was intended to be provocative by its very title – legal experts have turned towards the notion of the *'right* to assistance'.[6] The concept of having a right *to* – part of the second generation of rights – is well known in international public law, since we already talk about a right *to* development, a right *to* the environment and a right *to* peace.[7] However, such themes have neither prospered nor become part of positive law. As for the various *'rights to'* that can be found in the International Covenant on Social and Economic Rights, these are to be found in the context of international norms serving to guide internal relations. The concept of a *right to assistance*, destined to play a role in international relations, is not so easy to construct, even if particularly seductive.[8]

Nevertheless, when hunger strikes as a weapon, some sort of *reason* to act must be found. The solution perhaps lies in the abandonment of the more strict aspects of the concept of the 'right *to*'. If the legal norm is, by definition, binary – that is to say, based upon the binomial right-obligation[9] – then perhaps, in order to construct this binomial in terms of

5. Cf. the initiative by the Caritas network with regard to several Heads of State and governments in 1992. The President of the French Republic made it known that he 'knew'.
6. Cf. notably the UNESCO Symposium entitled 'The Right of Victims to Assistance', held in Paris on 26–27 January 1995.
7. Refer to the Charter of Banjul, adopted by the OAU in 1981, Articles 22, 23 and 24, respectively.
8. Cf. Marie-José Domestici-Met; 1995; *Propos sur le Droit à l'Assistance (Comments on the Right to Assistance)* in *Le Droit Face aux Crises Humanitaires (The Law in Situations of Humanitarian Crisis)*; Office of Official Publications for the European Community, Luxembourg.
9. See Michel Virally; 1960; *La Pensée Juridique (Legal Thought)*; LGDJ, Paris.

humanitarianism, the coupling of a subjective right with a subjective obligation should be renounced. Obviously, we need to look at the situation from an objective point of view, one similar to that permeating humanitarian law where certain objectives form absolute imperatives due to the higher values they protect. The proposition is relatively simple: surely assistance in the form of food to people whose very existence is threatened by a severe food crisis forms something of an objective obligation, the result of an imperative need by and for humanity? The idea has the merit, at least, of being in conformity with the spirit of positive humanitarian law, even if difficulties arise. First, in that food assistance does not benefit from any specific provisions in the relevant texts; second, in that neither does the content of any obligations relating to food aid and resulting from humanitarian law.

While food aid has become a significant way to protect non-combatants, an obligation to act against an artificially created famine also emerges.

FOOD AID AS AN IMPORTANT MEANS
OF PROTECTING NON-COMBATANTS

The basic legal texts pertaining to armed conflicts emphasise protection more than assistance and contain relatively few specific provisions for food compared to medical assistance.[10] And even this does not appear to concern all population types.

The provisions of the Fourth Geneva Convention of 1949 have a generally limited conception of humanitarian assistance. Article 23 essentially mentions medicines, sanitary equipment and religious items, as well as indispensable food, clothes and tonics reserved for children less than 15 years old, for expectant mothers and maternity cases. While Articles 55 and 59 address more general questions of food, these focus more specifically on occupied territories.

However, as soon as hunger becomes a weapon, food assistance takes on a different dimension. It can appear as the *sina qua non* condition for safeguarding that most essential and primary of human rights: the right to life, as dependent on food. Its contents become more significant for humanitarian law (A) and its jurisdiction goes beyond the direct beneficiaries (B).

---

10. Health care agents and centres enjoy a special immunity, for which there is no equivalent for food aid.

THE CONTENTS ARE PREMISED ON THE DIRECT PROTECTION
OF A FUNDAMENTAL VALUE: HUMAN LIFE

The relationship between human rights and humanitarian law is one of the most sensitive areas of international law. A 'hard core' of human rights is safeguarded by humanitarian law during periods of armed conflict. Although humanitarian law cannot guarantee their full respect, it at least underlines their fundamental value and tries to restrict the more severe violations that might arise in such perilous contexts.

One of the pillars of this 'hard core' of human rights is the right to life. It has been asserted within the most fundamental texts on international human rights law, among the most important of which features the Universal Declaration of Human Rights. This states that: 'Everyone has the right to life, liberty and security of person' (Article 3). The right to life can also be found in major regional Conventions for the protection of human rights,[11] and in the UN Covenant on Civil and Political Rights.[12]

What is even more significant is that there have been several attempts at declaring the right to life to be non-derogable. Even in exceptional circumstances where certain rights can be set aside – due to difficulties in maintaining order, for example – no deviation from the right to life is possible.[13] Such is the reason for including, if not the right to life *per se*, at least protection of the life of *non-combatants*, through the law on armed conflicts. The obligation to respect life, enshrined in the body of norms regulating activities which tend to cause death, is of particular importance.

A closer look at the right to life seems necessary, given that respect for human rights is not applied exclusively through humanitarian law, and even less through food assistance. In both the UN Covenant on Civil and Political Rights, and the European Convention on Human Rights and Fundamental Freedoms, the right to life tends to be situated within the context of capital punishment and other intentional violations of life. This said, it should be mentioned that a more concrete and positive concept of

---

11. European Convention on Human Rights and Fundamental Freedoms: 'the right to life of each individual is protected by the law' (Article 2); American Convention (Article 4); African Charter of Peoples and Human Rights: 'The human being is inviolable. Every human being is entitled to respect for his life...' (Article 4).
12. 'The right to life is inherent to the human being' (Article 6).
13. In the case of war, refer to Articles 15 and 27 of the European Convention on Human Rights; in the case of 'a public danger threatening the life of a nation', see Article 15 of the European Convention; Article 27 of the American Convention; Article 4 of the Covenant on Civil Rights.

the right to life has recently appeared in human rights law. The development of combat methods should further provoke an influence on humanitarian law – to the advantage of food assistance.

Two characteristics of the system of International Human Rights Covenants are of importance. First, the Human Rights Committee established to monitor the Covenant on Civil Rights has developed a 'jurisprudence'[14] (or body of law) in which the right to life appears to have significantly concrete implications. In this, States must not only abstain from harming life, but even more than this, they must guarantee life through various measures, among them the development of health and food policies. In addition, one of the paragraphs of Article 11 of the Covenant on Economic and Social Rights introduces the idea of 'the fundamental right of everyone to be free from hunger'.[15]

Following on from this, efforts to free all those against whom hunger is cynically used as a means of deportation and massive elimination surely become all the more important? Assaults on the ability of people to feed themselves have become more and more systematic over the past three decades, whether communities are being deprived of their resources,[16] food aid is being impeded[17] or – even more Machiavellian – conditions have been deliberately created to attract humanitarian aid with a view to then diverting it for the benefit of repressive forces.[18]

At least in theory, the law of armed conflicts has been able to provide a response to such activities. And food, which appears to be much more of a crucial stake than ever before, is now a theme of both humanitarian assistance and protection in the humanitarian law of armed conflict. The idea of protection confers a *status of immunity on those persons exposed* in the form of a prohibition to harm placed upon those in a position to exert power over enemy forces, prison camp authorities, the occupying forces

14. The term has been placed in inverted commas to remind the reader of the non-jurisdictional character of the Committee's work.
15. 'The State Parties to the present Covenant recognise the right of everyone to an adequate standard of living for himself and his family, including adequate food, clothing and accommodation...States...recognise the right of everyone to be free from hunger.'
16. By poisoning wells (as in Somalia), inhibiting crops by planting landmines in fields (whether or not with the intention of using hunger as a weapon) and by uprooting people and their systems of production and distribution, etc.
17. By blocking convoys, sometimes for fear that they might really be carrying weapons, sometimes due to problems of donor partiality, with certain donors systematically supplying one camp over another (an argument often used by the Bosnian Serbs).
18. Such was the case in Ethiopia under the Mengistu regime.

and so on. The notion of assistance, meanwhile, provides for services to alleviate victims' situations. Altogether, protection has priority over assistance, for if the former were really effective, then assistance needs would be minimised.

1 The international law of armed conflict has long contained rules for the protection of life in general.[19] Protection in the field of nutrition was introduced more than 20 years ago. Although it is usually claimed that humanitarian law always seems to be one step behind any relevant war, the law had prohibited the use of hunger as a weapon well before prohibitions on conventional weapons.[20] The relevant provisions appear in the Protocols to the 1949 Conventions, adopted in 1977: *'Starvation of civilians as a method of warfare is prohibited.'* (Protocol I, Art. 54 sec. 1); *'Starvation of civilians as a method of combat is prohibited'* (Protocol II, Art. 14, Sec. 1). The first of these texts has been supplemented by more detailed provisions prohibiting specific acts which might endanger a population.[21]

2 Similarly for assistance. The time when surgical aid provided to victims of war typified humanitarian assistance no longer exists. It has instead been replaced by mass migrations sometimes engendered by famine, but also generating famines through disruption to modes of living, natural environments and cultural rhythms. Indeed, the type of large-scale assistance that has developed over the past three decades[22] largely corresponds to the huge increase in wars primarily targeting civilians.[23]

19. In Article 32 of the Convention on the Protection of Civilians in Times of War, the High Contracting Parties *'specifically agree that each of them is prohibited from taking any measure of such a character as to cause...the extermination of protected persons in their hands.'* Similarly, Article 3a, common to all four Geneva Conventions in relation to non-international conflicts, stipulates that *'persons taking no active part in the hostilities...shall be and shall remain protected at any time and in any place against violence to their life and person.'*
20. Convention adopted in 1980.
21. 'It is prohibited to attack, destroy, remove or render useless objects indispensable to the survival of the civilian population, such as foodstuffs, agricultural areas for the production of foodstuffs, crops, livestock, drinking water installations and supplies and irrigation networks, for the specific purpose of denying them for their sustenance value to the civilian population or to the adverse Party, whatever the motive, whether in order to starve out civilians, to cause them to move away, or for any other motive.'
22. When East Pakistan declared independence to form the State of Bangladesh, the UNHCR began to be faced with the first major population migrations (in 1970–71). In 1977, the ICRC opened an Operations Unit and in 1992, with the question of the Kurds at the forefront, the United Nations and the European Union set up structures responsible specifically for humanitarian aid.
23. During the First World War, 5% victims were civilians, compared to 95% in the Bosnian War.

Moreover, Article 18 of Protocol II, adopted in 1977, does not appear to give less importance to food aid than to medical aid, since both 'foodstuffs and sanitary supplies' are mentioned. And it is in respect of internal conflicts that the massive humanitarian operations witnessed over the past few years have developed. Today, then, beyond the more vulnerable cases, food distributions form the corollary of a new norm of protection. Written in bold on one side of the coin is the prohibition of the use of hunger as a weapon. On the other side should inevitably be an expanded form of assistance offered to the whole of the targeted population.

In reality, the distribution of foodstuffs to those being deliberately starved has become the most common form of assistance.

A LEGAL REGIME WHICH GOES BEYOND
THE DIRECT BENEFICIARIES OF FOOD AID

It is tempting to propose that the right to life should be followed by a *right to* assistance, residing with victims. However, the definition of a *right to* assistance is fraught with difficulties and technical problems.

First, and this is a very difficult question: Who is entitled to food? Each individual, or the entire population? And how is the latter to be defined? To talk about the right of people to food, rather than the right of an individual to food, involves several difficulties, and even dangers. Why wait till the number of deaths reaches a point where it is pronounced a genocide before declaring that people were deprived of food? Should the population be homogenous, consisting of only one community, one ethnic group? Should these people be that of a particular State? These are just some of the problems with the concept of a 'people' being entitled to food. And even if the concept of a 'people' was substituted with that of a 'population', and one asked if such vulnerable populations had the right to food, two problems still arise. First, if the population is that of a guilty State, a country under embargo, does it still have a right to food?[24] Second and more seriously, do the guilty have a right to food – something evoked in the camps of Goma?

Such a right also requires a specific debtor, for otherwise who is to be under an obligation to provide food? Last, the right further requires a

---

24. The 'filtering embargoes' that have been imposed in several recent cases tend to meet with a positive response. But do such embargoes filter sufficiently? Are they sufficient to provide enough food for the population? In the case of Iraq everything seems to suggest that this is not the case (see the chapter on Iraq).

specific legal regime for its implementation. Yet, what fact or condition triggers the right to food? What legal mechanisms exist for those entitled to this right to lodge a complaint if they are not given any food?

In the particularly precarious context of contemporary conflicts, such questions highlight the inadequacy of the notion of the *right to*. The same might be said for the concept of 'refugee' as expanded by that of 'internally displaced', where in the 1980s and 1990s the granting of status came to be substituted by *prima faciae* recognition and where the need to prove persecution came to be substituted, in certain instances, by the granting of 'temporary status'.[25]

The era of huge and largely uncontrolled waves of migrants was hardly conducive to creating a link between a creditor and a specific debtor, a notion not in conformity with the spirit of humanitarian law anyway. The law is based primarily on concepts of necessity, the general interest and identification of those to be assisted and protected due to their current state of distress – whether civilians, injured combatants or prisoners of war.

However, a specific debtor for the right to food cannot be chosen any more than the right be made available to all.

A right that cannot be invoked against a specific debtor

Even if there were to exist a right to food, who would provide that food? The territorial State is one obvious candidate due to its duties vis-à-vis its population. Similarly and according to humanitarian law, this applies to an occupying State in an armed conflict. In the same way, neighbouring States through which any food might be transported should not, under humanitarian law, impede this transport. Yet what about all those States far away and in a position to decide whether or not food is actually to be provided to the relevant people/population? Are they under any obligation to stage such an operation or to take positive action?

The rights from which victims benefit under humanitarian law are both more and less than subjective rights. They do not have the full and complete character of property law which would allow 'unrestricted enjoyment and use of possessions'. Instead, they tend to resemble the attributes of sovereignty, seen as 'inalienable and sacred'. Hence, the inappropriateness of questions about entitlements to the right to food.

25. Those coming from former Yugoslavia.

An inalienable right

A sense of the imperative is created by Article 7/7/7/8[26] which stipulates that protected persons cannot 'renounce in part or in entirety the rights secured to them'. In the margin, the official presentation of the document also summarises the article with the words: 'Non-Renunciation of Rights'. Thus, it cannot be presumed that persons in danger of dying from hunger have either renounced the prohibition on the use of hunger as a weapon or the reception of assistance. Even should significant discouragement have incited them to do so, the sum is greater than its parts, and such persons cannot be alienated from the humanity of which they are an integral part.

This leads us on to one of the singularities of a system constructed around the preservation of life in armed conflicts: the peremptory character of the norms posed.

TOWARDS THE EMERGENCE OF AN OBJECTIVE OBLIGATION TO FIGHT AGAINST ARTIFICIALLY CREATED FAMINES

Why should such an obligation be linked to a particular debtor? If indeed there is an absolute need to help people at risk, and if this need precludes these people's ability to control their own destiny, why should the obligation to come to their aid be limited to only a few responsible persons?

Before looking at some of the more concrete aspects to be expected from identifying an objective obligation to provide food aid (B), a more theoretical issue must be assessed. This makes reference to the concept of *jus cogens*, which is frequently used in connection with humanitarian law (A).

Situating such an objective obligation within the regime of peremptory norms

Here, it seems appropriate to take a closer look at what exactly causes the rules on assistance to be peremptory and, subsequently, to situate foodstuffs in their relevant context.

All the rules which form part of humanitarian law are embedded in the notion of *jus cogens*. This is something already obvious in the articles

---

26. Article 7 of the Conventions on the Wounded and Sick of the Territorial Forces, on the Wounded and Sick of the Marine and on Prisoners of War, as well as Article 8 of the Convention on the Protection of Civilians in Times of War.

common to all four of the 1949 Geneva Conventions, with Article 6/6/6/7[27] which stipulates that special agreements can be concluded, but 'without adversely affecting the situation' of the relevant protected persons and, therefore, only as long as in the direction of an improvement to their status. Thus, the Conventions confer only a minimal status, which is apparently non-derogable despite the absence of the term. That notwithstanding, the peremptory character of these rules is further emphasised by Article 7/7/7/8, already mentioned in Part 1.

The same peremptory regime is again highlighted in a text not part of the Geneva Conventions, namely Article 60 (Paragraph 5) of the Vienna Convention on the Law of Treaties which precludes the exception of non-fulfilment on the grounds of an absence of reciprocity in the commitments taken concerning the humanitarian.[28]

These are just three aspects indicative of the objective force of norms relating to public order. In order that the supposedly essential function of such norms be fully exercised, they are, in the course of their lifetime, protected against any potential opposition that might threaten them. First, by derogation which creates a realm of inapplicability, or a sub-set in a field of applicability, where norms do not have to be applied. Second, by the exception of non-fulfilment, with non-fulfilment by one party being met with non-fulfilment by the other party. Third, by renunciation which allows the final beneficiary of a norm conceived in the interest of humanity to behave as if he were the only one to be affected by it.

Can it not, therefore, be concluded that the norms of humanitarian law are objective in all respects, and that, as a result, there exists an objective obligation to act in favour of populations threatened by starvation?

Although the criteria for non-derogability may be peremptory,[29] this should not overshadow other aspects of the peremptory regime of norms referred to as *jus cogens*.[30] Beyond the force that these norms may have, other aspects relating to the ways in which violation of them might be

---

27. That is to say, Article 6 of the Conventions on the Wounded and Sick of the Territorial Armed Forces, on the Wounded and Sick of Armed Forces at Sea, and on Prisoners of War, in addition to Article 7 of the Convention on the Protection of Civilians in Times of War.
28. 'Paragraphs 1 to 3 do not apply to provisions on the protection of the individual contained in the treaties of humanitarian law'.
29. Notably under domestic Civil Law, with peremptory laws opposing laws of goodwill.
30. A systematic study would make it possible to assess the relevant aspects; see Marie-José Domestici-Met 'Recherche sur le concept d'ordre public en droit international public' (Research on the Concept of Public Order in International Public Law'), thesis, Nice, 1979.

sanctioned, for instance, give grounds for thinking that action is required at the international level.

In terms of the specificities marking the objectivity surrounding the sanctioning of *jus cogens* norms, other examples can also be cited. These include the nullity affecting the act itself, the possibility of persons other than the direct victim of condemning the offence and the existence of penal sanction. The latter is characteristic of the norms of humanitarian law, as set out in the Conventions of 1949, and even more so with regard to the creation of International Criminal Tribunals.

The idea of protection at the international level, meanwhile, is in fact explicitly included in the regime of certain international norms. Similarly, for the role of members of the UN in the implementation of the principle: Prohibition on the Recourse to Force.[31]

The same idea can also be found at the beginning of the four Geneva Conventions, with the obligation to respect and *to ensure respect* for the Conventions being enshrined in the first Article common to all of them. Thus, while there may exist an objective obligation to act, subjects of the law act neither for themselves nor in response to a corollary '*right to*'. Instead, they are merely the instruments of a general will to preserve certain values, including life, physical integrity and human dignity.

Such concepts legitimised interventions for humanity in the 19th century, regardless of the distortions to which the concept might have been subject due to certain controversies.[32] Today, armed intervention for humanity is no longer lawful.[33] Yet this said, should there not exist other ways in which a subject of international society could act in the name of humanity to put an end to a situation at odds with the law? Were such a mechanism to exist, it could only be within a peremptory context: such an

---

31. For instance, Article 2, Para. 6 of the Charter according to which State Parties must endeavour to enforce respect for the principles of the Charter by non-member States.

32. There has often been talk about intervention on the basis of humanity as an operation carried out for the purpose of defending the nationals of the intervening party – which may or may not be the case. It has also been perceived as a first step towards colonial subjection, which is only a by-product. In fact, what singles humanitarian assistance out is its objective: to bring about, using force if necessary, the eradication of the cause of distress. This is what distinguishes it from contemporary humanitarian operations, even where these might be combined with a degree of military deployment, aiming only to limit the distress.

33. Due to the prohibition on recourse to force. Given that the only lawful use of force by States lies in legitimate defence, it is not surprising that the evacuation of foreign nationals forms, today, the typical kind of armed operation in the context of a local crisis. The integration made by part of the doctrine between intervention for humanity and the evacuation of nationals no doubt follows from this.

action cannot be left to the good will of the intervening party, nor impunitively impeded by the State in a position to take action. This concept, then, may be relevant in the context of food aid.

THE OBJECTIVE OBLIGATION WITH RESPECT TO ORGANISED FAMINE

Written law is to be interpreted as setting real obligations – at least negative – as regards assistance. However, the most difficult part will consist of defining a content adapted to the needs experienced due to the use of hunger as a weapon, without compromising the texts. This is the challenge to be met if the intolerable cycle of abstention is to be broken.

The existence of obligations in terms of assistance

Here, reference should be made to both the texts and their authorised interpretations.[34] In terms of international conflicts, the relevant reference texts are those of Articles 23 and 55 of Convention IV, and Articles 69 and 70 of Protocol I. One underlying idea emerges from these texts: the absence of authorities' discretionary power to physically block humanitarian assistance.

The general case already contains an obligation, that is: 'if the civilian population of any territory under the control of a Party to the conflict, other than occupied territory, is not adequately provided...'[35] then relief actions are to be undertaken. Article 23 of Convention IV stipulates that: '*each High Contracting Party shall allow the free passage*' of foodstuffs and so on – the wording being such as to indicate, in juridical parlance, the existence of an obligation. Article 70 of Protocol I also adds that '*relief actions...shall be undertaken*', with the future indicative tense here too indicating the peremptory nature of the norm.

In terms of territories occupied by a power other than the territorially sovereign State, the texts impose an obligation to provide supplies. Article 55 clearly declares that the Occupying Power '*has the duty of ensuring the*

---

34. Denise Plattner; 1996; 'Le régime des Conventions de Genève et des Protocoles additionnels en matière d'assistance aux victimes des conflits armés' (The Regime of the Geneva Conventions and Additional Protocols on Aid to Victims of Armed Conflict), in *Aide Humanitaire Internationale: un consensus conflictuel* (International Humanitarian Aid, a Controversial Consensus), by M.J. Domestici-Met (ed); Economica.
35. Article 70, Protocol I.

food and medical supplies of the population', including, if necessary, through importation of the products in question. The idea is taken up again in Article 69 of Protocol I: *'the Occupying Power shall...also ensure the provision of...'*

It is, however, admitted that the Occupying Power has a power of control and that for various reasons it may refuse access to victims. Thus, in Convention IV:

- Article 23 notes that: *'The Power which allows passage...may make such permission conditional on the distribution...being made under... local supervision'*. Furthermore: *'The obligation of a High Contracting Party to allow free passage...is subject to the condition that this Party is satisfied that there are no serious reasons for fearing...'*
- Article 59 notes that: *'all Contracting Parties shall permit the free passage of these consignments.'* Obviously, they should authorise this, but they also have to provide an authorisation.

Similarly, Protocol I confirms that assistance activities *'shall be undertaken, subject to the agreement of the Parties concerned'* (Article 70, Para. 1). Furthermore: *'Where necessary, relief personnel may form part of the assistance provided in any relief action...the participation of such personnel shall be subject to the approval of the Party in whose territory they will carry out their duties'* (Article 71).

However, although such a power of authorisation is by no means discretionary,[36] it should be mentioned that fairly important differences exist between the regimes governing international conflicts, looked at here, and internal conflicts. Article 3 common to all the 1949 Conventions only vaguely addresses aid to victims, even if possible to make a broader interpretation.[37] However, Protocol II is relatively restrictive:

'If the civilian population is suffering undue hardship...relief actions...of an exclusively humanitarian...nature...shall be undertaken subject to the consent of the High Contracting Party concerned' (Article 18). The latter gives priority to State consent over that of any rebel groups.

---

36. 'The actual text, without encroaching upon sovereignty...implies that the agreement should not be refused' (Commentaire Pictet des Protocoles CICR, Geneva; 1986; no. 2805 P841).
37. 'An impartial humanitarian agency, such as the ICRC, may offer their services to the parties to the conflict.' According to Patrice Jean, the offer 'to the parties' can be interpreted as made to only one party, for example. Following from this, if it is accepted by the rebels, such an offer can disregard the refusal of the government ('Fulfilment or non-fulfilment of international humanitarian law', in *International Humanitarian Aid: a Conflictual Consensus*; M-J. Domestici-Met [ed]; Economica; 1996).

Given the number of internal conflicts and the scale of large aid operations over the past few years, this is not insignificant. It is no doubt one of the reasons underlying UN efforts to strengthen provisions in the Law of Geneva relating to assistance.[38] Most prominent among these have been the well-known resolutions, 43/131 (1988) and 45/100 (1990), which can be considered as decreeing something similar to a directive for the interpretation of competencies provided by the rules of Geneva in relation to authorisations to be given for access to relief by victims.

In that humanitarian assistance is obligatory and that the conditions that might impede it are, in principle, regulated by humanitarian law, does this mean that implementation of this group of norms should take place at the international level?

The content of the objective obligation to fight against the use of hunger as a weapon

As already seen, it seems appropriate at this stage not to succumb to imagination or speculative interest. Instead, legal provisions already available should be closely scrutinised in order to make them an effective weapon of combat.

Written law emphasises the obligation not to impede the delivery of assistance (including food assistance) – a phrase preferred to that of 'shall not arbitrarily impede'.[39] This constitutes a negative obligation. Yet, in order to ensure supplies to 'those who are going to die of hunger',[40] the existence of a positive obligation must be proved – although as mentioned earlier[41] it would be difficult to define the relevant debtor State having the positive obligation to supply. Should this be the richest? The closest? All of them?

It is, however, possible to conceive of a State fulfilling the objective obligation by means other than the delivery of food. There are many potential modes of action which, while not provided for within humanitarian law, can all be used to respond to acts using hunger as a weapon.

---

38. Besides the wish to create a general international humanitarian law valid for natural disasters and all that one might define as 'circumstances of a similar order', and besides the hope, once taken on board by certain French doctors, of having accepted the idea of interference.
39. Others might say not to impede discretionarily or arbitrarily.
40. S. Brunel; 1997; Seuil.
41. Cf. supra introduction and Part I.

And one should be careful not to forget NGOs which, despite their generally limited subjectivity at international level, have had certain of their actions recognised.

In what follows, a classification of such actions will be presented, independently of the *corpus juris* which makes them possible.

Operations involving the provision of material resources. This essentially involves the delivery of basic foodstuffs. Assistance is one way of compensating for the non-respect of protection and a way which can, depending on its scale, go as far as to completely overturn such non-respect. In this, it would almost be as if the decision to use hunger as a weapon was being cancelled, due to its being a violation of a peremptory norm.

However, given the context – that is, the actual existence of hunger as a *weapon* – such an undertaking cannot be confined to logistical aspects alone.[42] As a result, the sending of food may well have to be accompanied by a security operation to ensure effective delivery of supplies. Such operations can only be carried out by the UN or one or several State(s) acting on behalf of the UN.

Given prevailing conditions of security, or rather of insecurity, in the areas where humanitarian aid is required, it tends to be difficult for NGOs to act without State or inter-State organisations. Thus, it is impossible to place them under an obligation to take action in certain areas, despite the right of initiative given to them by Article 9/9/9/10, common to the 1949 Conventions (particularly Article 10 of the Fourth Convention).[43] They can nevertheless be expected to at least try to exert their right of initiative – and once again, the language and the tense in which the Article is written evokes a sense of the peremptory, even if the operation must be '*subject to the consent of interested Parties to the conflict...*'

No initiative to supply aid should ever be abandoned, even if it appears obvious that it will be rejected. Such a refusal may lead to an intervention that no longer conforms with the criteria established by humanitarian law in this regard, whilst also leaving those intending to exert their full powers of sovereignty open to condemnation.

---

42. One might think of the rice sent by French schoolchildren to Somalia: while discharged at the docks, it did not reach the vast majority of victims.
43. The Articles mention the humanitarian activities of the ICRC, as well as any other impartial humanitarian organisation. Article 10 of Convention IV, in particular, mentions that such activities be undertaken for the protection of civilians and for assistance to be brought to them.

Diplomatic operations: The aim of diplomatic operations is to '*ensure respect*' for international humanitarian law, as agreed upon by State Parties in common Article 1.[44] With the drawing up of the 1977 Protocols, this crucial article has been replaced by Article 89 of Protocol I, which proposes ways and means to fulfil such a task at the international level.

The problem tends to be situated within the context of multilateral diplomacy and without using the words of collective security. It brings to bear a new commitment and the idea of working in liaison with the UN.[45] Under the orthodoxy of this obligation, States will have the choice of submitting a case to either the General Assembly (according to Article 11, Para. 2) or to the Security Council (Article 35). The increasing number of Security Council Resolutions on humanitarian aid during the 1980s,[46] together with the adoption of two texts to establish jurisdictions for the punishment of war crimes, should not therefore come as a surprise.[47] However, only Resolutions on humanitarian assistance itself have aimed to ensure respect for certain aspects of humanitarian law.[48] Litigation against the use of hunger as a weapon, meanwhile, falls outside the scope for the implementation of humanitarian assistance.[49]

However, another text can be applied in this context: *Article 8 of the Convention on the Prevention and Repression of Genocide* stipulates that the UN can be called upon to take preventive action. In this respect, hunger as a weapon may be seen to amount to genocide, with definitions of the latter including: '*The deliberate subjection of a group to conditions of existence that might lead to their partial or total physical destruction*'.[50]

---

44. '*The High Contracting Parties commit themselves to respect and to ensure respect for the present Convention under all circumstances.*' Refer to cf. G. Abi Sabi: 'Common Article 1 to the Geneva Conventions'.
45. '*In the case of serious infraction of the Conventions or of the present Protocol, the High Contracting Parties commit themselves to acting, both collectively and individually, with the United Nations and in conformity with the Charter of the United Nations.*'
46. Basing its competence on a threat to peace – in an extensive conception of the latter – and going as far as to write that humanitarian assistance is a way to maintain peace.
47. Resolutions 808 and 827 relative to the International Criminal Tribunal for former Yugoslavia, and 955 for the ICT for Rwanda
48. Those relating to the ICTs aimed at sanctioning *a posteriori* (as for Rwanda) and at exerting pressure with a view to re-establishing peace (former Yugoslavia).
49. Those exercised by States in terms of universal criminal competence or collaboration with international repressive jurisdictions can only claim to have a deterrent or retributive effect, as with any repressive action. This falls into the domain of sanctions/punishment, outside the objective aim of acting against hunger.
50. Article 17 of the Code of Crimes Against the Peace and Security of Mankind Project (A/CN.4/L.532). This is also evident in the Convention of 1948.

Given that the *right to life which, in the last instance, is the foundation of humanitarian law*, is multi-faceted – 'let live', do not let die – humanitarian law can be less and less confined to protection activities even if the latter are increasingly being violated. The nature of conflict and the way it has developed in using hunger as a weapon has led not only to the material strengthening of nutritional assistance, but also to deep reflection on its dignity, its eminent necessity and the tools necessary to guarantee that which it represents.

Since interference cannot be justified in such terms (given that the parameters of a *right to* assistance cannot all be identified), a different approach is therefore necessary, one that is diversified in terms of means of action and actors. Nothing should be neglected in the arsenal so far evaluated. There is nothing insignificant about putting the issues on the agenda of a subsidiary body. However, the approach needs also to be coherent, one that is inspired by a conviction that this is a pre-eminent objective to be attained: to save those who risk death. And this needs to be done with will and perseverance, in the conviction that this is for the benefit of mankind.

Such an observation is not at variance with the nature of law: one should not be imprisoned by the dichotomy between *right of* and *right to*.[51] The same law may comprise both aspects, and such is the case with the right to life.

---

51. Even if this corresponds to the general dichotomy marking civil, civic and political laws on the one hand, and social and economic laws on the other, the correspondence is not perfect. Proof of this lies in the notion of the right to a fair trial, for although a civil-political right, it is nevertheless a right *to*, rather than a right *of*. The right belongs to the first generation of human rights laws, such as liberty of expression, whereas the right to work or to social security belongs to the second generation. The phrases 'capacity to do' and 'power to demand' proposed by the doctrine in the middle of the 20th century (cf. the great 'classic' written by Georges Burdeau on 'Public Freedoms') are no doubt more able to express a complex reality than distinctions founded on a difference of preposition. The former supposes that the law in question is exerted by its holder with neither intervention nor public assistance; the latter supposes that the holder will gain from the active behaviour of the authorities against whom the right may be held. On the one hand, a simple abstention, inspired by liberalism, is required; on the other hand, public intervention is required. Thus, two concepts of society are juxtaposed, one against the other.

The 'filtering' embargo: an effective solution?[1]

MARIO BETTATI

The term *'the right to interfere'*, or in the original French *'le droit d'inger-ence'*, is somewhat journalistic, or at least political rather than legal. Jurists prefer to talk about the principle of free access to victims, destined to permit the delivery of humanitarian aid, particularly food aid, as well as obviously needed medicines. The principle of free access was introduced by the United Nations through a series of resolutions voted in by the General Assembly and followed by the Security Council. It took place on the initiative of the French government, more specifically that led by Michel Rocard (Prime Minister from 1988 to 1990), and has subsequently been developed by all governments.

The principle has often been criticised as imposing greater restrictions on countries of the South as opposed to those of the North. Fundamental to any explanation of this is, of course, the observation that, as it so happens, those who are hungry are to be found in the South while those who have the resources to feed them are to be found in the North. However, and it is here that misconceptions must be righted, the obligation does not only lie with countries in the South.

First, countries of the South where humanitarian action unfurls tend to be in a state of deliquescence where, in the absence of a State, reliable interlocuters may be difficult to find among the ruins of society. Hence, the principle of free access to victims is unlikely to weigh upon a government that is no longer competent.

Subsequently, the principle of ensuring humanitarian actors free access to victims falls upon States of the North who are under an obligation not to impede assistance, particularly when imposing international sanctions. This is where an interesting innovation comes into the picture, an

1. This text is taken from a speech given by the author during a conference organised by Action Against Hunger on the 15 October 1997, at the Sorbonne, Paris.

important qualitative change brought about by France in relation to the embargo.

An embargo is a means of taking retaliatory measures and, as such, has been recognised within international law since the 19th century. Embargoes simply consist of banning imports to and exports from a country; that is, closing the country's borders and inhibiting other countries from selling it goods or from purchasing its goods, so as to sanction the government or impose restrictions on it.

For a long time, the world took this for granted. However, some began legitimately to question whether such actions actually harmed a State's population more than the government initially intended them to be punished. Unfortunately, these same people were reprimanded for the example they had chosen, namely South Africa. When South Africa was under the embargo, I remember asking: 'Don't you think this will do more harm to black populations, victims of *apartheid*, rather than to a white government which is already over-medicated and over-nourished?' After all, we all knew that Professor Barnard had carried out the country's first heart transplant and that South Africa was highly developed in the field of medicine while, in contrast, the country's poor black populations were being deprived of external assistance. At the time, I was told that all African countries were in favour of the embargo and that, therefore, it had to be maintained. When South Africa was expelled from the International Red Cross Conference, I think I must have been one of the few people in France to be indignant, although as a long-standing anti-*apartheid* activist I could not have been suspected of indulgence towards Pretoria. It was simply too early to try to rectify the harmful impact of the embargo.

After a first attempt to permit the passage of medicines (at the time of the Rhodesia affair and with limited success), the idea was again taken up in 1990, given the emphasis of humanitarian organisations on the counter-productivity of embargoes and the proposal of a solution that I would call the 'filtering embargo'.

THE COUNTER-PRODUCTIVE EFFECTS OF EMBARGOES

After a series of debates between public and private sector humanitarian organisations (Unicef, UNHCR, FAO and NGOs) with governments of the time, it was noted that embargoes could prove counter-productive in at least two respects: the one humanitarian, the other political.

The perverse humanitarian effects of embargoes are now well known. First, they 'victimise' populations already enduring hardships imposed by disrespectful governments that the international community would like to punish. Second, they have the immediate effect of 'squeezing' a number of local economic activities, with a number of businesses going bankrupt and unemployment rising. Third, they widen the gap between the ruling classes, their needs already being largely covered, and the general population already largely below the poverty line. Fourth, they often cause waves of refugees driven by shortage and in search of subsistence to move to neighbouring countries. After the Gulf War, when sanctions were imposed on Iraq, for instance, Jordan was subject to one such influx. Fifth, embargoes can provoke a large number of diseases often known as *'iatrogènes'* by doctors; that is, diseases caused by their very treatment, in this case, by international political treatment of the Iraqi crisis which led to nutritional deficiency and infant disease. Wasn't it the *New York Times* that claimed that, at the beginning of the 1990s, 1,000 children were dying each month as a result of the embargo alone? Finally, embargoes cause an inflation which specifically affects basic necessities such as food and medicine: a survey by FAO on the effects of the embargo in Burundi revealed an inflation rate of 92% on food products. *From a humanitarian point of view, then, embargoes are catastrophic.*

The perverse political effects of embargoes are equally overwhelming. First, they cause illegal trade and the black market to flourish, much to the delight of the trafficants. In this respect, embargoes contribute to the criminalisation of the economy, through the emergence of parallel networks and the disappearance of the Rule of Law. Second, management of such embargoes comes at considerable cost to the international community due to the bureaucratic structure and resources required. Thus, to monitor the implementation of sanctions against Iraq, marine forces from 25 countries were mobilised in order to conduct, in 1996, 23,000 enquiries, 10,000 inspections and 600 seizures! A third political difficulty lies in the deterrent effect of embargoes: no-one has yet been able to demonstrate their efficacity. Some have argued that these were tangible in the case of Rhodesia: their word will just have to be taken for it. Fourth, and above all, for the countries to be punished, embargoes provide a good excuse for propaganda both internally and externally. Ruling powers tend to be successful in reconstructing a sense of national unity vis-à-vis the hostile exterior. Thus, populations might be rallied with 'See the misery you're suffering: it's their fault!', while the international community, meanwhile, might be railed with 'Look at the misery of my people: it's your fault!' Imagine: had Mobutu's Zaire been placed under embargo, people's misery would no longer have been attributed to corruption or abuse of foreign aid but to the embargo. Saddam Hussein was well aware of this potential and exploited it with dexterity.[2]

Thus, the issue became one of reconciling the sanctions that the Security Council wished to continue to implement, with respect for the humanitarian principles that emergency organisations required. A form of reconciliation was proposed by the French government by way of a fundamental change to the rules for embargoes, a change which largely went unnoticed by public opinion.

IMPLEMENTATION OF THE 'FILTERING EMBARGO'

Under Michel Rocard, the French government proposed to institute what I, at the time, labelled a 'filtering' embargo. When this was first proposed to the UN, a distinction had to be made between goods for which trade with the country in question had effectively to be forbidden (obviously including arms and anything else that might fuel a country's war machinery) and those which were absolutely vital for a population's survival. A decision was made to distinguish between goods which were humanitarian in

---

2. On 8 January 1998, on the basis of a report by the present author, the French National Consultative Commission on Human Rights (CNCDH) adopted a resolution relating to embargoes and according to which:
    § 2 [It has been observed that] governments targeted often use the embargo for propaganda purposes so engendering certain risks:
    a) at the domestic level
    –   a prolonged embargo risks losing its potential as a tactical measure by producing strategically counter-productive effects in that it inverts the burden of victimisation to the advantage of the government and encourages the latter to take even stronger repressive measures under the pretext of fighting against a petty crime linked to penury;
    –   the embargo often places humanitarian organisations in a situation of blackmail in as far as the sanctioned government exploits their arguments and takes advantage of their audience to seek a relaxation or removal of sanctions;
    –   the targeted government may be inclined to vent responsibility for the pitiful living conditions of its people on the Security Council – which thus becomes a designated scapegoat;
    –   it has happened that the government has used ration distributions as a way of controlling its citizens;
    b) at the international level
    –   the government tends to present itself as a victim of the international community in order to divert attention away from the causes initially justifying the adoption of sanctions.

nature (medicines, food, clothes, cooking utensils and so on) and which were not to be impeded, and goods which were humanitarian in terms of destination, which would be subject to minimum control (those needed to run humanitarian institutions, such as energy for hospitals, ambulances and civilian vehicles, and a minimum of furniture for homes, dispensaries and so on).

For Iraq, this system was introduced in 1990 by virtue of Resolution 661, and subsequently amended by Resolution 986 in 1995. A Committee of Sanctions was established (not only for Iraq, in fact, but for each country subject to sanctions: former Yugoslavia, Libya and Haiti among them) in order to filter or vet export demands to the country (by virtue of Resolution 661), and thus distinguish between goods that were and were not humanitarian. A real headache! I sat on one of those committees and suffered terrible problems of conscience. Some 11,000 requests in 1995! 16,000 requests in 1996, and each one having to be checked every day.

The Committee is based in New York and includes one representative from each of the Security Council's 15 member States. All entities wishing to transport something to the country under embargo have to make a request to the committee. Nine times out of ten, the procedure is simple, consisting of a simple check for conformity with the Resolution and a receipt allowing the products to pass. Sometimes, however, more questions obviously need to be asked!

Once, the Committee received a request for the authorisation of anaesthetics destined for women having to undergo ceasarians. At a first glance, the product appeared humanitarian in nature, so there would be no problem in sending it. In fact, the Committee was on the verge of accepting when one member drew attention to the quantities being requested. He noted that, taking local demographic figures into account, the number of pregnant women likely to undergo such an operation was such that each woman would have to consume several kilos of anaesthetics. The delegate then noted that this might well be 'too much'! He added, not without some irony, that these anaesthetics also contained elements useful in the fabrication of chemical weapons and that therefore such humanitarian aid was likely to be otherwise used, something not immediately obvious. Nevertheless, through a reduction in the quantity of the order, the Committee was able to fulfil its objectives.

Conversely, the Committee once also received a request for the import of marble plaques, something at first sight devoid of all humanitarian purpose. However, it turned out that this marble was not for the decoration of a bank or a palace, but for use as tombstones. The destination was humanitarian and, as a result, the marble was granted passage.

None of this is simple. With some 10–20,000 requests every year, the Committee is completely inundated with work, hence the costs mentioned earlier, together with the somewhat slow decision-making in certain instances, a slowness which can heavily penalise humanitarian action. Thus, while the objective of the reform may be altruistic, the work of the Committee serious and the idea a good one, embargoes have, paradoxically, never been so open to criticism. They never seemed more harmful than when made more humanitarian – the irony of the innovation.[3]

3. Hence, the CNCDH:
    § 3 Observes nevertheless that the functioning of the Committees is not as satisfactory as that expected by humanitarian organisations at their establishment. To note:
    a) the often considerable slowdown in aid distribution due to delays in the Committees' replies, where these are subject to a number of demands for derogation above and beyond their capacity to treat these;
    b) the complexity of procedures for processing demands which, despite recent efforts at simplification, nonetheless deter a number of humanitarian organisations wishing to send goods to populations of the sanctioned country;
    c) the lack of transparency in terms of the Committees' functioning which does not allow for those interested to fully understand the acceptance and refusal criteria for certain requests.
4. This progress has not, however, always been visible in the actions of governments seeking to establish embargoes on goods and services (arms aside). This is something that the CNCDH Resolution has also commented on:
    § 4 Doubting the deterrent effect of such measures on the behaviour of governments not respecting the fundamental rights of the human person and of international humanitarian law, invites the French government to do everything it can to:
    a) make known to the Security Council the need for significant attention to be paid, in the decreeing of economic sanctions, to:
        –   the duration of these, given that over a certain period, they can become a structural element in the economic life of the country;
        –   the evaluation of their humanitarian consequences;
        –   the search for embargoes that better target all that relates to exchanges in kind to reinforce the State's repressive apparatus;
    b) ensure, in the case where a decision has been taken to implement such sanctions, that these always include derogations for humanitarian purposes and that these be reinforced;
    c) propose an improvement to the Sanctions' Committees by:
        –   strengthening their means with a view to accelerating decision-taking;
        –   increasing transparency with regards to their functioning through a publication detailing the reasons behind any rejections;
    d) ensure that alternative solutions are used as often as possible and notably:
        –   to increase the use of methods currently insufficiently used, for the peaceful resolution of differences in conformity with the principles of the Charter of the United Nations and, notably, international procedures implemented for the defence of Human Rights;
        –   to promote implementation at the regional level;
        –   to recommend simultaneously the use of diplomatic, sports or other sanctions on leaders.

There has nevertheless been a marked improvement since the adoption of Resolution 986, for under Resolution 661 (still in force) approximately half of all requests are deferred in order to obtain more details, whereas with the 'food for oil' resolution the number of requests deferred by the Commitee has become significantly smaller. The latest report by the UN shows 90% of all requests being accepted, the remaining 10% being either rejections or requests still pending decision. Thus, the system functions in a much more satisfactory manner. Whatever the case, the initiatives of the French government, even though they have not solved all the problems – far from it – have served to modify the humanitarian outlook compared to the period 1950–90.[4]

The organised martyrdom of the Iraqi population: a life-saving embargo?

BERNARD GRANJON

For a large sector of public opinion, an embargo such as the one imposed on Iraq for eight years by the United Nations (for want of saying the United States) represents if perhaps not a good solution then at least an acceptable one. After all, since the international community found itself in the unfortunate position, both morally and strategically, of having to contain Saddam Hussein's expansionist appetite, was it not better to find a means other than war to avoid a war which would otherwise no doubt have been triggered by the tyrant himself, if left unopposed? In any case, surely, within the context of such an embargo, there must be a way of mitigating its impact in the 'humanitarian' sense – as with the 'food for oil' deal, for example? One might start wishing that mankind finally forget its cruel follies and settle all its conflicts with the same prudent wisdom that initially led it to impose such a sanction!

Unfortunately, the reality looks somewhat different, for behind this reassuring facade, this apparent non-violence, unfolds a form of punishment frighteningly blind and cruel. One that is all the more insidious given the declarations of virtuosity and goodwill that accompanied the greed, the hypocrisy and the lies that led to its implementation.

In reality, the embargo to which Iraq has been subject since August 1990 is absurd, or worse, it forms part of a quadruple scandal, the intolerable and repugnant character of which cannot be sufficiently repeated.

THE FIRST SCANDAL:
THE EMBARGO IS KILLING THE SAME CIVILIANS IT WAS
SUPPOSED TO PROTECT

Women and children in particular are being subjected to a martyrdom, long under-estimated or even ignored, and at present difficult even to assess properly given the dearth of organisations or humanitarian associations present in the field, and the prevalence of misinformation and exaggeration.

The Iraqi population is short of everything and, above all, of food. This is hardly surprising when one considers that, prior to the war, 70% of needs were covered by imports. While it is true that the countless lorries we saw circulating between Baghdad and Amman were not exactly empty and that certain shops or institutions had everything, or just about, such abundance is both limited and inaccessible to the vast majority of the population, held at bay from the profits to be made from speculation and smuggling (one anti-biotic treatment costs as much as five months' salary!).

It has been estimated that 32% of Iraq's 22 million population lives below the poverty line. As always in such cases, it is the children who are the first victims of premature births and deprivation and of ill-health and weight deficits, to the point where cachexia and death have become commonplace. According to a survey done by Unicef in Iraq, one million under-five-year-old children (out of a population of three million) suffer from severe malnutrition. The food deficit is sometimes further aggravated by lack of access to drinking water. In Bassora, in the south of the country, one million people have been thus deprived, due to a lack of spare parts to rehabilitate the water purification system!

The lack of food also goes hand-in-hand with tragically insufficient health care: nothing is available, not even those items most urgent. With no authorisation to import or power to purchase, there is no more milk for new-borns, there are no more vaccines, medicines, anti-biotics, disinfectants, anesthetics (patients have operations without sedation!), no syringes, radio tapes, film-processing equipment and, moreover, very often no electricity – not even in the hospitals!

The people of Iraq are dying and the children first. The mortality rate is difficult to quantify accurately due to the risk of local statistics being over-estimated. Nevertheless, estimates from a variety of different sources do exist, the results of which serve to corroborate as much as terrify. There seems to be overall agreement that infant mortality has spiralled from 32/1,000 to 124/1,000 within eight years. According to Unicef, the number of deaths per month among under-fives is calculated to be 4,500. While the UN estimated in May 1996 that the embargo had caused the death of 500,000 under-fives, FAO calculated the annual average of child deaths since 1991 to be 100,000, which would give a total figure of 750,000 children dying due to embargo-induced deprivation. Have the United States and the West not yet realised that this allegedly 'humanitarian' measure has already claimed as many victims among the paediatric population of Iraq alone as the 1994 Rwandan genocide?

It goes without saying that this appalling slaughter corresponds to a morbidity that is just as repugnant: the high rate of premature and low-weight births, followed by retarded growth in weight and height will all have frightening consequences later on for both the physical and mental development of those children affected. To take just one example: the UN estimates the percentage of children victim to serious weight deficit to be at 25%! This is not surprising though, given the massive upsurge in diseases affecting the general population (including tuberculosis), to the extent that advances once made in medicine might just as well have been relegated to the past.

The situation has been further aggravated in Kurdistan which is not only subject to the embargo imposed on Iraq, but also to that which Saddam Hussein himself has imposed in retaliation for their uprising, even if smuggling serves to somewhat mitigate the impact.

The suffering does not just affect the individual man, woman or child, for the very society which they comprise has been trapped beneath the wreckage. In the field of education, for instance, children are taught (if at all) in classes of 60 or 70 by a teacher having no equipment and no salary. What we are in fact participating in is the tangible disintegration of Iraqi society: witness the begging, the prostitution, the banditry, the corruption and crime, the suicide, the emigration (of one fifth of the population), the displacement (of three million people) – all of which are weakening the culture and religion which were once the guarantors of social cohesion.

THE SECOND SCANDAL:
THE EMBARGO ENRICHES AND COMFORTS THE OPPRESSORS
IT WAS SUPPOSED TO PENALISE

The regime's dignitaries lack very little. On the contrary, they have been indulging in all manner of trafficking linked to smuggling, the black market and speculation. The palaces and night clubs are always full of them shamelessly displaying opulence and insolent luxury and made all the more outrageous when juxtaposed with such misery. It was never more true that riches are most easily earned at the cost of others. One needs only to look at Saddam Hussein's personal fortune which is estimated, although difficult to really quantify, to be one of the largest in the world, with that of his clan following suit! The embargo has been craftily exploited by the Iraqi dictator as much at home as abroad: Saddam Hussein has managed to cloak himself in the image of a martyr and, in the eyes of his people, that of a saviour constituting the final bastion against American imperialism.

This same dictator, then, having lost all the conflicts that he himself had imprudently provoked, having ruined and sacrificed a whole population and forced them to labour under a yoke of steel, has managed to ingratiate himself within the country and enjoy genuine popularity and undeniable support from most of his people. Actually, this is not surprising when one considers that the Iraqi government, in its cynicism, instead of helping to relieve the martyrdom suffered by its people, only makes it worse by knowingly taking advantage of the embargo – an embargo which represents a miraculous source of well-being, popularity and stability. Neither does the government hesitate to exacerbate the extent of the deprivation by diverting the small amount of food and medical aid supplied by the few humanitarian organisations authorised to give it (a mere 1.4% of medicines ordered actually arrive at their destination!) or by refusing for years at a time to accept legitimate exemptions, such as the 'humanitarian exception' concerning medicine and food aid. The latter are not targeted, at least in theory, by the embargo, as stipulated in Article 22 of UN Resolution 687 concerning the 'food for oil' deal, accepted somewhat late in December 1996 and renewed in June 1997.

This aid, however, worth about one billion US dollars every 90 days once compensation payments are taken into account, is notoriously insufficient, providing only 6.5 dollars per month for each of the 22 million Iraqis in the country (who, in comparison, had 26 billion US dollars at their disposal in 1980!). Refusal to accept the assistance offered by a number of humanitarian organisations, including Médecins du Monde (in this particular case, because of its intervention in Kurdistan), is all part of the same exploitative philosophy.

THE THIRD SCANDAL:
THE EMBARGO IS FURTHER JUSTIFIED IN THAT IT INCREASES
THE WEALTH OF MOST NEIGHBOURING COUNTRIES

OPEC countries gain quite visibly from the situation. Imagine what the consequences would be if Iraq, with no restraints, was able to return to pre-war levels of production (approximately 10% of total world production) and exploit its enormous reserves (approximately 10% of world reserves) at a time when producing countries cannot even manage to sell at a level of production already limited in volume and reduced to a price less than that prior to the first oil shock. Whatever the case though, such a scenario can for the moment be dismissed, since Iraq no longer has the capacity to produce even the quantity of oil authorised!

Turkey cannot be disappointed, drawing substantial benefits from the taxes levied on Iraqi oil, for in order to facilitate control, transport of oil is authorised through one single pipeline which, miraculously, goes through its territory! Only poor Jordan remains excluded from the celebrations: its economy has been ruined by the embargo which has disrupted virtually all trade with a once powerful and prosperous neighbour.

THE FOURTH SCANDAL:
THE EMBARGO, IMPOSED BY THE UNITED STATES, IS
PRIMARILY SUPPOSED TO ENSURE THAT COUNTRY'S GRIP
ON WORLD ENERGY RESOURCES

How can one not help but think that the United States, through the influence this measure ensures over its protégés (Saudi Arabia, Kuwait, Turkey and the United Arab Emirates), is trying to reaffirm its control over the Persian Gulf countries due to the military and economic benefits that only such an action can give? Analysed in this light, a measure presented as the result of laudable intentions – that is, avoiding war – only serves vested interests, inspired by nothing else but a moral doctrine which smacks of petro-dollars!

WHAT CONCLUSIONS CAN BE DRAWN?

It is not the work of humanitarian organisations such as ours to devise a politico-military strategy: yet in the case of Iraq and its dictator, how can one avoid feeling like the doctor who sees prevention as the preferable strategy as opposed to any other? Who sees respect for ethics based on human dignity as being the most sustainable? For many years, all the powerful industrialised countries contributed to strengthening Iraq's position as the world's principal arms buyer in the hope that, apart from access to very lucrative markets, the country would help relieve the planet of a government of Iranian Ayatollahs, even at the cost of more than one million useless deaths. Saddam Hussein only started to become 'immoral' once he launched his attack on 'virtuous' Kuwait and, as a consequence, on American interests. True, the Iraqi regime represents a danger for the Middle East and beyond, but was this so difficult to foresee? The suffering caused by the Gulf War and the catastrophic embargo that followed could have been prevented.

Embargoes and other blockades, despite their apparent 'humanitarian' nature, are nothing more than disguised wars, hypocritical, intolerable and, moreover, inefficient. It is, therefore, all the more dangerous not to call them such. They only ever lead to one loser: the civilian population.

Humanitarian responses to situations of food insecurity and their limits[1]

UNDER THE SUPERVISION OF ISABELLE LE NORMAND

WHAT IS FOOD SECURITY?

Defining food security

According to the World Bank, food security can be most simply defined as: access by all people at all times to sufficient food, so that they might lead an active and healthy life. In the context of Action Against Hunger's programmes, such a concept can be operationalised in a variety of ways, including:

- the renutrition of a child admitted to a feeding centre in Burundi;
- food aid to the elderly through canteens in Armenia;
- support for subsistence agriculture to farmers in Sierra Leone;
- the fight against cholera among the displaced in Mogadishu, Somalia;
- the optimisation of Haïtian farmers' agricultural income;
- the construction of boreholes to facilitate access to drinking water for South Sudanese refugees living in Uganda.

The concept, broad as it is, corresponds not only to the presence of food supplies, but also includes the need for satisfactory medical and health conditions. For a population to have adequate food, four conditions are essential:

---

1. This text forms part of a joint contribution made by the heads of each of Action Against Hunger's technical departments in Paris, France, and coordinated by Isabelle Le Normand. It aims to provide a more concrete example of the way in which humanitarian organisations such as Action Against Hunger, specialised in the fight against hunger, identify and deal with food insecurity in countries in crisis in which they intervene.

    The heads of the technical departments in Paris are: Claudine Prudhon (Nutrition), Anne Berton-Rafael (Nutrition), Yvonne Greletty (Nutrition), Philippe Leborgne (Medical), Eric Drouart (Hydraulics), Jean-Michel Vouillamoz (Hydraulics), Patrick Danard (Hydraulics), Isabelle Le Normand (Food Security, Co-ordinator).

1   *Food availability.* Food must be both available *in situ*, whether at the
    local, national or regional level, and must reach families. However,
    availability can be limited by:
    –   isolation, which may impede the exchange of basic foods between
        areas of surplus and deficit;
    –   transport problems encountered by villagers in their attempts to
        procure food from the market or sell their produce;
    –   food prices, which may be too high for certain sectors of the popula-
        tion;
    –   insecurity affecting a region after conflict.
    Food availability is a necessary, but not a sufficient, condition of food
    security. More often than not, the availability of food is linked to
    problems of access to food supplies.
2   *Food accessibility.* Families must be able to procure foodstuffs through:
    –   mechanisms of *production*, notably agriculture and animal
        husbandry;
    –   mechanisms linked to *economic exchange* for foodstuffs. In an urban
        context, professional activities not associated with production
        (particularly in the informal sector) form one way of accessing food
        supplies;
    –   social mechanisms of *inter-community assistance* and/or *family
        support*;
    –   cultural practices, affecting the way in which food is distributed
        among family members within the household.
3   *Food intake.* The food ration must be sufficient both in quantity and
    quality. If this is minimal or the balance between the different
    components not ensured, the population may suffer from a food deficit
    and/or nutritional deficiencies. Depending on the magnitude of the food
    deficit together with the medical and sanitary context, physiologically
    vulnerable groups such as children may be affected by malnutrition.
    Those vulnerable will in fact be those having above-average require-
    ments due to a particular status (pregnant or lactating women, under-
    five-year-olds). Malnutrition may be the result of a crisis situation so
    severe that the population is overwhelmed. It can also be observed in
    other situations, such as that of a structural food deficit within a given
    geographical zone, or within more marginalised groups in developed
    countries.
4   *Absorption and assimilation of the food ration must be satisfactory.* The
    implication is that the population must be in good health and in a

healthy environment. In fact, the most common diseases, particularly contagious diseases (such as measles and diarrhoea), as well as those that are water-borne (such as cholera and malaria), form the principal causes of child mortality and exacerbate malnutrition. Thus, assimilation of any food taken will be all the more effective where sanitary conditions and access to clean drinking water are satisfactory. An improvement in the former, in particular, is also one means of preventing epidemics such as cholera or diarrhoeal diseases.

In times of crisis due to political conflict or climatic vagaries, various combinations of the above-mentioned conditions can be observed.

THE INTERVENTION CONTEXT AND POPULATION NEEDS

Two scenarios are assessed and illustrated: a conjunctural crisis that is political in origin and a structural crisis due to recurrent adverse climatic conditions.

1 A political conflict marked by insecurity or economic collapse can have the following effects:
   - food supply networks are no longer functional, such that markets are poorly stocked and prices prohibitive;
   - agricultural production is limited to regional or local level and essentially to subsistence farming due to a lack of inputs (seeds, tools, fertiliser and other products), either due to insufficient quantity or exorbitant prices;
   - family resources (food stocks or monetary equivalents) become exhausted. Other resources such as jewelry or furniture can be affected, but supply tends to exceed demand, causing prices to plummet and therefore limiting access to food;
   - at the same time, income from economic activities other than trading or farming (such as civil servants in government departments or other institutions, staff in private companies) becomes limited or may even be altogether eliminated. Indeed, the absence of a government and the shortage of available resources tend to make it impossible for State structures to work and in such a political context private sector activities may also experience important difficulties in continuing activities;
   - in the case of a crisis characterised by high levels of insecurity, the very lives of a population may be endangered, leading to population

displacement towards zones with better levels of security. Displacement may engender the migration of entire families or alternatively (in particularly insecure conditions) lead to family members becoming scattered all over the place. Whether or not the displaced are able to keep their belongings with them depends on the level of insecurity and the speed with which the conflict is spreading. Should this be possible, the belongings may then be exchanged for foodstuffs.

2 In structural crises resulting from adverse climatic conditions, repercussions will be strongest on agricultural production. As a result, certain effects will be similar to those provoked during a political crisis:
   – reduction in the availability of foodstuffs in local markets and price inflation. Regional exchange and/or the import of foodstuffs may go some way towards compensation for local food shortage. However, the state of transport infrastructure limits the delivery of food supplies, exacerbating food shortages in the zone affected. Moreover, depending on the extent of the crisis, productive regions may also be affected by the shortage. Finally and in the case of food imports, countries affected by this type of crisis, such as Chad, tend to encounter problems in terms of foreign exchange liquidity;
   – reduction in food stocks and family asset depletion, given the sale of the family's last few remaining resources to purchase food. Following on from this, the family budget tends to diminish dramatically, so limiting their ability to purchase food in a situation already characterised by shortage and spiralling inflation.

In order to reverse the negative effects of such situations, populations tend to develop coping and/or response mechanisms. Such mechanisms are very diverse, and tend to be the result of a compromise between population specificities and the environment in which the population finds itself. Hence, recourse may be had to:
   – in a number of agro-pastoral societies, the gathering of wild fruits, leaves or roots, enabling them to partially compensate for any food supplies exhausted or destroyed, such as millet or sorghum;
   – migration by the family head to the nearest town, to another region of the country or to another country to find paid work and so increase family resources. Such migration tends to be either seasonal or over a period of several years;
   – in a number of zones subject to recurrent climatic vagaries, rural populations may start to use crop varieties that have different

growth cycles and allow cultivation to be staggered, so permitting food to be grown throughout the season. In this way, they may limit the effects of the hunger gap or those of adverse weather conditions;
— resource mobilisation (whether of productive capital such as cattle and tools, or non-productive capital such as jewelry and fixed assets) may also be used as a means of temporarily compensating for the impact of a crisis;
— in a number of countries subject to recurring food shortages due to adverse weather conditions (drought, for example), daily food intake is voluntarily reduced, whether by all the family or only by certain members (often women). This is effectively a short-term measure to keep the level of food insecurity within limits and avert a more dramatic impact in the medium term.

WHEN POPULATIONS ARE THREATENED BY FOOD INSECURITY

The above said, when a structural crisis is very severe, or when a population has run out of sufficient resources to cope with an additional conjunctural crisis, communities may find themselves on a downward spiral in terms of food vulnerability. Families have neither sufficient assets nor the means to access the food supplies required to cover their needs whilst simultaneously corresponding to usual food habits. In such a situation, family food intake will no longer correspond to that prevailing under 'normal' circumstances – whether in terms of the number of meals and/or food quality.

In a number of precarious situations where the food shortage/deficit is relatively small, families will only be able to partially satisfy their basic food needs. This might be done by depleting family assets. However, in the medium term, without an improvement in circumstances or external intervention, their food deficit will only be exacerbated, so furthering their vulnerability in terms of food security. *Children, pregnant and lactating women, as well as the elderly, will be the first to be affected.* Such a deficit may become manifest in malnutrition, anaemia and so on. Once health and sanitary conditions, together with water access, are no longer satisfactory, the precariousness of the situation will only be accentuated.

Such a situation tends to be found within political conflicts where health structures or drinking water facilities are no longer functioning or are even non-existent. The latter is particularly evident in zones to which civilians may have fled and where huge gatherings increase the risk of epidemics. If external intervention is delayed (as in the political famines of Liberia and Burundi, for instance), the population's situation will only deteriorate. The result may be acute food shortage with numerous cases of severe malnutrition among children and adults, together with an increase in mortality rates.

Meanwhile, in areas predominantly affected by recurrent adverse climatic conditions, as across the Sahel, but having health care systems, the latter's effectiveness may be reduced due to isolation and a lack of financial resources. Such centres tend to have rudimentary equipment as well as a more general lack of material in terms of both quantity and quality. In such a context, seasonal epidemics such as measles or meningitis may worsen the effects of food shortages and exacerbate severe malnutrition levels among children.

Lastly, the risk of famine tends to be magnified in countries such as Somalia that are characterised by both persistent political conflict and erratic weather conditions. In such cases, severe malnutrition causing high mortality rates and further exacerbated by epidemics which become endemic (such as cholera) will be all the greater.

Confronted by such scenarios, activities implemented in the field have to be based on an analysis of the magnitude of the crisis together with the needs expressed by those affected. Such an analysis allows for the definition of an intervention strategy, which will be based on Action Against Hunger's own criteria and principles.

INTERVENTION CRITERIA AND STRATEGIES

Action Against Hunger's intervention criteria are based on the extent and nature of the needs, as well as the capacity of local communities (both populations and institutions) to deal with the situation. The scale of needs (whether vital or basic) and their coverage by other organisations (whether partial or total) depends on the context of the intervention. As far as possible, responses to population needs will be closely coordinated.

Action Against Hunger's strategy of intervention is based on the following principles:
1 Interventions are organised in such a way as to *directly* address the target groups considered vulnerable;
2 *Domestic policies* are taken into account in the definition and implementation of activities;

3   Populations (beneficiaries, institutions and organisations) *participate* in the identification, implementation and follow-up of responses;

4   Support is provided to the response mechanisms employed by these same populations so that they might *limit their dependence* on external aid. In this respect, food aid is considered as a means rather than an end. Envisaged as a short-term measure, it needs to be accompanied by activities which enable the population to redevelop mechanisms of access to food supplies;

5   *Training* is provided to facilitate the transfer of know-how at the local and national levels. As far as possible, efforts will focus on treating malnutrition within health centres;

6   On-going population *sensitisation* to health education (notably, vis-à-vis hygiene promotion), nutrition education and water quality;

7   Ensuring the *long-term* impact of activities and projects is a systematic objective;

8   Close monitoring of activities and of developments in the situation allows the response to be adjusted and continually *adapted* to population needs.

Technical criteria (or technical standards, such as the level of calories per person per day, or water requirements per person per day) form the minimum required to meet needs. Depending on the context, these standards may be adjusted and the strategy of intervention better adapted to the environment. That is, changes may occur in view of the presence or absence of a government or functioning State structures, the economic situation, the social and religious organisation of communities, the degree of isolation, food habits, and so on. Intervention methods and organisational requirements are defined according to the context within a minimum time period. In complex political conflicts, it is also imperative that any negative effects a humanitarian intervention might have should be considered, particularly if the intervention is a major one and especially when food assistance is to be provided.

The possible political repercussions of large-scale food distributions are taken into account when defining the method of intervention and the organisation required for this.[2]

According to the extent of the food shortage and the political significance of food aid within the relevant context, food aid can be envisaged as

2.   An example of this may be found in the chapter on Sierra Leone, where food distributions were at the core of strategies to gain and/or retain power.

either hot meals or 'dry rations' obtained in return for an activity or work ('Food for Work'). Distributions can be general, organised for the entire population, or targeted towards specific groups such as families having a socio-economic status that does not allow them to meet their needs, so rendering them vulnerable. In some cases, physiologically fragile individuals may be selected (the elderly, pregnant and lactating women, and children).

Any food distribution will also take into account the population's social structure so as to avoid undermining it. In this respect, it is preferable to involve village chiefs or representatives of groups of women or beneficiaries in general, throughout the various phases of assistance (registration of beneficiaries, distribution of rations, follow-up and monitoring).

In a severe crisis, characterised by a dramatic reduction in the daily food intake (sudden population displacement, isolation due to conflict between rival factions), distribution to vulnerable groups tends to form the focal point of Action Against Hunger interventions. The intervention is undertaken in close collaboration with nutritional recovery programmes for under-five-year-olds.

As far as nutritional recovery is concerned, as much use as possible is made of existing health care structures. However, if the extent of the crisis is such that the use of such facilities is impossible, specialised and autonomous units will be required and established as quickly as possible, more often than not with a capacity of more than 100 children per unit.

In most cases, activities are aimed at fighting against population vulnerability to food shortage, whilst strengthening food security mechanisms. The overall objective of Action Against Hunger programmes is to enable populations to *recover a given level of food self-sufficiency* either by intervening directly with regard to food availability and accessibility and/or by developing complementary nutrition, public health, water and sanitation programmes.

ORGANISING CRISIS RESPONSE MECHANISMS

In an acute crisis, food distributions aim to respond to the immediate food deficit affecting families. Nutrition activities, meanwhile, target those specifically affected by malnutrition – although also having access to the same food aid as everyone else. In this way, the effectiveness of any treatment for malnutrition is reinforced by measures to ensure a family's basic food requirements.

Nutritional recovery and food aid programmes tend to be undertaken with a view to the short term, and in expectation of an improvement in the conflict and/or agricultural conditions. Programmes giving support to agricultural rehabilitation are also developed so as to limit beneficiary dependence on food aid, while ensuring respect for human dignity. Depending on the level of access to land and farming inputs (seeds, tools, fertiliser and other products), the agricultural production subsequently achieved should allow families to either fully or partially meet their food requirements. As a result, food distributions can then be progressively diminished or limited to certain vulnerable families or groups of individuals. In this way, agricultural rehabilitation would have already been begun should any improvement in the political situation have taken place. The re-establishment of trade and commerce would then be able to follow, and so facilitate family access to foodstuffs. Concurrently, malnutrition rates would diminish and re-nutrition centres, in the medium term, be reintegrated into national hospitals. Activities undertaken in Tubmanburg, Liberia, illustrate such a situation, where movement was made from an extreme emergency to the resumption of economic activities following political resolution of the conflict.

On the other hand, should a political crisis persist in making it impossible for communities to satisfy all their basic food needs (despite agricultural programmes or trading), food aid has to be maintained – although targeted at certain groups – so as to prevent a deterioration in nutritional status. In a number of situations it may be difficult to guarantee continuous food aid, given high risks of insecurity or of politically motivated aid diversion. In such a situation, the malnutrition rate will be persistently high, with the treatment of malnourished children being dependent on NGO capacity to intervene (and hence on access to beneficiaries and the availability of funds to cover costs). Indeed, the number of malnourished children requiring treatment often tends to exceed the capacity of local health structures, making it difficult to integrate their treatment needs into these structures. Moreover, given a situation of food shortage, children discharged from a centre may often be re-admitted several months later.

Ordinarily, once their nutritional status/food intake has become satisfactory, children leave the centre to be re-integrated into their family environment. However, if the precariousness of this environment is exacerbated by food shortage, the same children risk being re-admitted to the centres several months later, should their nutritional status demand this.

Such a situation prevails in Somalia, where re-nutrition programmes effectively compensate for the absence or the inadequacy of food aid. In addition, the persistence of the Somali conflict has limited efforts to make health structures more independent. Medical programmes cover those areas accessible and as a result, at least in the medium term, may be unable to prevent the outbreak of regional epidemics such as measles. Finally, given a number of insecure displaced and refugee populations who have found themselves in a cultural milieu very different from their own, community participation – needed for the implementation and maintenance of water and sanitation installations – is often minimal.

This type of conflict may last for years. Yet, population self-sufficiency, independent health care within local structures, and community participation in their development can really only be envisaged once a political resolution to the conflict has been found.

In a context of structural degradation, budgets allocated by States to the Ministries of Agriculture, Health, Water and Education tend to be the first to be mobilised, with eventual and complementary donor support. Action Against Hunger programmes aim to strengthen national State policy by providing adequate technical and material support such that policies can actually be implemented in the field. For a transitional period, then, local-level technical staff may participate in projects to consolidate agricultural production, to assist in the functioning of the public health system and to develop water installations. Such temporary support is characterised by efforts towards joint programming between Action Against Hunger personnel and the authorities. It is completed by continuous training of local staff involved in the programme. Thus, in times of food shortage due to structural crises, nutritional recovery activities will, from the outset and as far as possible, be carried out in liaison with State structures (such as health centres). Food aid interventions, meanwhile, will be implemented in close collaboration with national structures followed by regional delegations. The zones to be targeted, the quantities to be distributed and the methods of distribution will all be discussed between the different partners involved in each of the relevant domains.

Once in contact with beneficiaries, activities focus on community participation and take-over of works or infrastructures completed, such as pumps, wells, irrigation systems and health centres. Technical or management training as well as nutrition and/or health education complete the intervention, so also facilitating sustainability. Community take-over can either be total or partial according to the interest, the involvement and the financial means of the relevant authorities and beneficiaries, as well as the costs incurred from the operation and maintenance of installations.

More generally, such programmes make sense only if the government involved in the intervention shows the political willingness to follow medium-term development efforts – translated more practically into the regular supply of material resources to local actors as well as continuous and regular technical support.

Given the diversity of contexts, Action Against Hunger places much emphasis on taking these different characteristics into account so as to develop a needs-adapted response. Nevertheless, such responses will be limited if the conflict, in the absence of a political resolution, lasts longer than initially expected.

NEEDS-ADAPTED RESPONSES: THE EXAMPLE OF LIBERIA

Liberia provides an example of a country that, at least during the crisis of April 1996, was characterised by the absence of a formal government.

The escalation of violence and 'minimum life-saving activities'

For almost seven years, Liberia has suffered from waves of political crises, only briefly punctuated by periods of calm. The crisis that arose in April 1996 is indicative of a political conflict marked by heavy fighting between the various factions in Monrovia. Events led to serious violations of International Human Rights and Humanitarian Law:
1 The international community became the principal target of massive pillaging, with NGO vehicles and other logistical equipment being used by the various warring factions in their fighting. Analysis of the situation revealed the unintended and counter-productive effects of previous humanitarian operations which had fueled the war effort by injecting large amounts of logistical supplies;
2 The civilian population was particularly affected by events, due to the intensity of the fighting which not only lasted for several weeks, but also caused massive population displacement to camps together with the loss of the few resources that families still possessed through the destruction of houses or shelters, pillaging and so on. Moreover, certain areas of the town, particularly the main markets, remained difficult to access, while the level of humanitarian aid, food aid in particular, was limited to the extreme.

Once this escalation in violence had ended, NGOs reduced their activities to a minimum level ('minimum life-saving activities'), due to limited resources and so as to prevent the adverse effects of the prevailing war economy. It was also imperative that a message be sent to Charles Taylor (leader of the main warring faction). After several months of reduced NGO activity, the humanitarian situation remained alarming, especially with regard to human rights violations and infringements of humanitarian law.

In certain areas towards the interior, the civilian population was subject to sporadic fighting and significant harassment by fighters vying for control over the region. In addition, a number of regions remained inaccessible to humanitarian aid, despite the fact that needs were steadily growing. As a result, cases of malnutrition and mortality also rose. Difficulties in accessing interior areas have always characterised the Liberian conflict: Lofa region, for example, remained practically inaccessible during 1993, 1994 and 1995. The intensity of the crisis in April 1996 considerably exacerbated the situation and led to alarming rates of malnutrition.

Date of survey	Overall acute malnutrition rate[3]	Severe acute malnutrition rate
Monrovia, July 1996		
Residents	15.3%	4.2%
Displaced	19.1%	7.1%
Buchanan, August 1996	47.6%	5.6%
Bong County, August 1996	26.8%	9.7%

Source: Action Against Hunger, 1998

The magnitude of the malnutrition witnessed is due to the April crisis and everything to which this led, including:
1 Destruction of the population's resources, including their homes, as well as theft of personal belongings (food and non-food items).
2 Disruption of food aid, followed by its limited return. Since 1995, food aid policies have focused on assisting vulnerable population groups (displaced camps, institutions) and the substitution of rice by ground wheat so as to prevent the negative effects arising from the distribution

---

3. Global and severe acute malnutrition is defined by the following criteria:

Expressed in Z-score (standard deviation)	Global acute malnutrition W/H < −2 and/or oedema	Severe acute malnutrition W/H < −3 and/or oedema

of large quantities of rice – until then, the mainstay of the agricultural economy. The 1996 crisis caused a disruption in the food aid given over a certain period of time, before the aid was re-introduced in a different form.

3 Insufficient agricultural production in the country. Liberia is characterised by a large urban population and an economy which is divided between the coastal areas and the interior of the country. The conflict has accentuated these differences, leading to an even greater division between, on the one hand, urban areas along the coast which are under the control of ECOMOG and, on the other hand, the interior.[4] The coastal areas of Liberia are very densely populated and are dependent mainly on food aid and private supplies. The interior zones, which are more sparsely populated, are subject to the erratic movement of front-lines and the changes in security conditions. Populations in these interior zones survive mainly on their own agricultural production (rice and cassava), their systems of animal husbandry having been the first to be affected by the conflict. Theirs is essentially a subsistence agriculture, which is in fact insufficient to meet family food needs due to isolation, simple farming techniques, the limited availability of agricultural inputs (such as seeds and tools) and harassment by fighters in the conflict.

ECOMOG's gradual development has further sharpened divisions, with food assistance coming to be concentrated in zones under its control (since relatively secure), to the detriment of the country's interior where distributions are parsimonious and sporadic. Moreover, the start of the hunger gap at a time when few resources were available and/or accessible made the risk of a deterioration in the food security situation all the greater.

4 Destabilisation of the country's economy, with numerous traders having fled the country, limiting the delivery of food supplies through the port of Monrovia.

5 Limited access by populations to zones having resources due to insecurity and isolation, both of which have combined to reduce exchange between coastal areas and the interior.

6 Civilian harassment by warring factions who would seize any food necessary to their own survival.

4. ECOMOG is the Economic Community of West African States (ECOWAS) observation group responsible for maintaining peace.

The international community was thus caught in a dilemma. While needs were rising, few zones remained accessible and humanitarian assistance was developing in such a way as only to aggravate the situation by unintentionally feeding the various factions.

Faced with a dilemma, efforts are made to coordinate activities and to take into account the more political aspects

In view of this dilemma, the various actors present in Liberia (NGOs, United Nations and donors) made a more concerted attempt to coordinate their activities. These efforts resulted in the elaboration of a new intervention policy, as outlined below:

1 Self-regulatory mechanisms were foreseen, notably with regard to the systematic evaluation of needs prior to any activity as well as the monitoring of activities;
2 Within those programmes necessary to cover vital needs, resources were minimised so as to avoid reinforcing the war economy;
3 Operations were decentralised and support was given to local capacities to ensure sustainability;
4 Witness statements were sought regarding human rights violations by those who were party to the conflict;
5 Support was given to local capacities in the promotion of peace;
6 In the case of food aid, it was decided that:
   – general food distributions would be stopped and recourse made instead to food aid targeting vulnerable groups. Where malnutrition rates were alarming, food aid was to be provided for the population as a whole according to a mode of intervention that was to limit any negative side-effects;
   – the most vulnerable zones were to be targeted first of all;
   – the food distribution process was to be monitored.

Given Tubmanburg's strategic position – in Bomi county and part of the diamond-mining area near Monrovia – it has always been coveted. Having become an area isolated by insecurity, its population was also forced to live under particularly precarious conditions. After the area had been isolated for several months, September 1996 witnessed the opening up of Bomi and Grand Cape Mount counties to humanitarian aid. This was the result of negotiations between local representatives of the UN's Department of Humanitarian Affairs and the various local leaders and authorities of the rival factions. In Bomi, a joint needs assessment of the population was conducted by the UN and NGOs. The findings were shocking: the entire population – children, adults and the elderly – was found to be suffering from malnutrition. Of an estimated 15,000 persons, 800 severely malnourished persons and 500 moderately malnourished persons were admitted to therapeutic feeding centres, and the number of admissions for the severely malnoursished was no doubt an under-estimate. Moreover, a retrospective mortality survey revealed that 30% of children under five years old had already died due to malnutrition.

The first step, then, involved a food distribution for 15,000 people over a period of two weeks, together with a food supplement for under-twelve-year-olds suffering from malnutrition. An intervention strategy was designed to provide a rapid response to population needs, whilst limiting aid abuse by the warring factions. The strategy consisted of:

1   The establishment of three therapeutic feeding centres for both children and adults suffering from severe malnutrition. Due to the gravity of the situation, simple nutritional protocols adapted to the context were put in place.

2   The provision of hot meals by kitchens in response to the entire population's needs. General dry-ration distributions would have risked increasing population insecurity due to rebel harassment such that daily meal distributions were seen to be more advantageous. The latter required limited storage, avoided economic repercussions on the market, and made daily movements of limited quantities of food less attractive. Moreover, only those vulnerable to food shortages came regularly, so enabling better targeting of the population. However, given that such forms of intervention can engender significant dependence in the medium term, the kitchens were used for only three months. The programme targeted women, children and the elderly, all of whom were physiologically the most vulnerable.

3   Monitoring distributions and follow-up of the population's situation was undertaken to ensure proper allocation and use of food supplies. Follow-up also made it possible to re-adjust programmes according to changes in the context and the nutritional situation. After surveys, several population groups were identified – including families made vulnerable by a lack of or limited assets (female-headed households, for instance) – and subsequently included in the newly adapted strategy.

4   Re-adjustment of activities as events took their course. With an improvement in the nutritional situation and security levels, food aid in

the form of dry rations was introduced for those vulnerable families identified. At the same time, agricultural rehabilitation programmes were undertaken so as to enable the population to meet their own food needs and reduce their dependence on food aid.

In April 1997, one year after the crisis, an important reduction in malnutrition was recorded in the area (with a global malnutrition rate of 4.1%, and a severe malnutrition rate of 0.9% – expressed as Z-scores).

The efforts led to effective co-ordination

Activities were made possible by the efforts of partners then present in Liberia:
- co-ordination between actors was facilitated by the fact that numbers were few and understanding good;
- the intervention strategy was defined in response to the humanitarian crisis, with larger organisational objectives taking second place;
- donors were particularly open to co-ordination efforts and contributed to the implementation of the strategy.

The case of Tubmanburg illustrates the capacity of organisations to effectively and jointly halt a humanitarian crisis in a context where resolution of the political conflict took place. However, in protracted conflicts, organisations find themselves confronted with chronic humanitarian crises forcing them to adjust activity capacity accordingly, as in Somalia.

Treating severe malnutrition

YVONNE GRELETTY

In poor countries, severe malnutrition is one of the most frequent underlying causes of child death. Children suffer from severe marasmus, from oedemas also described as kwashiorkor, or from marasmus-kwashiorkor. Given that such diseases affect the functioning of most of their organs, effective treatment depends upon appropriate and well-administered care. The practical advice that accompanies such care significantly increases the chances of full recovery. Such children need to be admitted to specialised nutrition units within hospitals (where a few dozen children may receive treatment) or to rehabilitation centres, also known as therapeutic feeding centres, where several hundred children may be treated.

Treatment for children who are severely malnourished may take place in several stages:

1 Treatment/ prevention of hypoglycaemia (low blood sugar level);
2 Treatment/prevention of hypothermia (low body temperature);
3 Treatment/prevention of dehydration (loss of body liquid);
4 Correction of electrolyte imbalance and micro-nutrient deficiencies (vitamins and mineral salts);
5 Treatment of infections;
6 Initiation of re-feeding (focusing on the dietary rather than the medical needs);
7 Restoration of body tissue (catching up with growth);
8 Ensurance of stimulation, surrounding the patient with attention and care, playing with him/her;
9 Preparation of a monitoring system for the patient once s/he has left the therapeutic feeding centre.

The different stages cover two phases:

- a first or initial phase during which the more severe forms of malnutrition are treated (1, 2, 3, 4, 5, 6);
- a second or rehabilitation phase, somewhat longer than the first.

Treatment methods are the same for marasmus (a type of malnutrition accompanied by heavy weight loss) and kwashiorkor (malnutrition accompanied by oedema) (7, 8, 9).

RECOGNISED EXPERTISE

After 20 years of experience, Action Against Hunger is today internationally renowned for its technical expertise in treating severe malnutrition. The organisation tries continuously to develop more appropriate products and more effective nutritional programmes, in collaboration with experts in the field from all over the world. This is done through what is known as the Scientific Nutrition Committee.

PRINCIPAL DEVELOPMENT STRATEGIES

Treating severe malnutrition

Action Against Hunger works with the Scientific Nutrition Committee to improve and evaluate treatments for severe malnutrition. Field visits by members of the Committee allow regular adjustment and constant improvement of the relevant treatment protocols.

For this purpose, specifically adapted products for treating severe malnutrition have been introduced and evaluated within Action Against Hunger programmes. Among them are:
- the 'F-100 high-energy therapeutic feeding milk', composed of skimmed milk powder, oil, sugar and a mixture of vitamins and minerals. The product has helped make the weight increases of severely malnourished children comparable to those of children being treated in specialised research units;
- the oral rehydration salt, 'RESOMAL', used in therapeutic feeding centres and composed specifically to prevent the risk of heart attack in particularly fragile and severely malnourished children;
- the special 'F-75' milk used during the first days of treatment when the child's status is particularly critical and under evaluation.

To better evaluate the effectiveness of treatments given in therapeutic feeding centres, the organisation has also developed a tool allowing mortality rates in its feeding centres to be estimated.

Meanwhile, given an awareness of the different constraints influencing programmes in non-emergency contexts, the organisation is also working on a strategy to facilitate the integration of treatment methods into national health care structures.

In order to be able to provide home treatment to severely malnourished children, the development and evaluation of specifically adapted products is also underway.

Treating moderate malnutrition

At a meeting held in February 1994, the Scientific Nutrition Committee developed recommendations concerning the composition of the different flours used in the nutritional rehabilitation of moderately malnourished children. These were made with a view to improving the proportion of lipids and proteins and the vitamin and mineral content. Minutes of the meeting were published in the international scientific press.

Following on from this, efforts were made to improve products in France and Kenya, with an evaluation of their effectiveness taking place within current programmes. In this respect, the effect of the lipid and fibre contents, together with the cooking time required before porridge consumption, have also been taken into account.

General distributions

When a population does not have access to food, a daily food ration tends to be provided by inter-governmental organisations or NGOs. At a meeting organised by the Scientific Nutrition Committee in November 1994 – bringing together several NGOs, international organisations and institutional donors – problems in the quality and quantity of food distributions were highlighted. Since then, Action Against Hunger has been making efforts to improve the quality of its food distributions, particularly as far as their mineral and vitamin composition is concerned. For this purpose, a special software programme called NUTCALC was developed to facilitate the calculation of a well-balanced food ration in terms of its nutrients.

Quality control

The quality of the nutrition products distributed to malnourished children is crucial. Action Against Hunger has established a food quality control system to assess the hygiene and nutritional value of the food. Terms of reference and conditions have been established for the different products used, together with methods to verify whether or not products correspond to these conditions.

Food aid: a temporary remedy

FRANÇOIS GRUNEWALD

SOME CRUCIAL QUESTIONS

Over the past 30 years, the increase in the number of emergency programmes has been such that food aid has become an integral part of media coverage. The question as to whether one is 'for or against food aid' might then seem somewhat incongruous. Indeed, it might even seem unbearable given the numerous images of famine that flicker across the TV screen. Nevertheless, real political stakes underlie this apparently simplistic question: important debates concerning humanitarian ethics and crucial questions pertaining to method.

The issue is one of finding relevant and operational angles and then addressing the questions: *why* food aid? *when* food aid? *what* kind of food aid? and finally *how* to go beyond food aid? While the equilibrium between supply (food resources) and demand (needs) remains delicate and heavily dependent on the trade and agricultural policies of countries in the North (see next chapter, by Sylvie Brunel) and given the depletion of previously abundant stocks, the fight against hunger by a significant sector of the world's population remains a daily struggle. Food aid, then, is a scarce resource and one that must be used sensibly and in the most appropriate manner.

It might be well to remember that in an emergency situation the imperative is first and foremost to save lives. Food aid covers a broad range of activities, from the large-scale distribution of foodstuffs to the implementation of feeding programmes under medical control and of various soup-kitchen schemes. Thanks to emergency food aid programmes, hundreds of thousands of tons of food have reached millions of beneficiaries over the past 30 years, from Somalia to Angola, from Sierra Leone and Liberia to Cambodia, from Sarajevo to Kabul. At the same time, however, people are increasingly becoming aware that emergency food aid can also be used to serve other purposes. It might, for example, be used to protect what remains of a society's productive capital in order to permit survival strategies while limiting the process of family destitution and agricultural decapitalisation.

It has also long been established that food aid can have adverse effects, such as the disintegration of local agriculture, the creation of new eating habits and the induction of a dependency syndrome. In development contexts, though, efforts are made to use food aid to stimulate development as a creative catalyst and, sometimes, as a tool for preventing looming food crises.

A very common approach is 'food for work' programmes, such as the rehabilitation of irrigation networks in Cambodia or of dykes in Bangladesh or road construction projects in Nepal. Food aid may also be used for price stabilisation programmes. More complex interventions, meanwhile, function according to the principle of aid monetisation where income generated through the sale of food should generate financial resources which can then be used for various other purposes, including project funding, supporting privatisation of the cereal sector, and supporting the country's balance of payments within the framework of structural adjustment programmes.

Programme justification, analysis of the 'relevant domains' together with the costs of different modes of intervention and deliberation about needs assessment methods and impact studies, as well as the adverse economic effects of food aid, are all to be found at the centre of debate. They can be analysed by looking at three questions.

WHAT IMPACT DOES FOOD AID HAVE ON RURAL ECONOMIES?

The concepts of 'grain for grain' (title of a well-know book by Johnson, T.; 1985) and 'food as a weapon' are not merely figments of the imagination. Peasant agriculturists have regularly been unsettled by food aid programmes implemented too late (sometimes with one season's delay), arriving in huge quantities leading to the total collapse of prices on local markets and filling up all storage space. While lessons from the experience of the Sahelian crisis (a severe drought in 1974) may well have been drawn, they will take some time to be assimilated into action and strategy. Yet to respond to crises, it is important that these strategies be well timed and in accordance with the magnitude of needs and the season, so as to prevent serious and perhaps irreversible damage. As part of an effort to counter such problems, use is increasingly being made of regional surpluses with food being purchased in areas near crisis regions. So far, the impact of the approach appears to be sufficiently positive for it to form the basis of future strategies.

With the end of the Cold War and the concomitant changes that are affecting this 'crisis-ridden planet', strategies to instrumentalise food aid have also evolved. Thus, food embargoes, for instance, are becoming more and more common, and one can just imagine the endless suffering that decision-makers must go through – with the fear of unrest weighing heavily upon them – before finally succumbing to such measures. They, after all, are seldom the ones to suffer from any resulting shortages. Yet at what human cost? Embargoes are obviously part of a panoply of methods available to the United Nations Security Council for exerting diplomatic pressure – but one should be careful not to abuse them. In such situations, humanitarian agencies must maintain their full latitude to act in line with the principles of independence and impartiality, and to prevent disaster. Current debates about Iraq, Serbia and Burundi, however, show just how complex the issues are.

WHICH WAY OUT?
THE PROVERB OF THE FISH AND THE NET 'IN ACTION'

Emergency food programmes need to be replaced as early as possible with activities for agricultural rehabilitation and revival of the local economy. In situations of food crisis, some organisations have long managed to integrate agricultural rehabilitation into their intervention strategies, using food aid to fuel this. Emergency rehabilitation covers two specific areas. First, support for positive coping mechanisms, for in the midst of crises populations do not remain passive. Instead, they develop crisis management and survival mechanisms that need to be sustained. Thus, on the basis of the combined approaches of nutritionists, agronomists, veterinarians and hydrologists, etc., integrated programmes can be developed to facilitate a population's return to a given level of food self-sufficiency even in conflict. Second, emergency rehabilitation needs to facilitate the transition from the emergency phase to post-conflict development – by assisting the first groups of farmers returning to areas abandoned during the conflict, for instance. In this respect, the periods when food aid is needed must also be shortened. A positive sign for both donors and humanitarian organisations is that, over the past four years, the budgets mobilised for such programmes have seen major increases.

WHAT KIND OF FOOD AID CAN BE USED IN DEVELOPMENT CONTEXTS?

Here, recourse may be had to several complex mechanisms. First, 'food for work' (FFW) programmes. Instead of free distributions, food aid is used here as remuneration for works carried out to stimulate the establishment or maintenance of collective infrastructures (irrigation networks, roads, etc.) or for policies contributing to the prevention of natural disasters (anti-erosion barriers, reforestation, etc.). The success or failure of such programmes depends upon the 'opportunity costs' of the labour force. If food is expensive and employment opportunities limited, FFW programmes become attractive. As soon as the number of options increases or remuneration for a day's work in other sectors exceeds the reward from FFW activities, FFW is no longer attractive.

Similarly, if the local labour force has to choose between agricultural work on the family farm (ploughing, sowing, etc.) and non-agricultural work (house-repairs, handicrafts, etc.) or FFW, then FFW tends to be rejected. In some cases, FFW has been used as a subsidy for institutions to pay their employees, such practices being justifiable in situations of conflict or immediate post-conflict, where the economy has literally collapsed, food supplies are scarce and wages very low or altogether unpaid. Nevertheless, such programmes should not be run for too long, since signs of the disastrous side-effects that they can have in the long-term have already been seen.

Food aid can be used for regulating food prices, both at the international level and at the level of beneficiary countries. At the international level, countless studies have shown that 'quantities distributed' can have a highly negative impact on 'cereal prices', magnifying the impact of price rises on the economies of vulnerable countries having to import their basic foodstuffs. This said, food aid from the European Union, since fixed in volume, seems to have less of a negative impact than food aid from the United States, which is fixed in value. In theory, price stabilisation programmes implemented using food aid tend to offset the effects of the laws of supply and demand: in times of surplus, purchases are made to prevent a collapse in producer prices, while in times of shortage stocks are released to prevent an inflation of basic foodstuff prices. Although such programmes are theoretically satisfactory, in practice they meet with a number of problems: they involve honesty on the part of the body or institution responsible for stabilising prices; storage and stock rotation costs are high and fraught with complex technical problems; and programmes are often affected by economic measures imposed within the framework of structural adjustment loans.

CONCLUSION

While success stories may be numerous, those of failures or of programmes having negative side-effects abound as well. The successes can all be attributed to a similar combination of facts: an early and credible warning was launched, food stocks were in existence and there was no political blockade; support for survival strategies was given rapidly and food aid was reduced in good time, so that it did not hinder agricultural rehabilitation. So many conditions...that are seldom united. In this respect, recourse must be had to the crucial issues of humanitarian ethics, programme effectiveness and strategic efficiency.

The imperative of monitoring and control

Food aid must be conceived as purely humanitarian and as destined only for civilian populations – not as fueling the conflict. To ensure that food aid is not used for other purposes it is of utmost importance to monitor the different stages of delivery and distribution. That aid reaches those who need it is a responsibility held first and foremost towards victims, but also towards all those around the world who generously support such programmes through taxes or donations. Humanitarian actors must be perceived as neutral, impartial and independent, so that any food to be given reaches all victims.

Programme quality as an ethical requirement

Rather than simply being based on the use of well-known institutional methods, food programmes must be based on a concrete analysis of victims' needs, taking into account any possible medium-term repercussions. Hippocrates' aphorism should be remembered: 'First of all, do no harm'. Beyond ideas of generosity, it is no use doing more harm than good through ill-conceived actions! Cost-effectiveness requirements should not be ignored either: the best programme is that which permits maximum impact at minimal cost.

Situation diversity versus response standardisation

There are neither average victims nor standard situations. Thus, adaptability to heterogeneity is necessary. The complexity of situations must lead to growing diversification rather than standardisation of programmes. Food aid should be taken out of its relative isolation and reintegrated into the broader context of food security, something which involves a search for quality as opposed to just quantity. In this context, the obsession with standards as advocated by certain NGOs is a fatal error. The approach should instead be finely tuned to local conditions and include an analysis of the specific needs within the recapitalisation process of household economies as well as support for agricultural production. Such a multi-sectoral approach would permit overall coherence vis-à-vis the globality of any crisis.

When it is cold, food aid will have only a very limited impact unless supplemented by the distribution of blankets! In appalling sanitary conditions, the impact of food aid will be extremely limited by diarrhoea. Fear also forms part of the landscape, such that the protection of civilians is also of major concern. What needs to be done if famine is the result of farmland being riddled with landmines or due to the pillaging of fields and granaries by soldiers? Should a food distribution programme be launched if it is only going to increase the risks for its beneficiaries?

Separating the humanitarian from media-politics and the politico-military nexus

Humanitarian aid in general and food aid in particular are now part of the government diplomatic strategy. They also correspond with communications strategies adopted towards the public. The search for funding often leads organisations to seek strong media support and coverage and to accept 'easy finance'. Such a trend has already left far too many victims dying of hunger in far-flung corners of the earth with no-one reacting – whilst elsewhere, agencies struggle to obtain a small share of programmes. Unfortunately, food aid convoys escorted by armoured vehicles have also become all too common. In the end, humanitarian aid implemented under the aegis of the military will simply be taken as part of them. One day they too could become targets, so putting an end to neutrality and the impartiality of assistance, and therefore to the principle of access to victims. Humanitarianism needs, therefore, to remain free from the traces

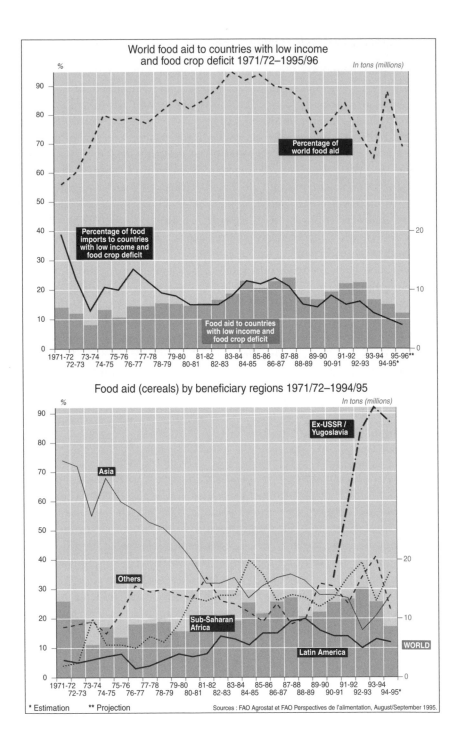

World food aid to countries with low income and food crop deficit 1971/72–1995/96

%

In tons (millions)

Percentage of world food aid

Percentage of food imports to countries with low income and food crop deficit

Food aid to countries with low income and food crop deficit

1971-72 73-74 75-76 77-78 79-80 81-82 83-84 85-86 87-88 89-90 91-92 93-94 95-96**
72-73 74-75 76-77 78-79 80-81 82-83 84-85 86-87 88-89 90-91 92-93 94-95*

Food aid (cereals) by beneficiary regions 1971/72–1994/95

%

In tons (millions)

Ex-USSR / Yugoslavia

Asia

Others

Sub-Saharan Africa

Latin America

WORLD

1971-72 73-74 75-76 77-78 79-80 81-82 83-84 85-86 87-88 89-90 91-92 93-94
72-73 74-75 76-77 78-79 80-81 82-83 84-85 86-87 88-89 90-91 92-93 94-95*

* Estimation   ** Projection

Sources : FAO Agrostat et FAO Perspectives de l'alimentation, August/September 1995.

of tanks. The risk of such a mix-up having a negative impact on access to victims is enormous.

Danger: insufficient world stocks

This said, food aid could also be strongly compromised by a situation of diminished availability. The move from 'humanitarian targeting' to 'media-political targeting' is only one step away. Becoming at best an operation for the media, at worst a political cloak, such programmes would no longer be humanitarian. Yet they should be. It is a question of human dignity, as much as for those who give as for those who, often humiliated, receive.

Who is going to feed the world?

SYLVIE BRUNEL

AVERAGE AMOUNT OF CALORIES AVAILABLE PER PERSON PER DAY

Country	1969–71	1990–92	2010
	(Calories / person / day)		
World	2,440	2,720	2,900
Developed countries	3,190	3,350	3,390
Developing countries	2,140	2,520	2,770

UNDER-FED/UNDER-NOURISHED POPULATION

Populations[1] having access to food below the nutritional threshold	1969–71	1990–92	2010
Habitants (in millions)	920	840	680
Percentage of total	35	20	12

1. Only relevant for developing countries
Source: FAO, 1997

'The missionary theory that postulated the universality (and hence the universal exportability) of our model of agricultural and food success still survives – although rattled (ad extra) by the failures of aid and undermined (ad intra) by the doubts which have given rise to the present impasse in which the more advanced countries find themselves. The theory was succeeded by the practice of market conquest, ideologically justified by the ineluctable advance of 'globalisation'. In this context, the discourse of the *great agricultural powers in relation to responsibilities to 'feed the world' (so that they might demonstrate their ability to live up to the ethics that come with their formidable productive potential), is crudely revealed for what it is: a false discourse. It is a discourse that simply hides a strategy of compensation for those marginalised from agricultural modernisation beneath a mantle of globalised generosity. At the same time, behind the classic discourse of co-operation, designating the 'latecomer nations' for whom the path to development has to be paved, a new discourse has begun to emerge. The latter apportions a part of the direct responsibility for difficulties being faced in Northern countries to the poor countries. Northern economies, so the argument goes, would be indisputably better off if the former did not try to disloyally compete with them, but instead, absorbed their surpluses. Such trends cannot, in fact, be countered by rigidly adhering to principles of co-operation, but rather by fixing, as a necessary pre-condition, the right of all people to development, and first and foremost, by taking active account of its main element: the right of all people to food.'*

The Right of Peoples to Food (p.107)
Bertrand Hervieu (Flammarion, 1996)

World food production is sufficient to feed the total world population, even once this reaches its peak. The more relevant question is *who* will feed the world tomorrow and *how*. Due to problems in the distribution of food production, some 800 million people have already been marginalised. Are we not in danger of moving towards a world that is increasingly characterised by an inegalitarian distribution of food? Where a handful of over-protected farmers ensure the food security of billions of individuals living in poor countries, at the mercy of a new 'green' weapon?

SUBSTANTIAL FOOD RESERVES

The spectre of generalised famine, disseminated by a few professional prophets of doom, hardly seems relevant if one takes into account the fact that, over the past 30 years, even in developing countries, world food production has continued to increase more rapidly than that of the world's population.

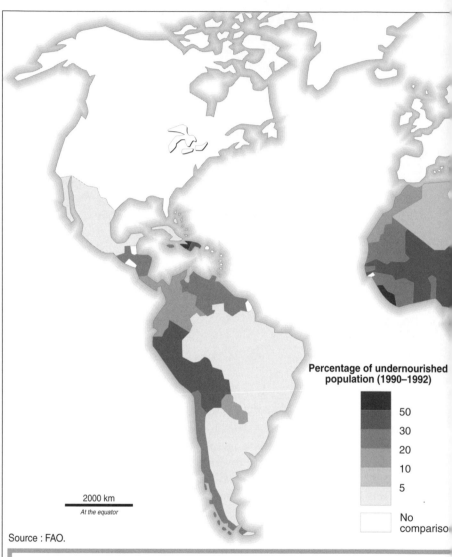

Percentage of undernourished population (1990–1992)

50
30
20
10
5

No
compariso

2000 km
At the equator

Source : FAO.

Incidence of undernutrition is defined as the percentage of the population which do
not have access to a sufficient quantity of food to satisfy its food energy (calorie
needs. Although one might predict a decrease in global chronic undernutrition, as h
been the trend for several decades, undernutrition is still widespread in particu
regions.

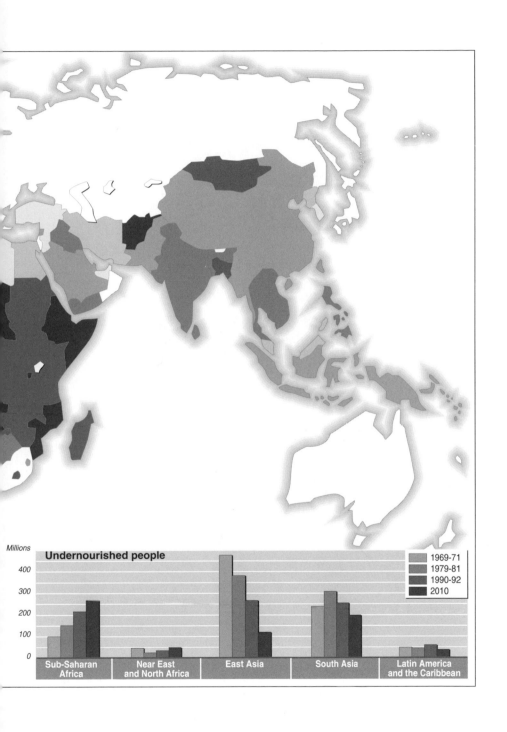

Millions

Undernourished people

400

300

200

100

0

| Sub-Saharan Africa | Near East and North Africa | East Asia | South Asia | Latin America and the Caribbean |

1969-71
1979-81
1990-92
2010

Is the future really so bright? 'Technically', a significant increase in food production is still possible, for even today there exists a considerable amount of resources both in developing and developed countries. This in a context where, according to most population experts, world population

World: agricultural production, population and production per inhabitant 1961–1992

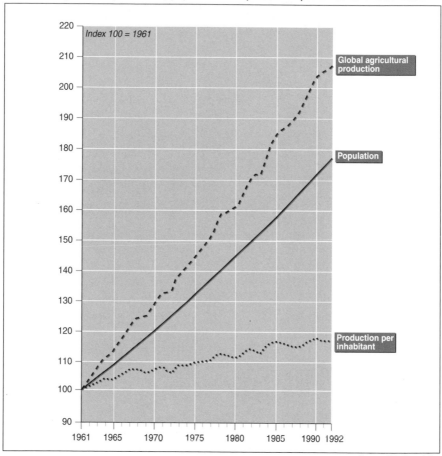

Sources : FAO, Alexandratos.

While the world's population doubled between 1960 and 1990, global food production more than trebled, increasing from 600 to 1,900 million tons, as a result of which the food ration available to each living person has increased by approximately 20%.

(which has grown rapidly since the early 1950s) is expected to gradually stabilise at around 11 billion by the end of the next century.

Interestingly enough, a mere 4% of land in the United States is sufficient to feed its entire population: so what does this say about the use of cultivable space worldwide? Pierre Leroy has calculated that if all the land currently left fallow in Europe were to be brought under cultivation, cereal production would increase by 20 million tons (corresponding to about twice the amount of grain imported by Africa in 1995). In rich countries, the threat comes more from overproduction than from shortage, something which has forced governments to resort to costly measures of subsidisation or the freezing of land-use.

In the developing world, meanwhile, FAO has calculated that 700 million supplementary hectares (equivalent to the amount of land currently cultivated) could be brought into cultivation without encroaching upon protected or inhabited zones. For the most part such land is to be found in Latin America and Africa.

In these two continents, intensified agriculture is still in its early stages. In Africa, on average, less than 11 kg of fertiliser are used per hectare, compared to 67 kg in Latin America and 129 kg in Asia. Meanwhile, only 5% of cultivated land is irrigated. In Latin America, huge tracts of land remain undeveloped due to possession by large landowners. In short, the potential exists for increased agricultural production in both continents.

That said, Asia should not to be forgotten. While it is admitted that regions affected by the Green Revolution in its early stages all tended to suffer from problems of land pollution and soil salinisation, agronomists were nevertheless forced to look at other ecologically less costly methods of production. It cannot be said, then, that the Green Revolution is over. Varieties of 'super-rice' currently being studied at the IRRI research centre in the Philippines could well increase yields from 10 tons – the amount currently obtained with the IR 36 variety (product of the first Green Revolution) – to 15 tons per hectare. It should be remembered that traditional yields bordered on 1.5 tons. The adoption of such new varieties on land already cultivated would provide food for another 500 million people. As discussed by Gilbert Étienne in the next chapter, malnutrition in Asia – essentially the result of poverty – could then be eradicated. On the one hand, government policies need only devote more attention to agriculture; on the other hand, they might also focus more strongly on the ecological and social future of more marginalised areas by implementing what CIRAD, for instance, has called the 'Double Green Revolution'.

Hunger: type, region and degree

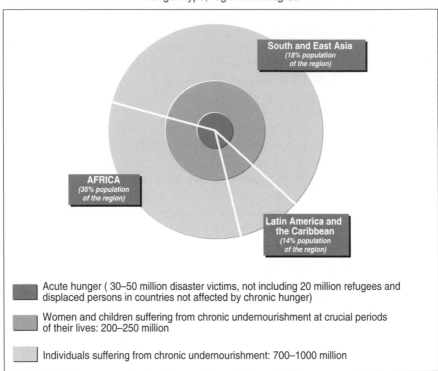

South and East Asia
*(18% population
of the region)*

AFRICA
*(35% population
of the region)*

Latin America and
the Caribbean
*(14% population
of the region)*

Acute hunger (30–50 million disaster victims, not including 20 million refugees and
displaced persons in countries not affected by chronic hunger)

Women and children suffering from chronic undernourishment at crucial periods
of their lives: 200–250 million

Individuals suffering from chronic undernourishment: 700–1000 million

Sources : FAO 1995 : Rosegrant *et al.* 1995 ; CAC/SCN 1995 ; UN 95 (Extract of WFP report 1996)

DISTRIBUTION PROBLEMS HAVE CREATED
800 MILLION MALNOURISHED

Feeding 11 or even 12 billion people is, therefore, a challenge which is by
no means impossible to meet. Yet in poor countries, some 800 million suffer
from malnutrition. *And here, the finger cannot be pointed at insufficient
levels of agricultural production, but rather at the inadequate and unjust
distribution of food resources.* If these resources were more fairly appor-
tioned, every human being in the so-called Third World, or the South,
would have access to 2,500 calories per day, more than enough to meet
their needs (generally estimated at 2,200 calories per person per day).

Hence, it can be concluded that famine is not part of some ineluctable
destiny: production is sufficient to cover needs practically everywhere.

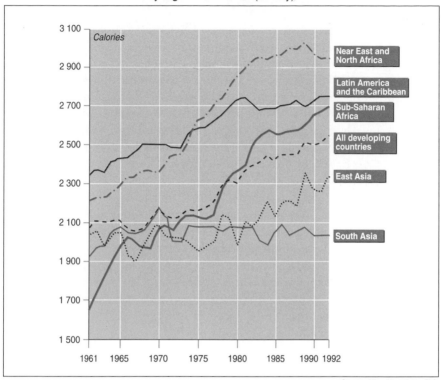

Evolution of food availability per inhabitant
by region 1961–1992 (cal/day)

Sources : Nikos Alexandratos, FAO.

Moreover, figures cited only take into account those resources available for direct human consumption (about 50% of world production), with another 25% being destined for livestock, 5% being conserved as seeds and a further 20% being lost due to problems of crop storage. Efforts here would also free more resources, without even requiring new methods.

GROWING FOOD DEPENDENCY IN THE SOUTH

Despite the possibilities, countries in the South are becoming more dependent on food imports every year, with imports jumping from 20 million tons at the beginning of the 1960s (around 2% of total cereal consumption) to 120 million tons at the beginning of the 1990s (around 10% of consumption). An increase to 160 million tons by the year 2010 is expected.

High demographic growth, increasing urbanisation, changes to social and political structures, weak support to agriculture and new food demands explain this growing dependency among developing countries:

– Rapid demographic growth in the South automatically causes a rise in the demand for food. Each year the world's population increases by another 87 million persons; nine-tenths of these live in developing countries. Demographic pressure is all the greater in rural areas where the farming techniques of small peasants have developed little due to a lack of economic or financial incentive. The result has been land competition and massive rural exodus.

– The corollary of rapid population growth in the South is urbanisation. Today, more and more of the world's huge cities are to be found in the South. Feeding such immense cities poses complex problems relating not just to supply and distribution, but also to price. For a long time, problems were avoided due to access to low-priced cereals 'dumped' by the agro-industrial powers of the North who were more than happy to get rid of their surpluses by taking over the South's markets. Indeed, such an objective was clearly stated in America's first legal text, Public Law 480, institutionalising food aid in 1954.

This aside, growing urbanisation has not necessarily been a bad thing for local agriculture. On the contrary, the existence of a large city often stimulates the surrounding countryside by bringing about changes in local – or even distant – rural activities, provided that there exists sufficient infrastructure to rapidly transport (and in good condition) the food required by the great city. This, however, is far from being the case in a good number of countries, particularly in Africa. Here, problems of isolation attest to the lack of exchange between surplus and deficit regions, and hence to problems of redistribution due to a lack of infrastructure and to problems of rural market organisation.

– *To a significant degree, the problem of food dependence in the South resides in weak, or even non-existent, agricultural and food policies.* In order to keep urban areas free of unrest, governments have long preferred to keep food prices in cities very low, and to do this they have had to resort to imports, to the detriment of local producers. Indeed, countless factors contribute to explaining the propensity of States in the South to disregard their own agriculturists: the accessibility and low prices of cereals on world markets, the utility of import tariffs in providing a revenue to help balance difficult national budgets as well as consumer demand for imported products judged to be more modern, more practical to use, and more reliable than local products – sometimes in terms of hygiene as well. This is not to mention the often deliberate policy of neglect for fear of potential political clout and agitation. Small peasants have, as a result, been abandoned with few if any outlets existing for domestic production, particularly when this comes from a proliferation of small producers, while the country's cities increasingly purchase their food from outside.

– Lastly, the rising volume of imports by the South can also be explained not – as often claimed – by under-development but by development. The Newly Industrialised Countries (NICs), for instance, are increasingly seeking cereals (particularly secondary cereals destined to feed livestock) as well as all sorts of more developed products from the rich countries. With a rise in living standards, consumerism is increasing and diversifying. The appearance of a new middle class is causing food habits to change. Today, demands are being made for three diversified meals per day, often with foods that do not form part of traditional diets (generally monotonous since based exclusively on local production). In the Ivory Coast, for instance, the question: 'Do you eat butter?' is one that might be used to identify the more well-off households.[1] As economic growth occurs, consumption habits are gradually coming to include dairy and meat products, fruit and vegetables, confectionery, frozen or ready-made foods and so on. And as imports combined with fashion trends and imitation products grow, the proportion of the population working in agriculture is becoming smaller and smaller, with productivity remaining low due to a lack of incentive.

THE DISTRIBUTION OF FOOD DEPENDS MORE ON FINANCIAL INCENTIVE THAN ON NATURAL ADVANTAGE

World food production is not distributed on the basis of regional climatic advantages, but rather according to the money that States are prepared to spend on agriculture. The poorer and more traditional a society, the greater the proportion of farmers amongst its working population, and the

1. Denis Resquiers Desjardin; 1989; *L'Alimentation en Afrique*; Karthala.

less these are taken into account in public spending priorities. Conversely, the more developed a society, the fewer the farmers and the greater their voice and prioritisation. Bertrand Hervieu sums it up well: '*A paradox, attested by history, must be confronted across the world: those societies that have attained self-sufficiency or even become great exporting powers have done so by and through a process which has allowed them to cease being agricultural societies...*' (*The Right of Peoples to Food...*; p. 51).

It is not a coincidence that rich countries, with an average of less than 5% of their working populations involved in agriculture, control two-thirds of the world's agricultural and food markets. The smallest 'revolt' in the West catches media and political attention, with subsidies usually being released immediately so as to calm the unrest. A few figures might make one dizzy: in terms of direct subsidies and direct assistance, the United States spends per year about US$37,000 per farmer, Japan US$30,000 and Europe US$20,000. Looked at in terms of dollars per hectare of cultivated land, public support reaches US$70 in the United States, US$950 in the European Union and US$13,000 in Japan! Altogether, rich countries dedicate more than US$200 billion per year to support agriculture.

Expenditure related to the Common Agricultural Policy (CAP) takes up more than half of the European budget. The income of each French farmer depends by as much as 60% on the various public aid packages. Another paradox just as striking is that the larger and more productive a farm, the more it is helped. In 1995, average direct aid for a farm of over 200 hectares in France averaged around US$112,000. Conversely, small farms with a panoply of activities that tend to be in close harmony with their environment (and which in France play a crucial role in preserving the countryside and rural life) tend to be less well favoured by the agricultural strategies of rich countries.

How can African, Asian or South American farms be expected to compete with such self-indulgence when their own governments not only refuse to recognise their right to domestic market protection vis-à-vis international competition, but instead promote such competition? When more than half of the population in developing countries lives off agriculture (two-thirds in Africa, increasing to four-fifths in Burkina Faso, Niger and Burundi – although the record is held by Nepal, where 90% of the population is employed in agriculture!), developing countries have only a mere 10% share in world food markets! As long as national currencies remain strong and imports that much more competitive (subsidised by their countries of origin), the majority of the population will be condemned to economic death, to rural exodus and to impoverishment on city outskirts. Huge modern agro-businesses, on the other hand, will continue to be all the more competitive, given links to the halls of power and their ability to defend their interests.

THE NEED FOR CEREALS MAY GROW

Since the mid-1990s, world agriculture has changed. After a period of significantly low world market prices – linked to structural surpluses from rich countries (the United States, European countries, Japan, Australia and Canada) and from some less developed countries (such as Argentina, Vietnam and Thailand) – prices began to recover sharply, as of 1995.

A series of bad harvests in the United States, the collapse of agriculture in Eastern Europe and the former Soviet Union and significant demand from China and the NICs all converged to put heavy pressure on cereal supplies. This was further aggravated by reform of the CAP in 1992, as a result of which 15% of land in Europe is now to be left fallow.

Such changes would appear permanent: there will be a constant increase in demand. On the one hand, agreements concluded in Marrakech in April 1994, under the auspices of the World Trade Organisation (WTO), make provisions for the progressive dismantlement of subsidies to agricultural exports (which should lead to an increase in world cereal prices). On the other hand, they also make provisions for the gradual opening-up of domestic markets to food imports – up to 5% of domestic consumption. While this might not have a huge impact on poor countries already heavily dependent on imports, it should have an impact on those countries protected from foreign competition, such as Japan, India and European countries, forcing them to purchase cereals on world markets.

Moreover, despite plummeting prices after the record harvests of 1998, cereals are becoming increasingly coveted. Importing countries of the South, however, will have to foot the bill which, according to FAO predictions, is expected to increase by 4 billion dollars a year, from 40 billion dollars in 1989 to 65 billion dollars by the year 2000.

WHEN RICH COUNTRIES WANT TO FEED THE WORLD...

The larger cereal exporters are modifying their strategies accordingly. After all, why continue to pay such enormous amounts of money to support agricultural revenue (which, in addition, contravenes WTO agreements), when the domination of world markets holds much more favourable financial prospects that are significantly less costly for national budgets?

The United States has finally unveiled its intention to feed the world – manifest in its new law on agricultural policy, the *Fair Act*, which aims to liberalise agricultural supply to the maximum. Putting an end to compulsory fallow land and replacing subsidies with direct assistance to production, the Act is aimed at turning farmers into autonomous economic producers, free to choose what to produce according to whatever might be of interest at that particular moment. America already controls more than one-third of the world's wheat market, two-thirds of that for secondary cereals and three-quarters of that for soya. Moreover, the major constraint so far encountered in the drive to conquer new markets – the numerous barriers protecting EU farmers from foreign competition – should soon be a thing of the past.

This said, however, the EU, under American pressure to dismantle its arsenal of trade barriers and in line with WTO agreements, is following in America's footsteps. Reform of the CAP, currently under review, breaks with the principle that governed EU agricultural policy since its conception, that is, the principle of food self-sufficiency at all costs. Following American trends, reforms provide for the replacement of subsidies by direct assistance to production, a significant reduction in intervention prices, and the replacement of compulsory fallow land with optional fallow land. It has been left to European farmers to find a means of compensating finance previously obtained through EU indemnities, through world market domination.

In the knowledge that changes in world demand play in their favour, the text under review for reform of the CAP has met with the approval of cereal producers, regardless of price reductions (20% for cereals). On the other hand, the text has also put meat and dairy farmers, together with maize, fruit and vegetable producers, on the defensive. For the latter, the reduction in intervention prices has meant greater vulnerability in times all the more uncertain due to 'mad cow's disease' and the advent of genetically modified crops – all of which change the equation. Small-scale mixed farmers are also becoming increasingly worried, for given the emphasis of the CAP on specialised and highly productive large-scale farms which might be more able to dominate world markets, what is to become of them?

Since early 1997, reform of the CAP has become a subject of fierce debate, particularly in France where the Minister of Agriculture, Louis le

Pensec, has taken a resolute stance against the reforms currently conceived by Brussels. It should be noted, however, that as the arguments are tossed from side to side, the future of the South has become a secondary issue. For leaders of the debate about EU agricultural policy, the question is not about who is going to provide food for the world and at what cost, but whether or not in feeding the world, farmers of rich countries will gain financially now that current measures of protection and support to production will soon be at least partially dismantled.

In this debate, and despite its importance to the South, farmers in the South would appear singularly unarmed and vulnerable – their interests have been utterly ignored, as in the Uruguay Round of negotiations where, as far as agriculture was concerned, debates focused exclusively on the confrontation between the United States and Europe. For the rich countries, there is no doubt that the millions of poor appear as mouths to be fed by them, in as much as their purchasing power makes them worthy of such interest; for *until very recently, the large European and American exporters had chosen to voluntarily limit their agricultural production to demands considered solvent, that is, backed by real purchasing power.* A non-solvent demand, then, could not be considered a real demand – such that the 800 million malnourished people cannot be considered of economic importance.

THE CRUCIAL QUESTION OF ACCESS TO FOOD BY THE POOREST

Over the next few years, therefore, the world's markets risk becoming the object of fierce competition between the major exporting countries, while millions of others continue to lack food. The decline in food aid since the steep increase in cereal prices is indicative of this. As long as food aid did not cost anything and allowed for the sale of large surpluses that would otherwise have been wasted, it was exploited largely to cushion urgent food deficits or to form part of a co-operation in kind that was motivated by commercial or geopolitical interests. Today, the free provision of cereals is expensive, as is their storage. World stocks are thus also collapsing.

Paradoxically, a significant proportion of the world's cereal stocks are held in developing countries such as China and India, both as part of deliberate policy (the desire for national food self-sufficiency) and unintentionally (poor management of surpluses, bottlenecks in transport and surplus redistribution systems). Cereal stocks in China are estimated to be about 80 million tons, with some sources even going as far as to postulate

500 million tons! India, meanwhile, has about 35 million tons – while at the same time being home to 70 million malnourished children!

The large developed countries no longer wish to finance public cereal stocks. The United States in particular no longer has any – or rather, those that it has are managed by large multi-nationals according to market logic. The privatisation of world cereal stocks has resulted in their reduction from 25% to 15% of world consumption (corresponding to about 120 million tons). As a result, humanitarian organisations such as the World Food Programme, hoping to rescue the world's starving, are increasingly having to meet market conditions to do this. At a time when hunger has become a preferred weapon in most local conflicts, such a development only aggravates questions concerning the management of humanitarian aid.

500 million malnourished in Asia: the unaccomplished Green Revolution

GILBERT ÉTIENNE

Asia is both the continent that has witnessed the most spectacular improve-ments in food production and also the one suffering from the highest number of malnourished. The future should be faced with caution: agricul-ture has not been encouraged as needed for 10–15 years due to lack of public investment. Meanwhile, the severe flooding in China and Bangladesh during the summer of 1998 underlines the vulnerability of countries where agriculture still plays a major role in the economy.

As a result of the Green Revolution, most Asian countries have been able to make considerable progress in terms of food production. Even so, much more remains to be done. Substantial areas of misery remain where under-nourishment, or should we say inadequate nutrition, is prominent. Despite a general slowdown in demographic growth, although to variable degrees, the number of mouths needing to be fed remains a burden. In addition, signs of a slowdown in production are visible in a number of countries and have yet to be remedied. Since the early 1980s, meanwhile, agriculture has been the victim of less attention and less capital investment from the leading elite. The importance of the agricultural sector and the farmers dependent on it has been overshadowed by economic reform, private foreign investment, trade liberalisation and technology transfers – both nationally in many countries and at the international level. Just to give one example: in the run-up to an important international conference on Asia in 1998, I couldn't even convince people to devote at least one debate to agriculture!

Such relative neglect is all the more deplorable given that, in Asia, agriculture still represents 20–30% of GNP and employs 50–70% of the workforce, with rural areas also being home to as much as 60–80% of the population depending on the country (the exceptions being Japan, South Korea and Taiwan).

COMMENTS

Today, for the first time in history, the risk of famines marked by mass starvation and the death of hundreds of thousands, or even millions, of people has disappeared. This is one reason for satisfaction. Only limited famines persist due to war or civil unrest. One might think here of the threat that looms over the Hazarajat in central Afghanistan – victim of a blockade imposed by the Taliban since 1997 – due to a civil war that is tearing the country apart.[1]

This victory over famine is the result of the Green Revolution and grain storage policies, together with various producer purchasing price regulations. At present, almost all States have grain reserves to mobilise in case of natural disaster, so limiting massive imports leading to sharp increases in cereal prices. Reserves might also be used to regulate market prices.

In China, and later Vietnam, agricultural decollectivisation and economic liberalisation breathed fresh air into the countryside, initially leading to extraordinary increases in production. However, inadequate public investment subsequently led to a downturn. That said, meat production has continued to grow, particularly in China, causing remarkable improvements in the diet of millions of people.

Contrary to the thesis widespread in the literature between 1970 and 1985, the Green Revolution was not just for the benefit of the rich. The average peasant and very small landowners were also successfully integrated into the movement, allowing them to meet their food needs and sometimes to generate a surplus for sale – even from half a hectare of well-cultivated land. The Green Revolution also brought about real increases in the wages of landless peasants, with employment possibilities similarly expanding as rural economies were stimulated. Secondary agricultural activities flourished, among them kitchen gardening, animal husbandry, small industry, trade, and improvements of roads and electricity supplies. In short, the Green Revolution gave impetus to a global process of rural development, characterised by increases in and diversification of production, expanded employment opportunities and a resulting reduction in poverty.

As such, the process is nothing new, having existed and promoted growth in Europe and Asia for numerous centuries. The only difference

---

1. For more details, refer to the chapter on Afghanistan.

today lies in technical performances which are more powerful and in a demographic growth that is much stronger than previously. In the past, population growth rarely exceeded 1% per year, except in the case of massive immigration, compared to present trends of 2–3% per year, although generally less than 2% in Asia.

In other words, in the agricultural sector the effect of growth on the poor – *the trickle down effect* – that has been so decried, or even denied for such a long time, is a reality which cannot be denied.

In India, for instance, landless peasants earn twice as much in areas affected by the Green Revolution than those doing the same work in areas of slow growth. They can, in addition, find more employment throughout the year. Even in Bangladesh, one of the poorest countries in the continent, there has been a marked decline in poverty in the more advanced district of Comilla. In China, meanwhile, peasant families from the more prosperous and well-developed districts can survive on 0.3–0.4 hectares of intensively cultivated land, together with support from a large variety of secondary activities. By 1980, in Indonesia, owners of half a hectare of well-cultivated land had already come to be considered as 'middle-class' peasants, some with even the means to buy a little scooter.[2]

Nevertheless, even in the more developed regions, vulnerable groups, the malnourished, female-headed households, the elderly with no family support – all those who, for whatever reason, were not able to be integrated into the movement – remain.

There are, then, still vast regions that have been excluded from the Green Revolution, a Revolution which is far from being an all-out remedy *(see box overleaf)*. Lack of rainfall and/or irrigation can significantly limit, or even block its impact and provoke major fluctuations in harvests: from 0–200 kg of grain per hectare to 500–800 kg. Vast areas of the continent – among them, the plateaux of Iran and Afghanistan, countless districts of peninsular India and the plateaux of both north-eastern Thailand and north-western China – suffer from an unfavourable environment charac-terised by lack of water and by poor soils increasingly subject to erosion. With around 100–150 inhabitants per sq. km or even less, these plateaux areas are far less densely populated than the plains, which tend to have about 500–1,000 inhabitants per sq. km or more. However, the differences

2. G. Étienne; 1995; *Rural Change in South Asia, India, Pakistan, Bangladesh*; New Delhi, Vikas; and J.L. Maurer; 1986; *Modernisation agricole...a Java*; Paris, Geneva; PUF Collection HEI.

THE KEY TO THE GREEN REVOLUTION

1 New seeds (wheat, rice, maize, sorghum and millet) that react genetically to chemical fertilisers and much more strongly than those used in the past. Varieties with shorter stems (to avoid problems of lodging) and often with short growing periods to facilitate two annual harvests on the same soil.
2 In many cases, new varieties + chemical fertilizers require more water (rainwater and/or irrigation) than traditional varieties without chemical fertilizers.
3 Genetically homogeneous, new varieties are more vulnerable to pests, hence the importance of pest control.
4 Wheat and rice varieties gradually lose their quality, so they have to be replaced every four or five years, thus necessitating continuous research into new seeds and their multiplication. Hybrid varieties (maize, millet and rice) must be renewed every year.
5 The use of a tractor is not crucial.
6 The same variety cannot be adapted to any kind of physical environment.

DEVELOPMENT OF YIELDS

Irrigated areas

kg/ha	Wheat	Rice
Good traditional crops	1,000–1,300	1,200–1,400
First phase of Green Revolution	2,000	2,000
Second phase	2,500–3,000	3,000
Current phase	3,500–4,000	3,500–4,000
Further possibilities	5,000	5,000–6,000

Husked rice = 2/3 of paddy

Transition from rainfed to irrigated crops

kg/ha	Wheat	Rice
Traditional non-irrigated crops	400–900	700–1,200
First phase of Green Revolution with irrigation	1,500–2,000	2,000
Then similar development to that above		

These data refer to average conditions over wide areas. They are quite a lot lower than results obtained at research stations in productivity are such that, compared to the yields gained from the Green Revolution, peasants in southern-central China, for instance, can produce more on 0.3–0.4 hectares than those cultivating 2 hectares on the plateaux of Inner Mongolia.

In the poorer regions, progress can only be limited and will, depending on the situation, be costly. It might consist of improvements through watershed development to prevent run-off and improve soils, anti-erosion and dry farming techniques. Two scenarios can be discerned: areas having outlets for their produce, such as big cities or towns undergoing development, and areas that are completely isolated. The 19th century Bombay hinterland (Maharashtra) is indicative of the first scenario. Numerous peasant families survived on the extra income received from a member of their family living in the nearby town, a trend which has become more important over the past 50 years. There has been a similar pattern in the northern rainfed plateaux of Pakistani Punjab and in the poor zones of Thailand and China. In China since 1980 vigorous growth has led to a 'floating' population of about 140 million people. For the most part, these are peasants from districts excluded from the Green Revolution, taking up temporary or permanent work in the towns. In short, then, an improvement in living conditions depends largely on the absorption of a growing sector of the population in the secondary (manufacturing) or tertiary (service) sectors.

While migration might be a hard experience – at least in the first phase, until such time as migrants manage to settle in areas other than agriculture – certain sectors of the population tend to be too isolated or overwhelmed by their poverty to follow the trend. For the isolated aborigine tribes of peninsular India, life is so hard that some of them are threatened by extinction. Glaring malnutrition has left adults lifeless and children with bloated stomachs. The few surveys undertaken have revealed deplorable health conditions and it is difficult to know how many people are affected, particularly as so many villages remain unvisited. Long hours walking through dense forest are necessary to find them.

Such conditions are less common in other parts of Asia. However, surveys conducted in China have revealed that in the isolated villages of Gansu province only one member of the family usually manages to leave the house during winter (very harsh), having to wear all available clothes to do so.

Besides areas affected by the Green Revolution and those having an unfavourable physical environment, a third category exists, grouping together very poor communities in potentially rich areas. The most typical examples can be found in the eastern plains of India and in Bangladesh. These beautiful alluvial plains, abundant in water (with both rainwater and irrigation possibilities), have acted as the grainstores of the area for more than 2,000 years. Today, following a period of economic decline that began at the end of the 18th century until independence in 1947, they constitute the greatest area of misery in Asia. Since independence, progress has been slow, with land pressure continuing to rise (Bangladesh has a national average of 1,000 inhabitants per sq. km) and market outlets other than those for agriculture slow to materialise. Under-nutrition, related to a lack of job opportunities, precarious health conditions and high infant mortality rates, remains the fate of landless peasants and small landholders. Is this surprising given that only 30–35% of land is irrigated, as opposed to the potential 80–90% that might be irrigated through surface and/or underground water sources?

Large-scale irrigation would help to extend the still limited Green Revolution. In a first phase, rainfed rice yields (husked) might increase from 500–1,000 to 2,000 kg/ha, and then in a second phase to 3,000 kg/ha or more. At the same time, more land could also be brought into cultivation during the dry season, so providing a supplementary 2,000–3,000 kg/ha.

THE TEMPTATION TO REFER TO STATISTICS

Since the beginning of the 1970s, economists and statisticians have been trying to determine the poverty line below which living conditions, even minimal, are not met. This they have done by looking at nutritional deficiencies (one of the most important criteria), precarious health, infant mortality, low incomes, under-employment and so on. According to FAO (1995), the number of people suffering from chronic under-nutrition is somewhere between 700 million and one billion for the Third World as a whole. Some 500 million of these are in Asia. Having little scientific value due to the degree of disagreement among experts, these figures remain somewhat dubious as to the real extent of the problem. In China, the National Statistical Office of Beijing has estimated that 65 million people live below the poverty line. The World Bank, on the basis of its own criteria, has put the figure at 350 million (out of a total population of 1.25 billion at the end of 1997). In India, the percentage of people living below the poverty line has been put at 19% but was revised to 37% in 1997. Who is to be believed?

Those who talk with the poor, instead of talking about the poor in offices stacked with computers and so on, have long shown that the poorer a family, the more difficult it is to determine the family's standard of living and to assess all the unquantifiable elements necessary. In fact, this had already been pointed out by the French ethnologist and expert on India, Louis Dumont, some 40 years ago. His equally well-known colleague, M.N. Srinivas, and other field researchers have all come to the same conclusion. Only very detailed and focused surveys might provide some understanding of the reality, although this is not always possible.[3]

Technical factors reinforce the difficulties. The nutritional standard of 2,450 calories per day per person proposed by FAO is similarly subject to variations of 300 calories or more according to the needs of people of the same weight, same sex and same age, and working under similar climatic conditions.[4] This said, there is no doubt that the numbers of malnourished in Asia remain so high that enough may never be done to fight poverty.

India, itself a sub-continent of 960 million people, reveals a wide spectrum of situations. With marked progress in areas affected by the Green Revolution – particularly the plains of the north-west and the deltas of the south-east – areas such as the basins of the middle and lower Ganges (Bihar, Western Bengal) remain precarious (the plains of Orissa being somewhat better off).

QUALITATIVE DIETARY CHANGES

Not only the quantity but also the quality of diets has changed. In the 1950s in South Asia, particularly in India and Bangladesh, lentils and other pulses were relatively important, even in the ordinary diets of the poor. This is no longer the case today. Progress in their production has been limited, mainly for technical reasons. Most of these crops depend only on rainfall and despite research which began in the 1970s the development of new high-yielding varieties has been hindered by a lack of water.[5] In India, only 10% of pulses are irrigated. Between 1950 to 1995, production was not

---

3. Cf. L. Dumont; 1957; *The Under-Caste of South India*; Paris, Mouton; and M.N. Srinivas; 1982; *Village Studies – Economic and Political Weekly*; August 1975. The reader might also refer to G. Étienne; 1982; *Developpement Rural en Asie*; Paris, PUF Collection, Tiers Monde.
4. P.V. Sukhatme; 1977; *Incidence of Undernutrition – Indian Journal of Agricultural Economics*; no. 3
5. Whereas research on rice, wheat and maize in Europe, the United States and Japan had begun 100 years earlier.

even able to double, moving from 8.16 million tons to only 14.12 million tons, whereas that for wheat jumped from 6.4 to 65.5 million tons and for rice from 23.5 to 81 million tons. As a natural consequence of this relative decline in supply, pulses have become a luxury for the poor, who are no longer able to afford them.

Other changes in diets have been positive. The spectacular increase in meat consumption in China has already been mentioned. In Pakistan, India and South–East Asia animal husbandry, fishing, kitchen gardens and fruit orchards are all on the increase, guaranteeing a more balanced diet for significant sectors of the population. Progress has been most marked among those who, having lived on extremely frugal rations 30 or 40 years ago, are now beginning to live better. Hence, the small Indian peasant now able to put sugar in his milk tea, the child of the landless untouchable now guaranteed a glass of milk every day and the Muslim who eats meat once a week rather than once a month, as before – all due to the Green Revolution.

Although the extreme monotony of diets is now being reduced almost throughout Asia – a trend already visible in Europe in the 19th century – there nevertheless remain those who have been excluded, whatever their number.

SPECIAL FOOD PROGRAMMES

Although China is trying to expand special measures targeting its poorer regions, the broadest range of programmes can still be found in India and Bangladesh.

In 'food for work' programmes, poor peasants participate in rural construction projects (such as terracing or the construction of roads, paths and small reservoirs) for which they are paid in cash or in kind (in grain, for instance). While by no means negligible, these activities are insufficient to meet needs. However, in an emergency situation (in regions affected by drought for example, and therefore threatened by famine) such activities do help the poor, as has often been seen in India. In such situations, local authorities are mobilised to avoid disaster, for in a democratic system such as that of India, it has become intolerable to let people die of hunger, risking an outcry in the State Assemblies or the Central Legislature.

Nevertheless, 'food for work' programmes, completed in routine fashion, still produce somewhat modest results. Studies and even official reports reveal wastage, misuse and poor quality construction.

Another type of programme is that of free school meal distributions, as in Tamil Nadu, for instance, or the sale of rice at extremely low prices to the poorest, as in Andhra. Although this has produced positive effects, the losses are not insignificant.

Other types of activities are also undertaken – in Pakistan, among other countries. On the whole, however, after dozens of years, such direct attacks on poverty do not appear particularly convincing, coming up against problems of management, magnitude of the task and wastage.

UNPREDICTABLE WEATHER CONDITIONS

Despite advances in irrigation and flood prevention, Asian agriculture remains vulnerable to erratic weather conditions. Unless the monsoons fill up the rivers and the reservoirs, irrigated land depending on surface water (canals) tends to suffer from drought. Moreover, a significant proportion of crops is still dependent on rainfall alone, with yields of 0–200 kg/ha for sorghum or millet.

For the continent as a whole, climatic conditions have been relatively favourable over the past 10 years or so. Since 1987, India has not been subject to a bad monsoon, as has Bangladesh. China, however, has had serious floods and drought. In 1998, floods caused by the Yang Tse were so dramatic they affected about 240 million people, with severe flooding in August 1998. Then very unusual floods hit north-eastern China (Manchuria), where precipitation is usually quite low.

Nature, then, remains dangerous. Since 1992, repeated and exceptional floods in Pakistan, punctured by periods of drought, have damaged the crops. However, relatively good weather conditions promoted bumper cereal harvests in 1997–98, leading to expectations about a reduction in cereal imports. In 1997, Indonesia was hit by considerable drought, apparently linked to El Niño, such that rice imports were expected to reach 4–5 million tons in 1998, as opposed to having usually been less than 1 million tons in recent years. The Philippines have also been affected. After having made positive progress due to the Green Revolution, the country was expected to import 800,000 tons of rice for 1998. China also experienced a significant drop in the 1997 maize harvest.

In this chapter, it is not possible to tackle the complex debates about climatic change. Nevertheless, attention needs to be paid to this issue. Even if the risk of severe famines has practically disappeared, those areas most vulnerable to natural disaster are obviously the poorest.

LOOKING TO THE FUTURE

Since 1997, there has been growing concern among the ruling elites in China, Indonesia, India and Pakistan about the effects of climate. From the Indus basin to the plain around Beijing, hydraulic works, irrigation canals and anti-flood dykes are increasingly being found in poor condition due to inadequate maintenance. The severity of the floods which have hit China several times in recent years, notably in 1998, can be partly attributed to the poor condition of the country's dykes. According to the Chinese Ministry for Agriculture, in 1993 two-thirds of the 246,000 km of dykes were found to be badly in need of repair. Major investments would be necessary to extend and improve rainfed crops. Much still needs to be done in terms of basic research, seed reproduction and supply. Thus, even if Asian agriculture has significant potential for further development, tens of billions of dollars of public investment would be required – not to mention the support of farmers.

China and India are already having difficulties gathering the necessary funds. As for Indonesia and Pakistan, given the serious financial crisis afflicting both countries, massive agricultural rehabilitation can hardly be expected to occur overnight. In the medium term, the future of Bangladesh appears more promising, following recent discoveries of considerable resources above and beyond those of already known natural gas deposits. As a result, the country might find more financial means with which to accelerate growth.

In conclusion, the future looks fairly bright: the catastrophic forecasts of a massive cereal deficit for the years 2020 or 2030 made by the American expert, Lester Brown, appear to have little foundation. What does give cause for concern, however, is the slowdown in agricultural growth and hence a slower pace in the reduction of both extreme poverty and under-nutrition.

Bibliography

This general bibliography, which does not claim to be exhaustive, supplements the bibliographies given at the end of some chapters.

Alexandratos, N.; *Agriculture Mondiale: Horizon 2010*; FAO.

Bettati, M.; 1996; *Le Droit d'Ingérence*; Odile Jacob.

Brauman, R.; 1993; *Somalie: le Crime Humanitaire*; Arlea.

—1994; *Devant le Mal, Rwanda, un Génocide Direct*; Arlea.

—1995; *L'Action Humanitaire*; Flammarion-Dominos.

Brunel, S.; 1991; *Une Tragedie Banalisée, la Faim dans le Monde*; Hachette-Pluriel.

—1986; *Asie-Afrique, Greniers Vides Greniers Pleins*; Economica.

—1996; *Les Problèmes Alimentaires dans le Monde*; Cahiers Francais (no. 278).

—1995; *Le Sud dans la Nouvelle Economie Mondiale*; Puf-Major.

—1997; *Ceux Qui Vont Mourir de la Faim*; Seuil – l'Histoire Immediate.

CIRAD; 1995; *Vers une Révolution Doublement Verte*.

Deldique, P-E.; 1994; *Le Mythe des Nations-Unies, l'ONU après la Guerre Froide*; Hachette.

Delpeuch, B.; 1992; *L'Enjeu Alimentaire Nord-Sud*; Syros-Alternatives.

Domestici-Met, M-J. (ed); 1996; *Aide Humanitaire Internationale, un Consensus Conflictuel*; Economica.

Emmanuelli, X.; 1991; *Les Prédateurs de l'Action Humanitaire*; Albin Michel.

Etienne, G.; 1995; *Rural Change in South Asia*; Vikas (New Delhi).

—1996; *L'Economie de l'Inde*; PUF-QSJ.

Gallais, J.; 1994; *Les Tropiques, Terres de Risques et de Violences*; Armand Colin, Collection U.

Gourou, P. and Etienne, G. (eds); 1985; *Des Labours de Cluny à la Révolution Verte*; PUF.

Guillebaud, J-C.; 1995; *La Trahison des Lumières*; Seuil.

Hunger Project; 1985; *Ending Hunger*; Praeger.

Interventions; 1994; *La Faim en Dix Questions Clés*; ACF.

Jean, F. (ed); *Populations in Danger – Annual Report of MSF*; La Découverte.

Julliard, J.; 1994; *L'Année des Dupes*; Seuil.

—1996; *Pour la Bosnie*; Seuil.

Kempf, H.; 1994; *La Baleine qui Cache la Forêt*; La Découverte.

Klatzmann, J.; 1991; *Nourrir l'Humanité, Espoirs et Inquiétudes*; Intra-Economica.

Kouchner, B.; 1991; *Le Malheur des Autres*; Odile Jacob.

—1986; *Charité Business*; le Pre aux Clercs.

Le Roy, P.; 1996; *Agriculture et Alimentation Mondiales: des Raisons d'Espérer*; Publications du Credit Mutuel.

—1994; *La Faim dans le Monde*; Marabout.

Ould Abdallah, A. and Smith, S.; 1996; *La Diplomatie Pyromane*; Calmann-Levy.

Prunier, G.; 1997; *Rwanda, un Génocide en Direct*; Dagorno.

Rufin, J-C.; 1993; *Le Piège Humanitaire*; Hachette-Pluriel.

—1991; *L'Empire et les Nouveaux Barbares*; Lattes.

Russbach, O.; 1994; *ONU Contre ONU, le Droit International Confisqué*; La
    Découverte.
Serageldin, I.; 1994; *Overcoming Global Hunger*; The World Bank.
Smith, S.; 1993; *Somalie, la Guerre Perdue de l'Humanitaire*; Calmann-Levy.
Swaminathan, M.S. and Sinha, S.K.; 1986; *Global Aspects of Food Production*;
    International Rice Research Institute, Tycooly International.
Unicef; 1994; *The Progress of Nations – Annual Report and Faim et Malnutrition
    dans le Tiers-Monde*; Unicef.
Vershave, F-X.; 1994; *Complicité de Génocide? La Politique de la France au
    Rwanda*; La Découverte.

Various reports from the UNDP, the World Bank, Unicef, FAO and UNESCO.

Acknowledgements

Although very much the effort of the organisation as a whole, this report nevertheless required more intensive work by some more than others in order that deadlines
be met. As a result, we would particularly like to thank:

Florence Daunis and Carole Dubrulle who, whether by telephone, fax or e-mail,
made sure that efforts were co-ordinated at field level by chasing up the various
programme directors working in hunger-stricken countries (where it was not
always easy to find the calm to write), so that they might send us their analyses
(often under somewhat acrobatic conditions).

Eric Bouvet, Véronique Burger and Hermine Cleret, professional photographers
who kindly gave us permission to use their work for the report.

Iesha Singh who translated and edited the English version of the report in collaboration with Isabel Brenner.

Sylvie Brunel who abandoned her own book-writing for several months, so that
she might devote more time to co-ordinating the organisation's report and so give
birth to the 'baby' so long-awaited by each one of us ... and, we hope, by you as well.

If you would like to know more about Action Against Hunger, contact our offices
in London or New York at the following addresses:

London: 1 Catton Street, London WC1R 4AB, UK
            Tel: (44) 171 831 5858; Fax: (44) 171 831 4259
            E-mail: aahuk@gn.apc.org

New York: 875 Avenue of the Americas, Suite 1905, New York, NY 10001, USA
            Tel: (1) 212 967 7800; Fax: (1) 212 967 5480
            E-mail: aicfusa@aah-usa.org

List of contributors

External

Mario Bettati	Professor of International Law, Dean of the University of Paris II
Marie-José Domestici-Met	Professor of International Law at the Faculty of Law and Political Science, University of Aix-Marseille III Director of the DESS: 'Emergency and Rehabilitation International Humanitarian Aid'
Gilbert Étienne	Professor at the Institutes of International Studies and Development Studies in Geneva
Bernard Granjon	Honorary President of Médecins du Monde
François Grunewald	Agronomist, Consultant
Ahmedou Ould Abdallah	Executive Secretary of the Global Coalition for Africa
Gérard Prunier	Researcher at the National Centre for Scientific Research (CNRS)

Members of Action Against Hunger

Anne Berton-Rafael	Nurse-Nutritionist
José Bidegain	President, Paris
Annie Blaise	Press Officer, Paris
Jean-Luc Bodin	General Director, Paris
Sylvie Brunel	Strategic Counsellor, Paris
Patrick Danard	Hydrologist
Florence Daunis	Desk Officer, Paris
Eric Drouart	Hydrologist
Thomas Gonnet	Desk Officer, Paris
Yvonne Grellety	Head of the Nutrition Department, Paris
Jean-Marc Jouineau	Desk Officer, Paris
Philippe Leborgne	Head of the Medical Department, Paris
Pascal Lefort	Desk Officer, Paris
Isabelle Le Normand	Head of the Food Security Department, Paris
Jonathan Littell	Country Director
Jean-Fabrice Pietri	Desk Officer, Paris
Claudine Prudhon	Nutritionist
Iesha Singh	Socio-Economist
Jean-Michel Vouillamoz	Hydrologist